How to Retire Happy, Wild, and Free

How to Retire Happy, Wild, and Free

Retirement Wisdom That You Won't Get from Your Financial Advisor

Ernie J. Zelinski

TEN SPEED PRESS
Berkeley | Toronto

Ten Speed Press
P.O. Box 7123
Berkeley, California 94707
www.tenspeed.com

Distributed in Australia by Simon and Schuster,
Australia, in New Zealand by Southern Publishers Group,
in South Africa by Real Books, and in the United Kingdom
and Europe by Airlift Book Company.

Published in Greek by Kedros Publishers, Athens, Greece.
Published in Spanish by Planeta De Agostini Professional
Y Formación, S.L. (Editorial Amat), Barcelona, Spain.
Published in Chinese simplified characters by CITIC
Publishing House, Beijing, China and in Chinese complex
characters by Yuan-Liou Publishing, Taipei, Taiwan.
Published in Japanese by Open Knowledge, Tokyo, Japan.
Published in Korean by Like a Wildflower, Seoul, S. Korea.
Published in French by Stanké Int., Montreal and Paris.
Published in Canada by Visions International Publishing
& Distributed by Sandhill Book Marketing, Kelowna, B.C.

Library of Congress Cataloguing-in-Publication Data
Zelinski, Ernie J. (Ernie John), 1949–
How to retire happy, wild, and free : retirement wisdom
that you won't get from your financial advisor / Ernie J.
Zelinski.
p. cm.
ISBN 1-58008-578-4 (pbk.)
1. Retirement. 2. Early Retirement. 3. Leisure I. Title.
HQ1062.Z448 2004
646.7'9—dc22   2004000580

Printed and bound in Canada
    4 5 6 7 8 9 10 — 09 08 07 06 05

Contents

Preface

Soon retirement day will have come and gone. For your many years of service to the organization, you will have received congratulations from co-workers, a gold watch, and perhaps even a book on how to retire happily. If you are one of the fortunate ones, a generous company pension, government social security, and investments will give you the opportunity to pursue many interesting activities. According to financial experts, you will have it made. Indeed, you should live happily ever after.

Not so fast! These questions beg your consideration: What will you do with your time if you have never learned how to enjoy your leisure? What should you say to your spouse — and perhaps your parents — if you are retiring before they can? How are you going to experience a sense of accomplishment and satisfaction without a job? How will you relate to your friends who are still working while you are living the life of an aristocrat?

Perhaps in retirement I will be tempted by the ultimate weakness of idealistic minds — which is to write a book.

Truth be known, after the novelty of the retirement lifestyle wears off in a month or two, you may feel that you don't have any reason to get up in the morning. Once you get up, you may feel you have nowhere in particular to go. There will be no regular coffee breaks with colleagues, no clients to call on, and no challenges to give your life shape and purpose. Eventually, you may end up asking yourself, "Okay, genius. What do I do now?"

In the Western world there is a big misconception about what contributes to a happy and fulfilling retirement. Many people have an idealized concept of how great and wonderful life after work is going to turn out. This vision can include no deadlines, no rush-hour traffic, no mean bosses, exotic travel, hanging around cappuccino bars, and sleeping in late every day. Let's not forget the freedom to do what you want, whenever you want to do it.

Retirement can be both exciting and demanding, bringing new challenges, new experiences, and new uncertainties. Regardless of how it turns out, retirement normally turns out far different from what people first envision. For some, it is a big disappointment. For others, it is merely a big annoyance. And still for others — much to their delight — retirement becomes an opportunity to live life like never before.

Regardless of how talented you are and how successful you are in the workplace, there is some danger that you will not be as happy and satisfied as you hope to be in retirement. This may be the case even if you end up having friends to spend time with, living the lifestyle you want to live, residing where you want to live, and having many interesting things to do. What may be missing is a sense of purpose and some meaning to your life. Put another way, you will want to keep growing as an individual instead of remaining stagnant.

Financial institutions program us to believe that we are set for a happy retirement as long as we follow their financial advice. Recently I received a pamphlet from a community college advertising a three-session retirement planning course called *A Prime Approach to Retirement Planning*. The course, created by a financial organization, covered a lot of topics — all of them financial. There was not one mention of anything related to how retirees should spend their time after they leave the workforce.

Although stockbrokers, bank officials, and other "retirement planners" overwhelm us with advertisements, solicitations, and advice on how to plan financially for retirement, they ignore other factors that contribute to a successful retirement. Similarly, for every twenty books written on retirement, there may be only one that has any worthwhile treatment of the important personal issues. The result is that many people spend forty years building an impressive retirement nest egg, but no time at all thinking about how they are going to enjoy retirement. Indeed, the biggest mistake you can make with your retirement planning is to concentrate only on the financial aspects.

> Retirement is the time when you never do all the things you intended to do when you'd have the time.
>
> — Laurence J. Peter

On the surface, a happy retirement doesn't seem that difficult to achieve. And it isn't for individuals who understand there's far more to achieving fulfillment in retirement than having wealth and good health. Indeed, there is no shortage of scholarly evidence that financial status constitutes only a small piece of the puzzle as to whether people will succeed and be happy in retirement. Apparently, most "retirement planners" either are not aware of this evidence or focus only on the financial so that they can sell more financially related products.

This is where *How to Retire Happy, Wild, and Free* comes into the picture. For the most part, this book offers retirement wisdom that you won't receive from your financial advisor. Contrary to popular wisdom, many elements — not just having a million or two in the bank — contribute to happiness and satisfaction for today's retirees. Indeed, physical well-being, mental well-being, and solid social support play bigger roles than financial status for most retirees.

Retirement is the perfect time to become the person you would like to be and do the things you have always wanted to do. No doubt doing everything you have always wanted to do sounds great. It won't happen by itself, however. This is true even if you have excellent health and a big pile of money in the bank when you retire.

> When men reach their sixties and retire, they go to pieces. Women go right on cooking.
>
> — Gail Sheehy

Planning is important. You must take steps to ensure that when the bell rings to announce your retirement, you're ready for what's in front of you. The time available for marital, personal, social, creative, and family activities expands considerably when the hours previously taken up with full-time employment cease. How you manage time is just as important as when you are in the workforce.

This I can assure you: You won't find genuine joy and satisfaction by spending all your time sleeping, relaxing, loafing, and watching TV, hoping to live up to the ideal of a true idler. Many retired people with nothing to do wind up depressed and hating retirement. In this regard, Florida physician Richard Neubauer concluded that many people experience a rapid decline in physical and mental health soon after retirement — often due to idleness and feelings of uselessness.

To retire happy, wild, and free, you must stay active. It's also important that you have goals and dreams. Retirement can be a time for life's best moments, provided that you take the time to plan what you are going to do with the rest of your life. Just as important, you must be motivated enough to follow your dreams, and change course if adversity intrudes to put a dent in your plans. The most fortunate of retirees are those who through good planning, experimentation, and risk-taking succeed in making retirement the best time of their lives.

In short, it's up to you to design a lifestyle that is as relaxing and invigorating as you want it to be. No one else is going to do it for you. Recreating yourself as a retired person will be challenging, but through patience and positive thinking, you can do it. The rewards will be more than worth it.

As a matter of course retirement is the last opportunity for individuals to reinvent themselves, let go of the past, and find peace and happiness within. Many people discover — much to their surprise — that retirement life following four or five decades of full-time work is full of new and exciting opportunities. For these individuals, their work was a barrier to the lives they wanted; now they're free to live life to the fullest.

> In retirement, I look for days off from my days off.
>
> — Mason Cooley

Despite the bad press that retirement sometimes gets, there has never been a better time to be retired in Western nations. One in every eight people is age sixty-five or older. More people than ever are retiring much earlier than age sixty-five. Today's retirees have far better health, a higher level of education, more income, and many more options for maintaining an active and productive lifestyle than the retirees who came before them.

Above all, this book celebrates retirement because it's the beginning of a new life. Retirement is an opportune time to get to know yourself better — psychologically, materially, and spiritually. Moreover, retirement allows you to do what you don't like as little as possible and what you like as much as possible. Whatever it is — a part-time career, family relationships, spiritual fulfillment, passionate pursuits, or the opportunity to hang around Starbucks writing a book — you must find those things that matter most to you.

The way I see it, you will have attained true freedom in this world when you can get up in the morning when you want to get up; go to sleep when you want to go to sleep; and in the interval, work and play at the things you want to work and play at — all at your own pace. The great news is that retirement allows you the opportunity to attain this freedom.

1

Thank Heaven for Retirement

Perhaps It's Time to Tell Your Boss, "I'm Outta Here!"

Learn to live well, or fairly make your will;
You've played, and loved, and ate, and drunk your fill:
Walk sober off; before a sprightlier age
Comes tittering on, and shoves you from the stage:
— Alexander Pope

Soon there may come a time when you won't want to work at your career anymore. You will have had enough of the pretending that happens in the typical workplace. Working at nebulous activities just for the money can go on only so long before you realize that you are in a state of mental inertia. You will start wondering why so many workers blindly accept confinement to rigid work hours, waiting until they are in their sixties or seventies to be put out to pasture — either by layoff or poor health.

You know it's time for retirement when you spend all your time reporting on all the nothing you are doing.

After focusing on the negatives of the typical workplace long enough, you will start looking at alternatives. As is to be expected, the thought of early retirement will appear highly promising. It will be easy to fantasize about the wonderful things that you can do once you retire — go on three cruises a year, spend a lot of time with your grandchildren, spend a year in a monastery, or live in Costa

Rica for a year. If you have recently been having similar fantasies, perhaps it's time to tell your boss, "I'm outta here!"

At the same time that you are contemplating your exit from your lengthy career, you will be wondering if you are the only one in the world who feels so dissatisfied. Believe me, you aren't. As people approach their mid-forties and beyond, the thought of retirement becomes more pronounced. Some feel less secure in their jobs while others find that the satisfaction they used to have is now missing. For people working in Western nations — such as Canada but not the United States — where corporations can impose a mandatory retirement age, leaving before they are involuntarily put out to pasture can enter their minds. This would make them feel more in control of their lives.

The numbers of people in their forties and fifties who want to leave their traditional careers may surprise you. "No one wants to hang around until they're sixty-five anymore," states Nancy Langdon Jones, a financial planner in Upland, California. "They're itching to retire." Career counselors indicate that the vast majority of people tire of what they do by age fifty or so, and have a secret wish of retiring by fifty-five. Few workers, however, meet that deadline, although more would do so if they had a plan.

On the other hand, some people do meet their deadline or, in fact, beat it. Ian Hammond of Montrose, from the county of Angus, Scotland, is an example of someone who was itching to retire and did so at an opportune time. After reading *The Joy of Not Working*, Hammond decided to quit his job. A plan of action helped him achieve his goal of doing something more productive with his life.

> Most people perform essentially meaningless work. When they retire that truth is borne upon them.
>
> — Brendan Francis

Hammond drafted his notice of resignation more than a year before he actually quit his job. The letter was posted in his electronic calendar manager as an "out-of-office reminder." He showed this notice to his boss and co-workers several months before his exit. Following is his notice of resignation, which he kindly agreed to share with readers of this book:

> I will terminate my employment on the 30th of September 1998 to pursue a more rewarding lifestyle which I intend to enjoy for at least the next several years. The technical content of the job has diminished for which I believe I show an aptitude and commitment;

this change is due to a corresponding increase in administrative duties, for which I am entirely unsuited and which are of little interest. The performance system places too high a reliance on managerial ability in what should be a technically-based environment, and as a graduate, there is an expectation that I will move through the company system and become 'Dilbertised' along with all the others; unfortunately I refuse to prostitute myself in this way and prefer to collect a modest salary based on my intellectual achievements, demonstrating ability rather than visibility. The time wasted in this job, whether in circular arguments, writing unread reports, or performing substandard work due to inadequate resources and poorly-trained staff, is worth more to me than the recognition and reward

> The best time to start thinking about your retirement is before your boss does.
>
> — Unknown wise person

that the company sees fit to deny me. It is with much pleasure that I announce that, after spending some time with my dad in Cornwall and with friends in France, I will overwinter in New Zealand for four months, camping and cycling. On my return I intend to pursue several interests:

- Study for an astronomy degree;
- Learn to speak Spanish and German fluently;
- Write and publish a travelogue, short stories and poetry;
- Read all the "classics;"
- Volunteer as an overseas science/French/English teacher;
- Study for an electronics degree;
- Cycle around the world;
- Compete in an international chess tournament;
- Play classical guitar to concert standard;
- Learn tourist Italian and Portuguese;
- Paint watercolors;
- Do ten things I haven't thought of doing yet!

If I achieve a third of these aims, I will consider my
time well-spent. The corporate work ethic and its
success depend on the uncritical thinking of those who
believe that they are making a difference and are being
recognized for it.

Best wishes for your future, if you want one.

Ian, 26th of May 1997.

No doubt most readers will find Ian's notice of resignation
inspiring. May I suggest that you use Ian's list of interests as a
model for creating your own list of activities to pursue in
retirement. Ian did, in fact, retire in September 1998. He first wrote
to me in April 2000 at which time he included the above notice of
resignation. Here is what he had to say:

Dear Ernie,

I have just read *The Joy of Not Working* for the third
time so it is about time that I congratulated you on
such a sensible book; it states the obvious, which isn't
to most people.

I came across the book whilst browsing one rainy day
waiting for a bus. I bought it after reading the first two
chapters — and missing the bus — since it confirmed
that there was at least one other madman who thought
like me. This is quite an achievement on your part;
although I'm an avid reader, your book was the only
book I bought in 1997 or since, because I use my own
town library.

Your book reinforced what I have thought for many
years about work and society, the purpose of life,
solitude, money, and motivation. My final job was as an
analytical chemist for a large company here in
Montrose, which is about to become a much larger
company; an example of merging which is in fashion
these days. I'm only a shareholder now and not an
employee what with all the
downsizing that will inevitably
result. The folks at work don't smile
much anyway.

> A career is a job that has
> gone on too long.
>
> — Jeff MacNelly

I've enclosed an "out of office"
reminder from my electronic

calendar manager which could be viewed for over a year before I finally left. I'm sure you've received similar stories from other technical people who could only progress as managers. My boss came across it one day appropriately enough whilst he was booking me for my annual appraisal! He ended up borrowing your book, and later we had a long chat during which he glumly handed it back saying it was all true.

> When work is a pleasure, life is a joy. When work is a duty, life is slavery.
>
> — Maxim Gorky

It felt good to give my employer a year's notice instead of the statutory one month, and the reception I received from everyone (except the upper echelons, of course) was genuine; it started a waiting-list for your book! The last six months were wonderful: others were given my modest managerial responsibilities and I was sidelined from new fast track projects, instead becoming an expert trainer/troubleshooter on call to anyone. It was almost a job worth living for.

It was a good job, but my life since has been better. I biked and camped around New Zealand, but for six months not four, because the scenery, climate and most importantly, the people, were fantastic (As a fellow cyclist I can recommend it to you as better than anywhere else that I've visited so far). I've also done similar two-month trips to the American Midwest and the Canary Islands, learning Spanish before the latter. I've done several watercolors from my New Zealand photographs, surprised myself with the results, and this year will attempt pastels too. I've seen more of my family and friends even though I've been travelling for half of my new life.

This summer I'm doing a two-monther around Ireland, studying electronics for the first time in a quarter-century, and seeing long-lost friends in Sydney, then biking around Australia for six months this winter. I don't know how I'd fit in work now!

All this on £6,000 a year, which is the income from my investments. What you say about money and the environment is very true, and I recycle or (better) reuse everything. My fruit and vegetable garden is not only a source of pleasure, but a way to help support my chosen lifestyle. I haven't put the dustbin out since I "retired"; maybe I should claim for a rebate.

If you ever come to Britain, let me know because I'd like to attend one of your talks. Failing that, I may travel in Canada one day and we could go for a bike ride. I'd even buy you that meal!

Keep in touch and thank you once more.

Ian

Obviously, Ian was prepared for retirement. He had the courage to quit his job and retire to a more leisurely lifestyle. As some lucky people are able to do, Ian retired happy, wild, and free. Note that the word "wild" has many connotations. In *How to Retire Happy, Wild, and Free*, however, "wild" signifies "happy-go-lucky" and/or "highly enthusiastic."

Keep in mind how much money Ian needed to retire happy, wild, and free. Six thousand pounds a year is certainly a lot less than what most financial advisors cite as a healthy retirement income. As this book will emphasize throughout, a happy, wild, and free retirement is based not only on a healthy relationship with money and our financial resources, but also on our friends, our community, our family, our life's purpose, our leisure activities, and our dreams. Above all, a happy retirement is based on a healthy relationship with ourselves.

When I retire, I plan to do absolutely nothing for at least a year or two.

How will you know when you are finished?

Retirement Should Put a Perpetual Smile on Your Face

While millions like Ian Hammond look forward to retirement, millions also fear or worry about it. A recent study by researchers David Evans and Terry Lynn Gall concluded that although most Canadian workers viewed retirement as a positive step, only about a third looked forward to it and adjusted well. In fact, 16 percent of those interviewed saw nothing good about it.

"We are a society not only obsessed with looks and youth, but also hard work ethics," declared Marian Marzynski, the producer of the PBS documentary film *My Retirement Dreams*. "For those who never slowed down from work, the idea of retirement can be frightening; they don't know what to do after."

> As to that leisure evening of life, I must say that I do not want it. I can conceive of no contentment of which toil is not to be the immediate parent.
>
> — Anthony Trollope

To some degree, most people worry about retirement. Many worry about not having enough money. Others worry about having to leave the comfort and community provided by the workplace. Still others worry about what they are going to do with their time. Of course, excessive worry about retirement can shorten your life expectancy so much that you need not be concerned about it.

Fear about retirement in today's world has become so pronounced that some people even want it totally abolished. Mind you, there have always been detractors ever since the concept of retirement was invented. Spanish cellist Pablo Casals concluded, "To retire is the beginning of death." Ernest Hemingway wasn't much more positive. "Retirement," declared Hemingway, "is the ugliest word in the language."

In the 1980s, the late Maggie Kuhn started a group in the United States called the Gray Panthers to fight what she termed "ageism." One of its goals was to get rid of traditional retirement. "Men and women approaching retirement age should be recycled for public service work, and their companies should foot the bill," stated Kuhn. "We can no longer afford to scrap-pile people."

Apparently, retirement is not held in high regard in other countries either. In *The Gift of Age*, a collection of essays on the challenges of aging, Ramasami Natarajan, sixty-nine, of Singapore wrote, "I was amused that the reaction to retirement in our part of the world was the same as the reaction to death. It was as though the day I announced my retirement, all my 'strengths' were stripped off me by some unknown force. I became a wimp in the eyes of the world."

"Enforced idlement" is what some North Americans opposed to retirement call it. Some go so far as to say that retirement is an invention of corporate human resources departments designed to get rid of old blood and bring in some youth and creativity. According to those who fear retirement, the biggest beneficiaries of retirement are corporations and financial institutions and not retirees.

Yet to fear retirement is to fear life. People all too often fear retirement because they focus on what they are giving up instead of what they are gaining. Instead of seeing retirement as something to be avoided at all costs, they should look at it as a phase of life that can be filled with joy, fun, challenge, excitement, and satisfaction due to all the benefits they can experience. For starters, here are a few of the benefits you get to enjoy once you retire:

> I think it [retirement] beats the heck out of life after death, that's for sure.
>
> — Martina Navratilova

- ➤ You can get up when you want to.
- ➤ You have no daily rush hour traffic to contend with.
- ➤ You don't have to deal with the jerks at the office anymore.
- ➤ Where you live doesn't have to be dictated by your employment.
- ➤ You have lots of time to do the household projects you have been putting off forever.
- ➤ You can spend winter in Florida, Arizona, or Hawaii.
- ➤ You don't have to wait for a bus on a sub-zero January morning.
- ➤ You get to set your own agenda.
- ➤ You have fewer headaches because life is simpler.
- ➤ You can have a lot more variety in your life.
- ➤ You don't have to report to a boss about your actions.
- ➤ You can go on a vacation when you want to go and not when your employer says you can.
- ➤ You have more time for more friends in your life.
- ➤ You can put more time into creative pursuits.
- ➤ There are no co-workers to get envious of your accomplishments.
- ➤ It's easier to be spontaneous.
- ➤ You don't have to work through lunch hour.
- ➤ You don't have to take tedious business trips involving being away from home, overbooked

flights, and being alone.
- ➤ Life is less predictable from nine to five.
- ➤ You can take a nap when the urge hits.
- ➤ You have plenty of time to eat out with friends.
- ➤ You have the time to do all the things you always wanted to do but never had time for.
- ➤ By doing things when everyone else is at work, you can be much more efficient and less hurried at the same time.
- ➤ You can take a carefree vacation without having to take some work with you.
- ➤ More than any other time in your life, you have the opportunity to put all areas of your life in proper balance.
- ➤ You can feel morally superior to working people because you have earned your retirement and they haven't.

The best part about retirement is that it allows you to stop doing what someone tells you to do; instead, you can start doing what you want to do. Eight years after he retired, sixty-nine-year-old Bobby Joe Anderson, former president and CEO of Puritan/Churchill Chemical Co. of Atlanta, Georgia, stated, "But once

> There is a whole new kind of life ahead, full of experiences just waiting to happen. Some call it "retirement." I call it bliss.
>
> — Betty Sullivan

you retire — and that's one of the things, if not the thing, I enjoy most — there's a minimum of binding commitments that I can't rearrange or circumvent or get around. I enjoy that after so many years of being very rigidly involved and committed to a timetable that I couldn't control."

A more positive view of retirement reveals a life much more rewarding than work. This is a life that retirees want to live instead of the life they had to live while employed. Active retirees find many interesting things to do, and more time to do them. Leaving behind the demands of a job allows for a more balanced life comprised of a broader range of interests, activities, routines, and relationships. Indeed, many new retirees become so busy that they don't know how they ever had time for work.

Provided that you take advantage of its benefits, retirement should put a perpetual smile on your face. Indeed, instead of fearing retirement, you should be enthusiastically looking forward to it. Perhaps you are already retired. In this case, with all the great things that you can regularly experience, each and every day should be a day that you declare, "Thank heaven for retirement."

To Not Plan for an Active Retirement Is to Set Yourself Up for a Difficult One

> To have his path made clear for him is the aspiration of every human being in our beclouded and tempestuous existence.
>
> — Joseph Conrad

For many people, retirement is something that is coming sometime in the future but they don't necessarily feel that it is imminent. The desire or need to retire, however, comes a lot sooner than most people expect. For some, retirement is forced upon them. Mandatory retirement at a certain age may not be a corporate policy but corporations use downsizing to get rid of older workers.

Workers, particularly those involved in specialized fields or intense manual labor, should also keep in mind that they may lose their ability to perform their jobs and be forced into retirement a lot sooner than they expect. As American boxer Sugar Ray Robinson stated about his retirement at age forty-two in December 1965, "You always say 'I'll quit when I start to slide,' and then one morning you wake up and realize you've done slid." The fact is, whether they retire voluntarily or otherwise, one day many people wake up and don't have a job to go to.

Most people have at least a vague sense that they should set aside some surplus cash now for retirement so they don't have to rely on meager government pensions sometime in the future. But when it comes to how they will spend their time, the majority of individuals are waiting for fate to show them the way. The more that these people expect from retirement without any effort on their part, the more likely that their retirement will be filled with boredom — even depression.

Retirement is an opportunity to do what you have always wanted to do but haven't got around to because of the demands of a career. Alas, the jackpot of retirement life may be something you fail to enjoy in the event that you don't plan ahead! You shouldn't get too concerned about retirement when you are in your twenties or thirties. But as you enter your forties and fifties — or if you are already retired — you should give it some consideration. Indeed, the quality of your retirement life will be immensely improved if you give it a great deal of serious consideration.

What to do with their lives once they leave their primary careers poses more of a problem for people than it ever did. Several decades ago, Franklin D. Roosevelt created the old-age retirement system in the United States. The magic age he set was sixty-five. It was a safe bet that most people would never collect their pensions because the average life expectancy back then was sixty-two. Thus, people approaching retirement didn't spend much time trying to decide what they were going to do once their careers were over.

The only major problem with retirement is that it gives you more time to read about the problems of retirement. If you can avoid this trap, you have it made.

Times have changed. Life expectancy at birth in the United States is now seventy-three for men and seventy-nine for women. Moreover, people who have reached fifty-five can add about another ten years to these figures. Comparable figures apply to many Western nations. This means that if they retire at fifty-five, there is a good chance that retirees will have three or more decades of life ahead of them. How to make these thirty or more years productive and enjoyable is not necessarily an easy task.

Given that you may have thirty or more years of retirement life ahead of you, to not plan for an active retirement is to set yourself up for a difficult one. Failing to plan financially may result in your spending most of your retirement days thinking about all the fulfilling activities you aren't able to pursue due to a lack of funds. Failing to plan emotionally may result in your working hard for many years, amassing a lot of money, and then wasting away your "golden years" in boring leisure activities. A recent AIG SunAmerica survey found that those who had prepared for retirement, irrespective of their wealth or income, tended to be the most satisfied.

Material well-being, personal growth, and relationships with a partner and family and friends all should be considered when measuring quality of retirement life according to David Evans, a professor of clinical psychology at the University of Western Ontario, and Terry Lynn Gall, a professor in the Faculty of Human Sciences at Saint Paul University. In 2002, Evans and Gall assessed 109 men six or seven years after they retired. The men ranged in age from sixty-one to seventy-five. Some had been managers, others laborers. Evans and Gall found that missing friends from work, being bored, and having trouble adjusting to change adversely affected these retirees more than a lack of money or poor health.

Ideally, workers should start planning their retirement interests and activities several years before they actually retire. Yet many people who are forced into early retirement due to family responsibilities, health reasons, or corporate layoffs are totally unprepared. With no idea of how to spend their time, and no foundation for a new identity, some sink into deep depression. A few never recover and die within a year or two after leaving the workplace.

> Retirement at sixty-five is ridiculous. When I was sixty-five, I still had pimples.
>
> — George Burns

Although working longer and harder than other people may appear to be the way to a happy retirement, the opposite is true. A reduced work schedule so that you can develop many interests outside of work will pay dividends that are just as big — possibly a lot bigger — for your retirement as a larger mutual fund. What's the point of being monetarily rich in retirement if you don't involve yourself in interesting activities that provide you with a sense of fulfillment?

It's wise to start thinking about the personal side a long time before you actually retire, particularly if you are a workaholic with few interests outside of work. "The more your life revolves around work, the more of a shock retirement will be," states John Osborne, a retired educational psychology professor in Victoria, B.C., who teaches a course on how to be happily retired. "It's like having a portfolio that's not diversified, and it's not until your job is gone that you confront the reality. It can be like falling into space."

Breadth of interests is important. Retirement will feel empty if your interests aren't varied. While you are working, it's important to develop many eclectic interests outside of your career. Just one interest, such as golfing, will not be enough to fill your days. Ensure that you have a varied combination, from writing, to playing golf, to visiting friends, to taking a course unrelated to your job. As we will cover in greater detail in chapter 2, it's also important that you choose at least one major activity that provides some purpose and a sense of achievement.

A valuable exercise is to make a list of the ten favorite interests and activities that you would like to pursue in retirement. At the same time, write down how much time you are presently spending on these activities. Leisure consultants and pre-retirement planners state that if you are not spending any time pursuing these activities before retirement, it is unlikely that you will spend much time on these activities after you quit work.

Retirees must choose activities that are right for them. Something highly enjoyable to tens of millions of retirees may not even be moderately fulfilling to many others. Take golf, for example. John Wilson retired in 1999 at the age of fifty from being an insurance executive with Mutual of New York in Kansas City, Missouri. Playing a lot of golf certainly couldn't make him happy. He had this to say: "It is the most boring game in the world. I only played it because it was the corporate thing to do. I would have worked until sixty-five in a second if I knew that I had to play golf in retirement."

> Our plans miscarry because they have no aim. When a man does not know what harbor he is making for, no wind is the right wind.
>
> — Seneca

Early retirement wasn't all that enjoyable to Wilson because he missed the challenges his career provided. Surprisingly, he even missed something others see as a prime reason for giving up a job — a lot of stress. "That may sound like a stupid answer, but when people ask me what I miss the most, it's the stress of my old job," Wilson told a reporter in 2002. "When you have seventy people working for you and they're pulling at you all day long, and you're scrambling to meet deadlines, you think: 'I'm in charge; I can handle this.' Suddenly, nobody's hanging at your door anymore. And the only stress you have is the stress of being retired."

Instead of golf, running a ranch was more appropriate for Wilson since he was always an outdoor enthusiast, an able horseman, and, in his words, a cowboy at heart. After Wilson bought a ranch outside of Kansas City, he had to deal with the stresses of unpredictable weather, the fluctuating price of soybeans, and an unstable market for cattle. Nonetheless, this is exactly what he needed for a happy retirement. "Nobody would describe farming and ranching as a low-stress, low-risk business," he stated in 2002, "but I'm loving it."

Fortunately, like John Wilson, you too can turn retirement into a highly satisfying time of your life. To be solidly in the driver's seat, however, you should put as much time into planning retirement as you did into planning your career. Planning for retirement involves taking inventory of not only your finances, but also your skills, your health, your friends, your family, your marital status, your interests, and your dreams. You must design a retirement plan based on your personal situation and then implement it to the best of your ability.

Best of all, a realistic retirement plan can help you while you are still working, according to Ronald J. Manheimer, executive director of the North Carolina Center for Creative Retirement: "It may make retirement more attractive when you have a sense of what is on the other side. It can make your last days and months and years of work more enjoyable, knowing that you are working toward something you feel positive about."

You Are Never Too Young to Retire

Several Australian studies conclude that the best indicators of whether individuals will find retirement easy are their ability to cope financially, their satisfaction with life as a whole prior to retirement, and their ability to retire at the time preferred. In the event that you are still working, but looking forward to retirement, it's important to pay close attention to all three factors, particularly the last one.

> There are so many other interesting ways to spend your time. I feel like early retirement is a gift, but it's such an incredible gift. It's a gift I need to use.
>
> — Martha Felt-Bardon

Retiring at the right time is not always the easiest thing in the world to pull off. Even so, some people are able to retire much closer to the ideal time than others. In 1996, Dianne Nahirny retired from full-time employment so that she could escape from the hectic pace of the corporate world. Interestingly, the Hamilton, Ontario, resident was only thirty-six at the time. More interestingly, she had never made more than $20,000 a year.

Nahirny has neither inherited a fortune nor won a lottery nor capitalized big time on the stock market boom of the late 1990s. Nonetheless, she lives relatively well and has money in the bank. Occasionally, she takes a part-time job that allows her savings to grow. Presently, Nahirny writes a weekly personal finance column for the *Hamilton Spectator*, and recently she wrote a book called *Stop Working . . . Start Living.*

Although Nahirny had to forego some luxuries that a bigger and more regular paycheck can provide, she has no regrets. She spends her time reading, gardening, horseback riding, and pursuing any new interests that may arise. In 2002, six years after her retirement, Nahirny reflected upon her decision to retire at a relatively young age. "This is the best thing that I've ever done. I'm sorry I didn't do it sooner."

Like Nahirny, millions around the world dream of escaping the work world many years early. Increasingly large numbers of people in nations such as Australia, Canada, and the United States are able to do so. Although it is not uncommon to see people attempting retirement in their mid-thirties, early retirement is largely seen as something you do in your late forties or throughout the fifties.

In practice, reasons for why people retire at any particular age will reflect voluntary and involuntary circumstances and can be influenced by individual, family, and corporate factors. Some people retire early by choice; others are forced into it. Rising income levels, changes in government pensions, early retirement packages, corporate downsizing, and a declining retirement age are all contributors to early retirement. A person's own health or that of a partner can also play a part.

> Retirement means doing whatever I want to do. It means choice.
>
> — Dianne Nahirny

Of course, people who have employer-provided pension plans, particularly those in the public sector, are more likely to retire early. The reason is that many corporate pension plans have an early retirement provision whereby workers can collect their pension sooner rather than later. For a few workers with thirty or more years of service, retirement with a full pension at fifty or fifty-five is possible. It makes no sense to work full time for $60,000 a year when they can retire on a company pension that pays $40,000 a year. They would effectively be getting paid only $20,000 a year (or about $10 an hour) for continuing to work.

Notwithstanding that many people may still be working after they "retire," they still intend to leave their primary careers. My educated guess is that most of the people who intend to shift to more enjoyable work intend to do it on a part-time basis. The fact remains, millions of Americans and Canadians, like their counterparts in other Western nations, want to retire early. Although employers and governments may not relish so many early retirees, I believe this is good news. Simply put, people shouldn't be working in their primary careers if they long to do otherwise.

Perhaps after calculating your financial assets and potential retirement income, you have concluded that early retirement is an option for you right now. By opting for a simpler lifestyle like Dianne Nahirny has done, you can leave your present job at a reduced pension and get rid of your present line of work forever. Particularly if you feel — like Ian Hammond did — that working for your company is not that enjoyable anymore, you are never too young to retire. Indeed, as retiree Maurice Musholt stated, "The younger, the better."

Retiring Too Late Means You Don't Get Another Chance to Do It Right

Fear no more the heat o' th' sun,
Nor the furious winter's rages.
Thou thy worldly task hast done,
Home art gone and ta'en thy wages.
— William Shakespeare

Some people seriously contemplate retirement but have a hard time getting around to it. At seventy-seven, actor Paul Newman was one of these people. Newman had threatened to give up acting, race-car driving, political activism, and control of the Newman's Own food brand, whose proceeds go to charity. "I've been trying to quit almost everything I do for the last ten years and I've managed to quit absolutely nothing," stated Newman. "And unfortunately, I'm busier now than before."

> Few men of action have been able to make a graceful exit at the appropriate time.
>
> — Malcolm Muggeridge

Newman proclaimed that he had seriously considered retiring "because I felt entitled. A man my age should be resting, he should be lying down. He should be supine most of the day. But it just hasn't happened that way." No doubt there is nothing wrong with putting off retirement if you are having a great time in your job and enjoying many extracurricular activities like Paul Newman was at seventy-seven. It's another matter altogether if you are putting off retirement because you are trying to amass a million or two while working at a job you dislike. Clearly, the ideal time to retire should not be based solely on some huge nest egg you are hoping to acquire.

Allow me to share a story about a friend of mine. Gabriel was in his early sixties when I first met him. Frugal as could be, he still wanted to retire wealthy. The company for which Gabriel worked had a mandatory retirement age of sixty-five. By his early sixties, Gabriel had amassed a net worth of about $1 million, which included two rental properties and a nice retirement home in White Rock, B.C. However, Gabriel had convinced the company to hire him as a consultant so that he could continue working full-time for another three or four years beyond his official retirement day. His primary reason was that he wanted to acquire more wealth for his golden years.

After fifteen years at it, I hate this job with a passion!

Cheer up, Frank! Only eighteen more years of misery and you can experience pension heaven.

Sadly, a week and half after I last talked to him, Gabriel, a healthy and energetic sixty-five at the time, was killed in a car accident in Paris. The moral of this story is straightforward: Regardless of how much wealth you acquire, you never know if you are going to live long enough to enjoy it. Eventually retiring at seventy-five with $10 million in the bank won't do you much good if you die a month later.

So, when is the ideal time to retire? There is no ideal time to retire but you don't want to put it off longer than you have to. It's possible to be too optimistic with your retirement dreams about how much you intend to achieve once you eventually leave the workforce for good. Being overly optimistic makes them pipe dreams.

Perhaps you are like many people who plan to work well into their seventies or eighties, and then retire to ten or twenty years of enjoyable leisure activities. In this case, you have to allow for the fact that your health may not hold out long enough for you to keep working. In Australia, a third of men and a quarter of women gave their own or a partner's poor health as a reason for retirement.

Of course, ill health will also mitigate your ability to enjoy leisure activities when you leave the workforce. This does not make for a happy, wild, and free retirement. As American newscaster, correspondent, and journalist Charles Kuralt told *Time* magazine in 1994, "I would like to explore some side roads in life while I am still in good health and good spirits." (Unfortunately, Kuralt passed away in 1997.)

Regardless of where you live in the Western world, the following U.S. government statistics should give some indication of what your chances for optimum health are as you get older.

Percentage of Americans in Very Good or Excellent Health

51 to 59 years old	50 percent
60 to 69 years old	42 percent
70 to 79 years old	33 percent
80 to 89 years old	25 percent
90 years and older	26 percent

Health is not the only factor that may play a role in how much you may be able to enjoy your retirement. People who retire early have more time and energy to devote to finding out which interests and activities are challenging, satisfying, and enjoyable. They can make mistakes and still wind up with sufficient time to pursue the truly satisfying activities. Late retirees don't have this luxury.

Although some people may look upon early retirees as irresponsible slackers, especially at a time when workers are in short supply, these early retirees are in a position to make retirement a lot more productive. Younger retirees are generally not only healthier, but also much stronger than those who retire at a later age. This means early retirees like Ian Hammond can engage in more arduous activities, such as cycling across New Zealand — something that might be too difficult or impossible if they were to retire fifteen or twenty years later.

If you want to travel extensively in retirement, you should do so while you are still able to enjoy it. Travel requires a high degree of mental and physical energy. There is a significant difference between traveling when you are in your sixties and traveling when you are in your twenties. As you get older it's harder to adapt to the physical and emotional challenges of travel. Indeed, this is one of the reasons many people retire in their fifties and not in their sixties or seventies.

> It is seldom that an American retires from business to enjoy his fortune in comfort. He works because he has always worked, and knows no other way.
>
> — Thomas Nichols

Generally speaking, young retirees have more zeal and are more adaptable to life's big changes than older retirees. In other words, the younger you are when you retire, the better you will be able to adapt to such a big change in your life. In the event that you wait until you are eighty, you aren't likely to do much about the negative aspects of retirement. In all probability, you will spend most of your time in a rocking chair — watching TV and waiting to die.

Ultimately, it's best not to allow culturally grounded norms and values to shape your expectations and beliefs about the "right" time to retire. Think about all the things you have put on the

> What can a man do who doesn't know what to do?
>
> — Milton Mayer

back burner for so many years. Voluntary early retirement gives you a chance to pursue new areas of study, work part-time in an area that interests you, or move to a warmer climate. It's a great opportunity to pursue your goals and dreams while you are still young, energetic, and healthy enough to enjoy them. In addition, retirement may be your last shot at being the person you would like to be.

Let this be a warning to you: Retiring too early doesn't pose too serious a problem; you can always go back to full-time work and give retirement another go sometime later. On the other hand, retiring too late means you don't get another chance to do it right. Put another way, if you put it off too long, upon your retirement you may find out that the best time to pursue your dreams and enjoy life to the fullest was twenty years ago.

You Can Have Your Retirement Cake and Eat It Too

"Retirement can be the best job you've ever had," declares retiree George Fulmore, who teaches a five-session evening class called "The Art of Retirement" in the San Francisco Bay area. Fulmore claims that "there's no excuse not to like retirement." Mind you, he qualifies this statement by adding, "But it's not for everyone." In fact, Fulmore has had people in his class shout, "I'd go back to work in a minute if I could."

By no means are all individuals ready for full-time retirement even if they have been highly dissatisfied with their jobs and have sufficient financial resources to live without a paycheck. Retirement can become an early death sentence for those who end up watching TV most of the time. Even fishing all day on a favorite lake can get boring after a week or two. Indeed, many retirees, after six months of total leisure, have become so bored that they go back to full-time work.

A research study released in 2001 by Cornell University psychologists found that, particularly for men, employment after official retirement is beneficial for their psychological well-being. Those who retire from their primary career, but then find some sort of other work, are the happiest and suffer the least depression. On the other hand, men who retire and don't go back to work experience the most unhappiness and depression. Surprisingly, the researchers didn't find much difference for women who go back to work after retiring versus those who don't. No reasons were given for this important difference between the sexes.

Whether you yourself are ready to fully retire will be determined not only by how much money you have available, but also by your age, your health, how much you like colleagues at work, whether your spouse wants you to retire, how much you believe in the work ethic, and your attitude towards leisure. Deep down you should know whether, in fact, you are ready to leave the workplace for good. In case you have some doubts, following are some signs that may give you a clearer picture:

> A society that gives to one class all the opportunities for leisure, and to another all the burdens of work, dooms both classes to spiritual sterility.
>
> — Lewis Mumford

Strong Signs That You Aren't Ready for Full-Time Retirement

- ➤ You have been unhappy all your working life and have been waiting for retirement to make you happy.
- ➤ You have no nest egg because you have been expecting a big lottery win to fund your retirement dreams.
- ➤ Planning a vacation is more fun than taking it.
- ➤ Vacations have always taken a back seat to work commitments.
- ➤ You have no hobbies or other interests outside of work.
- ➤ Your best friends are people that you work with and that you don't like all that much.
- ➤ All of the social functions you attend are work related.

➤ The thought of spending a lot more time at home with your spouse makes you extremely anxious or dejected.

➤ Your spouse has always wanted you to get a life outside of work, but you haven't gotten around to it.

➤ You don't know the meaning of sabbatical, let alone having ever actually taken one.

➤ On weekends your spouse constantly complains about your getting into her or his hair.

➤ You persistently think of work, even when you aren't on the job.

➤ You are proud to be a workaholic even though you know workaholics aren't that productive.

In short, individuals without hobbies and other interests outside of work are poor candidates for full-time retirement. They have overidentified with their work roles for so long that they don't know who they are without them. Outside the mainstream of the workplace, they are sure to have an identity crisis that leaves them feeling lonely, lost, and dejected.

Based on his observations of people attending his course, George Fulmore believes that some retirees need at least three to five years to master "The Art of Retirement." Sadly, some people never do find happiness in full-time retirement. Without a doubt, workaholics are most likely to be the unhappiest individuals of those who take traditional retirement.

After some reflection, you may have concluded that you are willing to try retirement, but you still like the positive aspects of employment. Work has provided your biggest challenges and your greatest satisfaction over the years. In fact, work has become the basis of

> Leisure tends to corrupt, and absolute leisure corrupts absolutely.
> — Edgar A. Shoaff

your identity. It may not be an identity you want to give up. Even if you have been a ditchdigger with somewhat of a tenuous work identity, this identity will not be easy to give up — particularly if you don't have another one to adequately replace it with.

The workplace has also provided you with a structure and routine. Many people go from leading a lifestyle that is highly structured, moderately purposeful, and reasonably fulfilling to a lifestyle that has little structure, no purpose, and no fulfillment.

> There is no wisdom without leisure.
>
> — Jewish proverb

Unless you are able to create some new structure and routine through leisure pursuits, it won't be long before you are missing some of the workplace structure and routine that previously felt confining and boring.

The degree to which you are able to give up the positive aspects of work will determine whether you are prepared to retire cold turkey in the traditional sense of the word. Semi-retirement may be a better alternative. It's a way to have your cake and eat it too. You can have a freer lifestyle and still enjoy the positives of having a job. Here are several reasons why many of today's retirees opt for semi-retirement:

- They love their field of endeavor.
- They want to feel productive.
- They can't think of anything else to do.
- They like the companionship of like-minded colleagues.
- They like being around bright people.
- They like the social aspect of work.
- They love building and creating in a work environment.
- They want to get out of their spouse's hair.

Especially for self-employed individuals with a love for their work, being semi-retired is a way to continue their lifelong passion, whether it's writing books, painting pictures, or running a restaurant. Other individuals can give up their prime-time careers and retire into something else. They may move into self-employment, consulting, contract work, job-sharing, community service, or a combination of these.

For some people, the worst part about retirement is that their career expectations were never fulfilled. By remaining in the workforce, they can still strive for their dreams. Instead of hanging on to shattered dreams and unattained goals, semi-retirement allows them to pursue a new career with new challenges that may help them eventually realize some real accomplishment and satisfaction in the workplace.

Semi-retirement is a way to change gears from full- to part-time work, while at the same time gradually changing one's lifestyle. As indicated earlier, individuals who are busily involved in a wide variety of activities while employed full-time are well prepared to do well in retirement. People who haven't had the chance to develop a number of interests while in the workforce may look at semi-retirement as a way to prepare for full-time retirement by gradually introducing more and more leisure pursuits into their lives.

> Much work is merely a way to make money; much leisure is merely a way to spend it.
> — C. Wright Mills

Of course, the issue of finances is ever so important. Can the retiree afford to retire full-time or does she need part-time work to maintain a comfortable lifestyle? A Rutgers University study found that 76 percent of baby boomers want to retire before sixty, but only 29 percent think that they will have enough money. Semi-retirement will allow many of these workers to experience the benefits of early retirement with a much smaller nest egg because they have a supplementary income and are able to keep some of their company benefits.

A Major Dilemma: Life Is Short — and So Is Money

Clearly money has something to do with life
- In fact, they've a lot in common, if you enquire:
You can't put off being young until you retire.
— Philip Larkin, *Money*

A major dilemma faces many of us as we try to decide when is the best time to retire. It involves our finances. This dilemma is best summarized by the words of Bertolt Brecht: "Life is short, and so is money."

Everyone has decisions to make about money and what each is willing to sacrifice in the pursuit of it. Virtually all freedom-minded individuals have a magic number in mind that would allow them to retire early, move to that village in some laid-back country, and take it easy for the rest of their lives. To some, the monetary surplus is only $250,000; to others, $5 million is required to guarantee a full, relaxed, happy, and satisfying retirement lifestyle.

Ironically, too much of an emphasis on saving for retirement can undermine your chances of experiencing a happy retirement. Although virtually everyone needs a modest amount of money for essentials and a few luxuries from time to time, people who spend all their time and energy on building a huge nest egg often forget how to live happily in their working lives. They compromise their health, they neglect their friends, and they don't develop interests outside of work. Once they retire they realize that no amount of money can buy excellent health, great friends, or the ability to enjoy leisure activities. Sadly, they wind up even less happy in retirement than they were in their working lives.

No doubt the people with the best opportunity to fulfill their dreams in retirement will be the ones with the biggest nest eggs. Especially for those individualistic people who want to pursue expensive activities or hobbies, such as adventure travel or collecting African-American art, having a sizeable retirement fund is important. Having said this, not everyone wants to pursue expensive hobbies or live a lavish lifestyle.

Individuals looking forward to retirement must determine what sort of lifestyle will make them happy and how much money they will need to support it. They must then take steps to ensure that they will have enough money to support this lifestyle. An AIG SunAmerica study found that satisfaction is positively related to the number of years individuals save for retirement. More than 60 percent of those who saved for twenty-five years or more reported being extremely satisfied with their retirement. Just over half of those who saved for fifteen to twenty-four years were extremely satisfied, and only 46 percent of those who saved for less than fifteen years were extremely satisfied.

> Increased means and increased leisure are the two civilizers of man.
>
> — Benjamin Disraeli

Most financial planners today believe that retirees need to "replace" at least 80 percent of the income they made in their working years. Some financial planners even say that retirees need a higher income than they made in their careers. Indeed, in 2002, Washington-based benefits consultants Watson Wyatt Worldwide warned retirees that they may need to replace 105 percent of their working income if they hope to maintain their living standards.

It shouldn't take a genius to figure out that a rigid retirement replacement ratio — whether it's 80 percent or 105 percent — is irresponsible and misleading. If you earned $800,000 a year the last five years before you retired, surely you can get by on only 25 percent of this when you retire. On the other hand, if you earned only $5,000 a year before you retired, it may be a little difficult getting by on 150 percent of your pre-retirement income.

If these so-called financial experts were attentive enough to question the logic behind the 80 or 105 percent replacement ratio, they would see how ludicrous it really is. To be sure, if you want to live in Monte Carlo, go to five-star restaurants every night, and fly to Aspen to ski several times each winter, you will need not only a million, but five or ten million. The fact is, even most millionaires, let alone the middle class, don't want to live in this style. Most middle-class people will be content to live as well in retirement as in their working years — many will even be content to live at a lower standard of living.

To be fair, not all "experts" are hung up on a high replacement ratio for retirement income. "It's staggeringly stupid advice in Canada and bad in the U.S. as well," stated actuary Malcolm Hamilton in response to the Watson Wyatt Worldwide study and the 105 percent replacement ratio. Hamilton has adopted a position that retirees need replace only 40 percent to 60 percent of their working income. "I see no great inherent merit in a system that tells people to live at a low standard of living while working so they can be rich in retirement. And that's what a 105 percent target accomplishes," said Hamilton, who works for Mercer Human Resource Consulting in Toronto.

It wasn't until after I worked hard for thirty-five years and retired with $10 million to my name that I realized that money doesn't buy happiness. What can I do now to make me happy, Doc?

How the heck should I know? Get out of here, you freak. You're depressing me!

There are other financial experts who agree with Hamilton. "One of the faults of the financial planning field has been that we keep saying you need $1 million to retire," says William Gustafson, professor of family financial planning at Texas Tech University. Another expert was even more vociferous about this matter. "I get so furious with that," American financial planner Nancy Langdon Jones recently told a *USA TODAY* reporter. "There is no formula that will fit everyone."

Statistics Canada has found that, in practice, most Canadians retire on 62 percent or less of their working income. Not surprisingly, the percentage falls as incomes rise — it's just 45 percent for those making more than $70,000 a year. Here are eight good reasons why the large majority of retirees, whether they live in Canada, the United States, or other Western nations, can live on far less than 80 percent of their pre-retirement income:

- ➤ Most retirees have their homes paid off and no longer have to pay a mortgage.
- ➤ Retirees no longer have the expenses associated with employment such as daily commuting and the need to purchase clothing suitable for a work environment.
- ➤ Because their income is lower, and they wind up in a lower tax bracket, retirees pay much lower taxes than they did when they were working.
- ➤ Retirees can move to a new location where the cost of living is lower.
- ➤ Retirees' children are grown up so they don't have to pay for their education anymore.
- ➤ Retirees can get seniors' discounts on practically everything they buy.
- ➤ Retirees don't have to earn extra income to set aside for retirement savings.
- ➤ In their later years, most people are not as insecure and ostentatious as they used to be; thus, they don't need material goods to validate themselves in the eyes of others.

> You can be young without money but you can't be old without it.
>
> — Tennessee Williams

The importance of these factors shouldn't be underestimated. *MoneySense* Magazine concluded that tens of thousands of middle-class couples will see their standard of living increase dramatically, despite having their overall income decline. Surprisingly, even with only 50 percent or less of their previous income, most middle-class couples will be able to live in greater style and comfort in retirement than they have ever lived before.

Take, for example, Ronnie Sawdonik and his wife Patricia Robinson. When both were working as schoolteachers in Calgary,

Alberta, their combined income was $128,000. Now that they have retired to Nanaimo, B.C., they live extremely well on only $47,000 a year. "And we're not skimping," according to Patricia. Ronnie and Patricia own two cars, are able to travel, and have no problem purchasing season tickets to the theater and symphony.

Notwithstanding the AIG SunAmerica study cited earlier, which found that satisfaction is positively related to the number of years one saves for retirement, Michelle O'Neill, vice president for strategic consulting at the Harris Poll organization that conducted the survey, declared, "The happiness of people in these categories was not necessarily linked to how much money they had made or had. Rather, happiness was linked with feeling financially prepared for whatever retirement lifestyle they wanted."

The point is, many people can have a happy, wild, and free retirement with a modest amount of money to their names. To put money in proper perspective regarding how much it counts towards a happy retirement, allow me to cite another retired individual who wrote to me. Here is the letter that Robert Radford sent to me from Ta Ta Creek, B.C.:

> The key to a happy retirement is to have enough money to live on, but not enough to worry about.
>
> — Unknown wise person

Dear Ernie;

I just finished absorbing your book, "The Joy of Not Working," a few pages at a time, over the past two months, having renewed the book twice at the Kimberly Public Library. Thank you for supporting Barbara's and my belief that our way of life is a lot more "successful" than many of our friends, relatives and acquaintances, who think we are nuts, would have us believe. Thank you, also, for putting into perspective some outlooks on money, a commodity which we never seem to have enough of but which neither Barbara nor I can bother worrying about.

I am 67 years old, Barbara is 56, we have 16-year-old twins (Sarah and Joshua), none of us has a job and we just moved from Ontario to Ta Ta Creek in November 1997. We are living in a solid log house, without furniture, in the trees on the western side of the Rocky Mountain Trench, eking out rent, utilities and food from four small pensions which I have managed to accumulate over a diverse career, and are thoroughly enjoying the fresh air, marvelous scenery, different animal species and wonderful people in this part of the world. I am a volunteer pianist with the Valley Community Church in Wasa, Barbara is a volunteer with the Crisis Line in Cranbrook, Josh is a volunteer producer with the Kootenay Cable TV, and Sarah has her art for sale in Marysville. I am currently working to get some significant reforms in the Canadian parliamentary system, Barbara is working to self-publish a book which I wrote many years ago, Josh is working to create special computer graphics for TV lead-ins and Sarah is working to establish an animal shelter.

Your book verbalized and organized many of the life-style factors which we have exemplified in our own lives and it was reassuring to get a positive evaluation of these factors from an impartial source. I had two brothers who deplored the instability and irresponsibility of my chosen lifestyles. One was very wealthy, with an unhappy family, who was old at 45 and also eventually died of cancer. I, too, as an electrical engineer was financially comfortable with an unhappy family. But when my wife and four children left me, I found Barbara and a way of life which led me into financial bankruptcy and a happiness and satisfaction which I had not been aware was available to me. Your book pointed out ways for us to now add financial independence to our lifestyles.

If there is any way in which you think we might be able to contribute to the valuable work you are doing in our society, please do not hesitate to get in touch with us.

Sincerely,

Robert Radford

> The day, water, sun, moon, night . . . I do not have to purchase these things with money.
> — Titus Maccius Plautus

Most financial advisors paint a picture of a penniless and destitute retirement for those with less than a million or two in their retirement portfolios. They emphasize higher earnings instead of lower spending as the key to having money to retire. Obviously, Robert Radford and his family don't have a lot of funds. They are, nevertheless, remarkably active and happy. The way I see it, Robert Radford has retired happy, wild, and free, much like Ian Hammond of Scotland.

Retirement planners who tell us that we need large retirement incomes to be happy should pay more attention to genuine, interesting individuals such as Ian Hammond and Robert Radford. These experts would learn a lot about what truly contributes to a happy retirement. To repeat, a successful retirement encompasses not only adequate financial resources, but also all other aspects of life — purpose, family, friends, interesting leisure activities, creative pursuits, and mental, physical, and spiritual health.

> I'd like to live like a poor man with lots of money.
> — Pablo Picasso

Of course, if you are a shallow person who believes that you need the latest SUV, a large house, and the latest fashions to overcome low self-esteem and be happy, you will require a great deal of money for your retirement years. Just be clear, however, that you won't attain true happiness, nor peace of mind, this way — just as you haven't all your working years. You will continue to fool yourself on the surface, knowing deep down that there is an emotional and spiritual void within you that can never be filled, regardless of how much money you acquire.

When it comes to having sufficient money for retirement, everyone is on a different page. Some people need a million or two to retire in lavish comfort and style. Others need a few hundred thousand to lead a modest lifestyle. Still others have few needs and wants and can retire in their mid-thirties with relatively little money.

All things considered, it's up to you, and not anyone else, to decide when you are financially ready. In the event that you don't like working very much, and would like to retire as early as possible, heed the words of Robert Benchley, who put it much more eloquently than I ever could: "The thing to do is to make so much money that you don't have to work after the age of twenty-seven. In case this is impractical, stop working at the earliest moment, even if it is a quarter past eleven in the morning of the day when you find you have enough money."

If Deep Down You Know You Are Ready, "Just Do It!"

We start early in the morning,
And work until we have to go to bed.
If this is all there is to living,
We would all rather be dead.
— Workplace Graffiti

Today, many people at a relatively young age are fleeing full-time work to live a lifestyle of their own choosing. You too may be able to realize the dream of a happy and productive retirement long before the typical retirement age of sixty-five. You don't want to retire so early that you outlast your money, but then again, you don't want to retire so late that your health doesn't allow for a happy retirement. Should it be the case that you are financially ready, you must still decide if you are mentally ready.

> Liberty is being free from the things we don't like in order to be slaves of the things we do like.
>
> — Ernest Benn

You have to know yourself well to make the right decision. Take your time. The key is to use a rational decision-making process that gives consideration to your health, your finances, your dreams, your family situation, and your present-day well-being. Here are four steps of one decision-making model you may want to use:

1. Write down all the pros and cons of retirement. Look for hidden disadvantages. It's all too easy to focus only on the advantages.

2. Decide whether the pros outweigh the cons. What net benefits do you receive by retiring? What benefits do you lose that may turn out to be far more important than meets the eye?

3. Find objective assistance from not only your spouse but also from friends and professionals. These people will be able to support you in your decision to retire; alternatively, they can ask insightful questions to make sure you aren't making the biggest mistake in your life.

4. Make the decision. If the pros win out over the cons, it's time to go. As the Nike ad says, "Just do it!" If things don't work out, it's not the end of the world. You can find another job, possibly better than the one you have now.

I notice that only one employee out of 200 in this company ever smiles while at work.

She's taking early retirement next month.

To be sure, it takes courage to retire early, particularly if you don't have to. Ian Hammond, mentioned earlier, showed great courage to give up a high-paying job and retire at a time in his life when most people would be afraid to retire.

You may be wondering how Ian made out. Ian, in fact, let me know what he was up to in June 2001 after I had written to him for permission to use his letters in this book.

Dear Ernie,

I have been biking Australia for seven months and only opened your letter this week whilst visiting my dad, who had kept my redirected mail. Of course you may use my letters; if they help to get your point across they will have served a useful purpose.

Australia isn't a "pretty" country, but it was a good experience, especially freecamping in the bush, meeting characters in the outback, and seeing landscapes in the National Parks which were unique not only to the world but in many cases to one part of Australia. There wasn't much in the way of history and most places were pretty nondescript, but the museums and galleries, particularly in the capital cities, were superb. If I ever return (there are a lot of places to see) I'll bike a smaller region in more detail to avoid the long, flat, straight, boring roads between nowhere and nowhere. At least I saw two friends at the start and end who had emigrated and then married and who I was not likely to see otherwise.

As a postscript to my letters, the company I used to work

for has now become a bigger company worth £110 billion with 100,000 employees worldwide in 150 countries. Unfortunately, the manufacturing/R&D site in Montrose doesn't figure in this latest example of multinational mergers, so it is to be sold with half the workforce being sacked. I'm glad I've had a three-year head start on this half and that at least I retired on my own terms with good feelings on both sides.

Best wishes for your future (which you don't need),

Ian

In case you have decided to opt for early retirement, semi-retirement, or traditional retirement after reading this chapter, congratulations. You are on track to becoming a different person, living a new way of life. It's important to do everything within your power so that you can enjoy a retirement filled with vitality and joy.

There are four fundamentals for attaining personal fulfillment during retirement:

1. Finding who you truly are and being this person

2. Recreating your life through personal interests and creative pursuits, possibly through a new, part-time career

3. Making optimum use of your extra leisure time

4. Maintaining physical, mental, and spiritual well-being

Despite these challenges, most people make a successful transition to semi- or full-time retirement and couldn't even faintly imagine going back to work full time. If you are definitely sure that a flexible lifestyle is what you want more than anything, and you can handle the freedom and risk that comes with it, then retirement should be no major problem to you. In fact, it should be a breeze compared to full-time employment.

> Work is what you do so that sometime you won't have to do it anymore.
>
> — Alfred Polgar

2

Retirement: A Time to Become Much More than You Have Ever Been

Retirement Can Set You Free

An elegant sufficiency, content,
Retirement, rural quiet, friendship, books,
Ease and alternate labor, useful life,
Progressive virtue, and approving Heaven!
— James Thomson

Upon retiring as Secretary General of the United Nations, Peruvian diplomat Javier Pérez de Cuéllar remarked, "I am a free man. I feel as light as a feather." As a matter of course retirement can set you free, or, like work, it can imprison you. Ultimately, it's up to you.

Being retired gives you the freedom to do what you want, when you want, and with whom you want. Part of the equation for handling all this freedom is your ability to be creative and to become a highly independent person, if you aren't one already. You must have

> It is often safer to be in chains than to be free.
> — Franz Kafka

interests and a purpose that are your own. It is a mistake to rely on your spouse's interests and purpose — or anyone else's for that matter — to give you meaning and fulfillment in retirement.

Perhaps you see retirement as the last opportunity for a full, relaxed, satisfying, and happy life. To end up successfully retired, however, you must have sufficient confidence in your own ability

37

> When people are free to do as they please, they usually imitate each other.
>
> — Eric Hoffer

to live life without any interference or guidance from someone else. Freedom is not always as easy as it appears. Saul Alinsky warned us, "The greatest enemy of individual freedom is the individual himself."

Once most people attain it, freedom is no longer the panacea it's made out to be. In fact, freedom becomes wasted opportunity. Lord John Boyd Orr articulated this point much more eloquently than I ever could with his classic statement: "If people have to choose between freedom and sandwiches, they will take sandwiches."

Surprisingly, even highly intelligent and abundantly skilled people have a difficult time making the transition to retirement and the personal freedom that they gain with it. Retirement responsibilities are fundamentally different from those experienced when working for an organization or corporation. Thus, individuals who have had someone else plan a major portion of their waking hours are at a loss when there is no one else there to do it for them.

"Even people who plan carefully for retirement cannot fully anticipate the actual experience because it's not just the end of employment," states John Osborne, a retired psychology professor in Victoria, B.C., who now teaches a course on how to be happily retired. "It's the loss of a life structure that has been central to a person's existence."

The first few months of retirement can be difficult particularly for people who didn't have an excellent work/life balance in their careers. Suddenly all those hours that used to be taken up by work are open for leisure activity. For some people, this is a frightening and challenging situation. Getting used to freedom and having to make their own decisions on what sort of activities to pursue can tax uncreative minds. For that matter, it can even tax a few creative ones.

The true sense of freedom that comes with retirement is best experienced by the self-reliant individuals of this world. People who fit this profile are adventurous and willing to take risks. Because long ago they chose to live their own lives with minimal interference from others, they experienced at least some measure of freedom in their working lives. Being independent thinkers, they are aware of the possibilities for how to enjoy life that most working people are too busy or too ignorant to spot.

Soul-searching is one of the keys to retiring happy, wild, and free. Retirement forces you to rethink who you are, what your interests are, and what your priorities are. More leisure time is an important aspect of quality of life, but so are freedom, creative pursuits, fun jobs, and enhanced health from not having to work at a stressful job. Retirement can provide you with this higher quality of life.

> Freedom is always and exclusively freedom for the one who thinks differently.
>
> — Rosa Luxemburg

Above all, retirement gives you the freedom to find your real self; it provides many opportunities for a new lease on life. Pursuing intellectual, creative, or spiritual goals is the road to personal renewal and renewed energy. Indeed, many people have spent practically all their waking hours for several decades working at their jobs, not knowing who they really were. Much to their surprise, after they retired, they discovered their true selves and what they really wanted to do with their lives.

"It's never too late," concluded George Eliot, "to be what you might have been." In this regard, retirement gives you the time and freedom to become more than you have ever been. In fact, it may be your last shot to become the type of person you have always wanted to become. Why not take advantage of it?

To Have No Aptitude for Leisure Is to Have No Aptitude for Life

> *Life is mostly froth and bubble.*
> *Two things stand like stone:*
> *Dodging duty at the double,*
> *Leaving work alone.*
> — Unknown wise person

For better or worse, there are few rules to guide you when you retire. This luxury of being able to do things at your own pace should be treasured and not ignored. Provided you are creative — a talent everyone can develop — you can discover outlets for self-expression that are more exciting and fulfilling than any of your past work-related challenges and accomplishments ever were.

The degree to which you can handle leisure will determine the overall quality of your retirement. Indeed, lots of leisure time is good for you provided that you indulge yourself in challenging and productive activities. "Leisure consists in all those virtuous activities by which a man grows morally, intellectually, and spiritually," declared Marcus Tullius Cicero, the great Roman statesman, orator, and philosopher. "It is that which makes a life worth living."

Plato and Socrates, two early Greek philosophers, also sang the praises of being leisurely in a productive way — that is, taking as much time as possible away from working life to self-actualize and grow as a human being. In spite of the fact that in today's workaholic world Plato and Socrates would be arrested for vagrancy, their philosophy merits serious consideration.

> They intoxicate themselves with work so they won't see how they really are.
>
> — Aldous Huxley

As Plato and Socrates pointed out, work is often an escape from freedom. Work, for the uncreative, is an easy and acceptable way to fill in a good portion of their lives which they couldn't do on their own. Learning to be productive with one's free time takes initiative and creativity — two things most people haven't developed.

One of the great advantages of retirement is that you are free of the pressures you had to face at work. You don't have to accomplish as many things as possible to impress the boss and achieve a higher raise. You are free of the deadlines, and free of the performance measures, that corporations impose on workers. Best of all, you are free from the need to continually achieve.

Unfortunately, giving up the need to achieve may not be as easy as it appears. After many years in the workforce, it's common for people — especially workaholics — to have become so engrossed in work that they aren't able to function without it. Not only are they unable to deal with the lack of work routines, they also have a hard time functioning without the sense of achievement — false as it may be — that comes from being involved in work.

According to researchers, the transition from work to retirement can seriously affect one in five individuals, leaving them in a state of mild to severe depression. Marilyn J. Sorenson, a clinical psychologist and author of *Breaking the Chain of Low Self-Esteem*, claims that low self-esteem is often the cause of post-retirement depression. "Many people with low self-esteem become overachievers," she says. "Driven to prove their adequacy, they throw themselves into their work."

Not surprisingly, in our workaholic world, some experts suggest that it's better for achievement-oriented individuals to work long and hard hours well into their seventies or eighties than to choose the alternative of retirement or semi-retirement. Ohio State University business professor Marcia Miceli claims, "It may be more beneficial to help achievement-oriented workaholics find ways to spend time doing what they enjoy — working." This sounds like a good solution on the surface; unfortunately, it may not be in the long-term interests of achievement-oriented individuals. This defensive, delusive, and dangerous practice can lead to failure and disillusionment.

In this regard, Richard Ryan, a researcher and professor of psychology at the University of Rochester in New York, has verified what wise people have been saying for centuries: The endless pursuit of status, power, wealth, and fame by achievement-oriented individuals begins and ends in unhappiness. According to Ryan, this is true whether the pursuit takes place in Russia or North America. In a lecture titled *Be Careful What You Wish For*, Ryan admitted that he was actually surprised by the results of his own research because he had expected achievement-oriented individuals to fare better on the happiness scale than they did.

> Leisure is the most challenging responsibility a man can be offered.
>
> — Dr. William Russell

Professor Ryan claims that his research conclusively shows that people driven by wealth, status, fame, or power — known as extrinsic goals — are generally dissatisfied with their lives. Worse, they are much more prone to a variety of psychological disorders. In fact, people who chase extrinsic goals are insecure and obsessed with how they measure up to others. "I think the issue of why people compare themselves to others comes back to needing to feel worthy," states Ryan.

The problem is that achievement-oriented individuals never feel worthy regardless of how much time they spend working. They keep on pursuing more and more money, fame, status, and power, hoping one day to acquire enough to make them happy. In an attempt to get ahead of others, they work harder, better, and longer. Even with $10 million in the bank, they will put off retirement indefinitely in a prolonged quest to prove their worthiness and achieve at least some measure of happiness.

Obviously, this lifestyle is not conducive to true satisfaction and a sense of well-being. Professor Ryan's research indicates that loving relationships, personal growth, and involvement in the community are the elements that can make an insecure person feel worthy. These elements will also ultimately provide satisfaction, contentment, and peace of mind — true happiness, in other words. "One summary of this," remarks Ryan, "is that the best things in life do remain free. But we're being told that's not the case and it's an easy cultural myth to buy."

In the event that you have been an achievement-oriented person all your working life, it behooves you to pay some attention to Professor Ryan's findings. Sure, you can go into denial, discount what he says, and keep on working in an attempt to prove your worthiness and find some happiness in the process. The million-dollar question is: Do you just want to get by in life, or do you want to become the person who you can be? There's a big difference.

> The best intelligence test is what we do with our leisure.
>
> — Laurence J. Peter

This is the time to revisit the classic saying: "Doing the same thing over and over again and expecting your life to change is a good definition of crazy." Given that as an achievement-oriented individual you stand virtually no chance of experiencing true satisfaction and happiness some time down the road, why remain on the same road? The truth is that you weren't born a high achiever. You allowed yourself to become one by not paying enough attention to the truly satisfying elements in life.

It's time to rid yourself of the values and moral virtues of hard work. You must get the work ethic out of your system and replace it with the enjoyment ethic. To the surprise of most workaholics, the Old Testament (Apocrypha. Ecclesiasticus 38:25) tells us, "The wisdom of a learned man cometh by opportunity of leisure: and he that hath little business shall become wise." This is not to say that work is bad for you. Later I encourage you to work part-time, but mainly for the enjoyment of work and not because it is more virtuous to be working than to have a life of leisure.

Unfortunately, the work ethic can be a powerful force that prevents some people from enjoying retirement. The freedom and the opportunity of leisure often bring on guilt feelings. This happened to James Paul Bauman of Oliver, B.C., who recently wrote to me. Bauman gives us a few hints on how to deal with this problem.

Dear Ernie,

I recently read your book *The Joy of Not Working.* I am very grateful for its message. Spirit sent it my way when I needed to learn its lesson. It gave me timely spiritual release. Thank you for writing it.

I'd long been laboring under some residual guilt feelings regarding my chosen lifestyle. I moved to a very simple life after I got separated several years ago. I wanted to have time to do all the things I'd rather do with my life, such as writing. As a result, I have been very fulfilled writing several books on economic freedom.

One big advantage of having chosen vagrancy as an occupation is that I have become very good at leisure. This makes me much better prepared for retirement than you guys will ever be.

While I passionately love and believe in the simple, quiet life I lead, and have thrown off much of the guilt that came attendant with living radically differently from everyone else around me, and having so much free time to enjoy, I nevertheless retained an uneasy guilty feeling that I must work long hours, for no better reason than to excuse this lifestyle. I even avoided going into my local town during normal working hours, lest I appear as a "welfare bum." Silly, yes, but it's not always easy to go against years of social ingrainment.

On my spiritual path I am learning to accept myself wholly. The need for freedom in all aspects of my life has led to a natural way of being which has often met with disapproval from others, and sometimes niggling residual fears and guilt of my own. But I've been overcoming these. The self-validation I've been receiving, including that which I've found in your book, has been overwhelming. Thank you!

Gratefully yours,

Jim

Jim Bauman's story shows that in spite of some guilt that may arise, a lot more leisure and freedom can place your life on the happiness track. You can become a different person living a new way of life. The good news is that people who change their ways by spending more time on interesting leisure activities — by themselves, with their spouse, with children and grandchildren, and with quality friends — end up feeling worthy and no longer need to zealously pursue extrinsic goals.

What Plato and Socrates were effectively telling us was that to have no aptitude for leisure is to have no aptitude for life. Regardless of whether you choose semi- or full-time retirement, you can reap many benefits from learning how to enjoy plenty of leisure time to the fullest. It is worthwhile to summarize the many benefits retirees get from more leisure time:

> - It's much easier to be spontaneous.
> - There is more opportunity for personal growth.
> - There is more time and opportunity to develop friendships outside the workplace.
> - People's health improves due to increased physical activity.
> - Higher self-esteem can be developed from pursuing fulfilling creative pursuits.
> - People experience less stress and a more relaxed lifestyle.
> - A great deal of satisfaction can be attained from being involved in challenging activities.
> - There is much more opportunity to create a variety of excitement and adventure.
> - A sense of high self-worth results from handling freedom.
> - An increase in the overall quality of family life is likely.
> - For those who have hated their careers, a bad day on the golf course will always feel better than what used to be deemed a good day at the office.

> If the soul has food for study and learning, nothing is more delightful than an old age of leisure.
>
> — Marcus Tullius Cicero

In your search for happiness in this world, don't ever underestimate the value of increased leisure that retirement brings with it. Abundant leisure is one of life's great treasures. Thus, the words of William Lyon Phelps: "Those who decide to use leisure as a means of mental development, who love good music, good books, good pictures, good plays, good company, good conversation — what are they? They are the happiest people in the world."

Create a New Identity
Because Your Old One Won't Do

Retired is being tired twice,
I've thought,
First of working,
Then tired to not.
— Richard Armour

As already emphasized, retirement allows you the freedom to be the person that you have always wanted to be. Paradoxically, you may not know any longer who it is that you exactly want to be. Work may have chipped away at your true identity until there is only an identity associated with the work world. This will have suppressed all the other wonderful aspects of your true self.

> It is always the same: once you are liberated, you are forced to ask who you are.
> — Jean Baudrillard

To ensure that you make the most of retirement, it's worthwhile to check whether your identity needs a little enhancement. How you eventually define yourself during retirement will likely be much different than how you define yourself during your work life. Not surprisingly, people whose work lives have centered around their jobs will experience the greatest change in identity while making the transition to retirement.

Most people hardly know how much they are defined by their jobs until they give them up. The late Italian-Jewish writer and chemist Primo Levi observed, "The bond between a man and his profession is similar to that which ties him to his country; it is just as complex, often ambivalent, and in general it is understood completely only when it is broken . . . by retirement in the case of a trade or profession."

Many retirees find it extremely difficult to accept that they no longer are "productive" in the traditional sense of the word. So much of their identity has been tied to their work activities and being productive that retirement represents major losses — of power, status, and self-worth. An identity that doesn't have work as its foundation isn't something that they can accept easily. Sadly, to them being free of the corporate grind is a major catastrophe instead of an opportunity to expand their limited identity.

> Identity is a bag and a gag.
> Yet it exists for me with all
> the force of a fatal disease.
>
> — Judith Rossner

Unfortunately, we live in a culture where "What do you do?" and "How much money do you make?" are more important than who we truly are. The root of this problem is that in industrialized nations, such as the United States, Germany, Spain, Canada, and Japan, we have allowed ourselves to be conditioned by society, corporations, and educational institutions to believe that visible work equals visible dignity. Most of us strongly believe that we are supposed to be working continually through our adult lives, if for no other reason than to fill the hours between 8:00 A.M. and 5:00 P.M. with some structured activity.

Working at something that is extremely boring — even if the activity has absolutely no purpose to it — is seen to be much more noble and productive than taking it easy and enjoying one's life. How sad indeed! Ironically, this happens in societies that consider themselves the most intelligent and advanced ever.

Job functions and titles shape not only how people spend a good portion of their time, but also how they are regarded by others and themselves. To lose work as part of their identity is not a problem for people who have developed a well-balanced life that includes many foundations other than work; it is a serious problem, however, for people who define themselves primarily through their jobs.

Preposterous as it may seem, the work world constitutes a tragic case of many mistaken identities. The identity problem is so pronounced that Barbara Udell, Director of Lifestyle Education at the Florida Pritkin Longevity Center, states, "Many professionals miss their personal career space and some have been known to rent office space after they have retired to maintain their routine and sense of importance. They'll tell their friends, 'Call me at the office,' just so they have a place to go."

Career identities keep people in bondage because these identities hide their true selves. People weren't born into this world as doctors, lawyers, teachers, or laborers. These are things

Frank, you've been given an early retirement. Don't look at this as being fired or laid off, however. Think of it as a great opportunity to recover all your authentic traits — and your heart and soul — that you lost while working here!

that they decided to become to earn a livelihood. Of course, some of the higher status careers may have also been chosen for their prestige quotient to give individuals a "better" identity.

After several years in the workforce, workers let their careers become their whole identities instead of just a minute part of much more comprehensive and wholesome identities. Barbara Udell adds, "For most of us, who we are, is based on what we do. If we become too dependent on this mind-set and our job ends, we lose our sense of identity. So before, or soon after retirement, we need to redefine who we are in a positive and meaningful way. Recycle yourself."

To redefine and recycle yourself in retirement, you must challenge and change certain assumptions about yourself, including how much you need to have a work identity in order to be a complete person. The point is, if you got by without a work identity for the first eighteen or twenty years of your life, you can certainly get by without one for another twenty years — or for however long you live after you retire. Thinking that you need a career identity to be a whole person is to deny yourself happiness and peace of mind.

What you have to accept is that your work identity is a distorted self-image of how the rest of the world, and you, look at yourself. This identity or self-image is not the real you. It has covered up your true identity for so long that it has obscured your authentic self. Your authentic identity transcends this work identity, resulting from or forged by influences that your mind should have filtered out a long time ago.

> An identity is questioned only when it is menaced, as when the mighty begin to fall, or when the wretched begin to rise, or when the stranger enters the gates, never, thereafter, to be a stranger.
>
> — James Baldwin

Ekhart Tolle advises in *The Power of Now*, "The mind is a superb instrument if used rightly. Used wrongly, however, it becomes very destructive." Your mind has been destructive indeed if it has created a false identity that is solely associated with your career or job. This identity is false because it is nothing more than a fiction of the mind. Your mind has had a destructive effect on your true self because it thinks that your career encompasses all of you. Sadly, when you retire, there is nothing left for your mind to identify with. To your mind, you are nothing.

You must transcend your own mind and societal thinking to discover and get in touch with your true identity — or "essence" as some spiritual leaders call it. In fact, getting in touch with your essence allows you to get closer to that state some people call enlightenment. When you are able to do this on a daily basis, you will no longer need a job or career to define who you are. You will experience much more peace of mind and happiness — with or without a job.

> Work with some men is as besetting a sin as idleness.
>
> — Samuel Butler

Luckily, you amount to a thousand times more than the sum of your work and always have. You just haven't realized it because practically everyone else in society is going through life thinking that they are their work. To get a better idea of your true identity, first ask yourself what sort of person you would want to be if work was totally abolished in this world. Write this down. Also record your five best traits. These traits can't have anything to do with work — such as ambitious, well-organized, or hard working.

After you have written down what you would want to be in a non-work world and listed your five best traits, you will have a better idea of who you really are. You should realize that your essence is the feeling of being whole and has nothing to do with what you did or did not do for a living. All things that truly matter to human beings are not based on any superficial identity — work-related or otherwise. Your true self is based on the experience of being human, and the joy and peace of mind that accompany the experience of being human.

The truth is that your essence encompasses much more than your work and always has. Being in touch with your deeper self reveals that a career by itself doesn't make you a whole person; neither do possessions, status, power, or net worth. Your true self is based on more profound things, such as your creativity, kindness, passionate pursuits, generosity, love, joy, spontaneity, connectedness to others, sense of humor, peace of mind, inner happiness, and spirituality. A new, healthy identity based on these traits will make retirement a joy to experience.

Think about it. Retirement is the time to live your life in the manner you have dreamed of living. It is the time to get in touch with your inner life. It is the time to reflect upon your values and discover what is important to you. Above all, it is the time when you have more time to devote to yourself, to do what you want to do.

Given all the opportunity that retirement offers for you to be your true self and become much more than you have ever been, there is no need to hang on to a work identity that will limit you. Perhaps to make up for the loss of a job title, you will still want a new name or title to express to others what you do in life. Of course, you don't want your title to simply say "Retiree." One dictionary defines a retiree as "one who has retired from active working life." You want your new title to reflect a much more wholesome and expansive you.

Have some fun with this. You can tell people that you are a "Connoisseur of Leisure." This is what I have done during my many years of unemployment and semi-retirement. I even had a T-shirt made up with Connoisseur of Leisure written on it. Telling people that you are a Connoisseur of Leisure will likely result in their asking you why you aren't working. Just declare that you are too prosperous — more so mentally than financially — to work at a full-time job.

> The real meditation is . . . the meditation on one's identity. Ah, voilà une chose! You try it. You try finding out why you're you and not somebody else. And who in the blazes are you anyhow? Ah, voilà une chose!
>
> — Ezra Pound

If Connoisseur of Leisure doesn't suit you because you intend to work part-time, try being a "Connoisseur of Life." As a Connoisseur of Life, you can tell people that you only work when you want to, and only on projects that make an important difference in this world. "I do work on special and interesting projects, but only at my leisure" is a good response to someone's question "Don't you work?"

If you believe in the power of affirmations, here is one that you can recite every morning to help you get your former work identity out of your system:

Affirmation for the Connoisseur of Life

I am now a Connoisseur of Life. I am too prosperous to work long and hard hours. I have earned my prosperity and deserve the right to enjoy a creative and satisfying lifestyle. I am too spiritually evolved to have an identity based on my work, possessions, and net worth.
Instead, my identity is based on more profound things, including my creativity, my generosity, my spontaneity, my sense of humor, my peace of mind, my passion for new experiences, my happiness, and my spirituality.

There is one more thing that you can do to help yourself make the transition from being a working person to one who is retired.

Have some new business cards — "personal life cards" is probably a better term — made with your name, phone number, and address. You can add a descriptive tag such as Connoisseur of Life; New Age Aristocrat; Chartered Member of the Happy, Wild, and Free; or President of the Too Prosperous to Work Society. When you introduce yourself to people, your card will project a healthy identity — and an inspirational one at that.

> Be what you is, not what you ain't, 'cause if you ain't what you is, you is what you ain't.
>
> — Luther D. Price

Again, retirement is an incredible opportunity for self-discovery. You get to find out who you really are and who you would like to be. Although this may be scary for a while, eventually you will find your true identity. You will think new thoughts about yourself and find different activities to give you a sense of achievement and satisfaction. Best of all, you will create a healthy new identity conducive to pursuing a lifestyle that makes a big difference in your life and that of others.

Being on Purpose Is Easy If You Have One

It's great to go from a busy working life to the laid-back lifestyle that retirement provides. Two essentials for successful retirement are sufficient funds to live on and sufficient things to live for. You may have the funds and a list of interests, hobbies, and leisure activities that will keep you busy. Nonetheless, if you want your retirement to be satisfying, these activities may not be enough. You may need an overriding purpose.

While describing retirement, George Bernard Shaw concluded, "A perpetual holiday is a good working definition of hell." Shaw was right in that retirement can be hell for those who don't put any purpose into it. On the other hand, for people who have some major purpose to their lives, retirement can be heaven.

A major purpose can take the form of a personal mission, a true calling, or a passionate pursuit. Kevan H. Namazi, a gerontologist at the University of Texas's Southwestern Medical Center in Dallas, stresses that an important purpose will help retirees remain happy well into their eighties, nineties, and beyond. "The most successful old-old people," states Namazi, "are those who have an important connection, a hobby, or something that gives them a zest for life."

In this regard, George Bernard Shaw ended up enjoying his later years because he retained a great sense of purpose until he died at the age of ninety-six. Indeed, he continued to write into his nineties. To the end, Shaw published brilliantly argued prefaces to his plays, flooded publishers with books, wrote numerous controversial articles, and regularly sent cantankerous letters to newspaper editors.

A major purpose is available to all retirees who are willing to discover one. Putting purpose into retirement is only unattainable to uncreative and unmotivated people who are unable to think and act on their own. That's why they need to inhabit a workplace eight or more hours a day where an employer provides them with some purpose, as shallow as it often is. It was Andy Rooney who said, "Making duplicate copies and computer print outs of things no one wanted even one of in the first place is giving America a new sense of purpose."

If you would like a higher purpose than is available in a Dilbertized work world, retirement is where you can find it. To be sure, purpose is an individual thing. What one person views as an important purpose in retirement may seem a trivial pursuit to many others. I'll use the example of Tom R. Durkan, Sr., to make my point. Tom wrote to me after reading *The Joy of Not Working*.

> The great and glorious masterpiece of man is to know how to live to purpose.
> — Michel de Montaigne

Dear Ernie:

Have bought 6 of your books, have kept two and have given the rest away. Your book has been very helpful.

Sold my business over two years ago and am living in New York and doing fine. Keep busy reading, going to movies and plays and walk 3.5 to 4 miles in the morning and another two assorted miles walking around New York.

Have no money problems. Have no strong goals other than keeping my health and keeping busy, both of which I have been able to do.

After two years, am open to new horizons. Am 76 years young and still chase after attractive women when I am in the mood. Whether I catch them or not is not the important thing.

Once, again, congratulations for putting together an outstanding book.

Sincerely,

Tom R. Durkan, Sr.

All things considered, it appears that Tom is truly enjoying his retirement. Based on most people's standards, he's living the good life. With excellent health and no money problems, indeed, he is happier than millions of retirees. For some retirees, there would be something important lacking if they led a life similar to Tom's. The main ingredient that would be missing is a sense of higher meaning.

Gail Sheehy in *New Passages: Mapping Your Life Across Time* advises us, "The secret in the search for meaning is to find your passion and pursue it." The fact is, many retirees need a higher purpose to make their lives complete. But who am I to say? Perhaps Tom's mission or passionate pursuit is chasing after attractive women. (On second thought, I may just make this my primary passionate pursuit when I am in my seventies.)

> Everything in the universe has a purpose. Indeed, the invisible intelligence that flows through everything in a purposeful fashion is also flowing through you.
>
> — Wayne Dyer

Whether Tom needs a higher purpose in retirement is not the issue here. Tom may well fit the profile of individuals identified as "Comfortably Contents" in an AIG SunAmerica study of retirees. Comfortably Contents look forward to traditional retirement. They want to relax and spend their time indulging in recreational activities. Beyond recreational goals, their major goal is to have no goal.

The major issue here is whether you need to experience being on purpose to make retirement feel worthwhile. Of course, being on purpose is easy if you have one. Whether it's chasing after members of the opposite sex or making the world a better place, a major purpose will add a lot to your satisfaction and happiness.

The nature of your career may determine how much purpose you require in your retirement years. If your job is repetitious in nature, you may be content merely with leisure activities that provide some routine, structure, and a sense of community. Ms. Daphne Chong, the coordinator of the Chua Chu Kang Fei Yue Retirees Centre in Singapore, says most of its members are from the lower-middle income brackets looking for a place to while away their time. "They have simpler needs and are happy as long as there is entertainment."

Ms. Chong adds, "Retirees who are more highly educated tend to look for enrichment elsewhere." In other words, if you have had a responsible and fulfilling career, it is unlikely that you will find happiness and satisfaction playing bingo, watching TV, napping, and window shopping. These passive activities are okay for filling some of your time, but you will require other activities that provide risk, challenge, purpose, and accomplishment.

Even people who fill their days with many interesting activities don't find the happiness and satisfaction they had hoped to experience in retirement. They are doing many of the things they have always wanted to do. Yet they sense that there should be more to retirement. Playing golf or debating controversial issues with the regulars at the local coffee bar for four hours every day of the week seems rather irresponsible and superficial after doing it for four months straight. Deep down these people crave far more meaning, purpose, challenge, excitement, and adventure in their lives.

> Nothing contributes so much to tranquilize the mind as a steady purpose.
> — Mary Shelley

Studies have shown that there are significant differences between retirees who feel retirement is easy and those who find it difficult or have mixed feelings. The more people are satisfied with the purpose and meaning in their lives, the easier they feel retirement is. As is to be expected, personal and emotional life are greatly enhanced when there is purpose and meaning to one's existence.

Benjamin Franklin advised us, "Leisure is time for doing something useful." Unless you put some purpose into daily activities, you may end up constantly questioning the meaning of life. This invariably leads to depression, which some retirees regularly experience. An overriding purpose is a great antidote for depression; you get to feel useful, committed, and productive.

Purpose in retirement involves pursuing activities that express our true selves. Clearly, it's not easy for everyone to discover a retirement purpose that is their own. Ingrid Bacci, in her book *The Art of Effortless Living*, states, "For all our culture's so-called individualism, most people have very little true sense of themselves, or of a purpose to their lives that they can eagerly espouse. It is no wonder that, if we focus on externals and find our validation primarily in what we do and in what we get for what we do, we will never find ourselves."

Put another way, many individuals (I use the term loosely in this case) don't have an important purpose because their focus has been on superficial pursuits, such as material possessions, status, competition, and wasteful consumption. They have been so programmed to work hard and earn a lot of money that they totally forgot who they are now that they have reached retirement age. They don't recall what they deeply care about or what really turns them on. Ironically, they may have more than enough money to do what they want, but they are not quite sure what it is.

You too may have allowed yourself to become so engrossed in your career and amassing material possessions that you have forgotten what makes you feel fulfilled and truly alive. Indeed, work and the pursuit of material things may have estranged you from who you really are. Thus, one of the most important aspects of defining a purpose for your retirement is to find out who you really are.

> Singing has always seemed to me the most perfect means of expression. It is so spontaneous. And after singing, I think the violin. Since I cannot sing, I paint.
>
> — Georgia O'Keeffe

Discovering who you really are is essential because purpose is created from within. Again, I refer to purpose as having an important mission, a true calling, or a passionate pursuit. Clearly, your purpose in life won't appear on its own. If you haven't found your purpose, it's important to take some time — a few days or weeks or even months — to explore your deeper self. Otherwise, you may never find your true purpose in life.

Here is a list of questions that you should ask yourself in the event that you are having difficulty discovering an important purpose in life:

- ➤ What is extremely important to me?
- ➤ What makes me happy?
- ➤ What made me happy in my childhood and my teens that I would like to do again?
- ➤ What made me happy in my career that I would like to continue doing?
- ➤ What would make me a much happier person? Having a lot more money or becoming famous can't be one of them.
- ➤ What talents or skills am I most proud of?
- ➤ What field of endeavor invariably challenges me in new and exciting ways?

- What makes me feel most creative?
- What special talent have I neglected while putting in long and hard hours in my career?
- What would I like to do that I have always wanted to do, but never got around to doing?
- How would I like to make the world a better place in my own way?
- What sort of legacy would I like to leave?

Write these questions down in a notebook, leaving sufficient room for several answers for each question. Then take a few minutes to spontaneously record your answers to the questions without stopping to think about them. Keep going no matter what you write down. You don't want your rational mind to interfere with your answers. Remember, your rational mind has a habit of disguising the real you.

Carry this notebook of questions around for the next two to four weeks and add to your answers. Every day take fifteen minutes or so to contemplate the questions further without interruption from outside distractions. Given enough time, you should eventually have sufficient information about your needs and wants to help you discover at least one important mission, true calling, or passionate pursuit for your retirement years. Most people, in fact, should discover more than one.

> Each of our acts makes a statement as to our purpose.
>
> — Leo Buscaglia

There is no end to the scope and variety of activities that can constitute an important purpose for retirees. It depends on the individual. Following are several examples of pursuits that individuals have found worthwhile:

Activities with a Major Purpose

- Go back to university or college to get a degree for the sake of learning and not for getting a job.
- Photograph nature in all areas of the world including Africa, South America, and Asia.
- Work to eradicate social problems.
- Help educate disadvantaged children.
- Learn more about solar energy and help promote it as a great benefit to humanity.

- ➤ Travel to at least fifty different countries and learn about the people, history, economy, geography, and customs of each country.
- ➤ Organize a protest group for some specific political pet project.
- ➤ First, retire happily. Then, teach a course on how to retire happily.
- ➤ Write science fiction.
- ➤ Record the history of your hometown.
- ➤ Write and publish several books of poetry.
- ➤ Become a public speaker about the benefits of preserving the environment.
- ➤ Start and operate a bed-and-breakfast place — not for the money, but for the fun of it.
- ➤ Help friends and family succeed in life.
- ➤ Indulge in a quest to prolong youth.

Don't ever underestimate the power of having an overriding purpose, or several of them, for your retirement years. A life without purpose can lead to disassociation from life; a life with an interesting purpose can lead to an incredible love of life. As the following example indicates, retirees can assure themselves a fulfilling life when they identify their passions and devote a good part of their waking hours to pursuing these passions.

> I think I must write a book. It has been my cherished dream and I feel an influence that I cannot resist calling me to the task.
> — Charles W. Chesnutt

Before his death in 1997 at the age of eighty-four, Red Skelton showed much more zest for life than most people in their twenties and thirties. One reason is that he had a personal mission to entertain people and make them happy. After he turned eighty, he still averaged seventy-five live performances a year. Moreover, Skelton had other passionate pursuits which meant that he consistently got only three hours of sleep, going to bed at 2:30 A.M. and rising at 5:30 A.M. Besides performing at concert halls, he spent his time writing stories, composing music, and painting.

As Red Skelton showed us, a passion for one or more pursuits is a vital force for getting the most out of retirement. Whether it's traveling to exotic places, or trying to make it as an artist, or learning several new languages, or sailing around the world to learn more about it, or running the New York marathon, your passionate pursuit will enrich you like no other leisure activity can.

Being involved in activities with a major purpose will not only keep you mentally and physically active, it will also provide you with emotional and spiritual fulfillment.

Finding and Pursuing Your True Calling Can Make Retirement the Best Time of Your Life

If you would like to work part-time in your retirement years, the optimum is to have your mission or overriding purpose take the form of a job that expresses who you are — your true calling in other words. Whether your true calling involves being a teacher of some important knowledge to children, or being an inspired artist, your retirement will be filled with satisfaction and happiness. To be sure, finding and pursuing your true calling can make retirement the best time of your life.

For retirees who find their true calling, semi-retirement is a time to work for the love of work rather than for the love of money. Going to work when one knows one doesn't have to work can be satisfying in itself. More important, working at a job one loves instead of a job that one loves to hate is highly rewarding.

A few individuals are lucky enough to have had their career work and some passionate pursuit be one and the same. Thus, they can continue happily working part-time in their field well past retirement, without having to discover their true calling. Unfortunately, this is not true for most of us.

Somewhere along the way, you may have had a sense of what you really would love to do. Instead, you chose a career or job considerably different from what could have been your passion. Over the years, you may have repressed this dream of a career with more meaning because you concluded it was an unattainable fantasy. Now that you are retired or about to retire, why not give your best shot to pursuing this higher avocation?

> Every moment comes to you pregnant with divine purpose.
> — Fulton J. Sheen

The good news is that many retirees are highly successful at discovering and pursuing a true calling in life. They make a career at one thing or another for years without drawing any attention to their accomplishments; however, once they retire, a non-career pursuit brings them happiness that they never felt was possible. The reason is that working at a dream job with some meaning to it gives them the opportunity to be creative and produce something that is valuable to humanity. Moreover, the love of their work makes them extremely good at what they do.

What we need in order to experience the same high degree of fulfillment — to paraphrase Stephen Stills — is to love the job we're with. In the event that you have no idea what your true calling is, other than to ensure that you don't work at what you did all your adult life, it's worthwhile to put in the time and effort to discover it. Utilize your answers to the list of questions on pages 54 and 55 to design your dream job with a purpose and meaning to it. Once you know what it is, try to find such a job. If you can't find one exactly like this, find one close enough. Alternatively, you can try creating this job by becoming self-employed, starting your own business, or volunteering in that area.

> The only failure a man ought to fear is failure in cleaving to the purpose he sees to be best.
>
> — George Eliot

If you are unable to find your true calling by utilizing the set of questions on pages 54 and 55, keep trying by utilizing other means. There are a lot of good books written in this area. You want to make sure that you end up working at something that you love instead of something just to kill time. You may have to think outside of the box to come up with some new job or business venture that matches your interests and deepest desires. Your new career may not appear to be a logical one to others, but it will be to you.

In their book *Whistle While You Work: Heeding Your Life's Calling*, authors Richard J. Leider and David A. Shapiro suggest that people ask themselves three important questions:

1. What gift do I naturally give to others?

2. What gift do I most enjoy giving to others?

3. What gift have I most often given to others?

According to the authors, by answering these questions, people are likely to reveal their calling to themselves — and ultimately move toward new realms of success and fulfillment. The authors define calling as "the inner urge to give our gifts away in service to something we are passionate about in an environment that is consistent with our values."

You may also find Dorothy Cantor's *What Do You Want to Do When You Grow Up: Starting the Next Chapter of Your Life* helpful. This self-help tome is directed at retirees, wannabe retirees, and mid-life job swappers. Cantor outlines practical ways for readers to figure out strengths and interests so that they can set out a blueprint for the last third of their lives. It's especially useful to people in middle age who have the sense that golf and bridge and visiting grandchildren can't be all that there is to retirement.

> I haven't strength of mind not to need a career.
>
> — Ruth Benedict

In addition to books, a course or seminar on how to successfully change careers may help you find your true calling. Check out the community colleges and universities in your area to see if they offer programs similar to the Un-retirement Option at the North Carolina Center for Creative Retirement in Asheville, North Carolina. The Un-retirement Option is a program that caters to retirees who want to ponder new careers, explore the changing workplace, and decide how they are going to reenter it.

With sufficient time and effort devoted to self-discovery, many retirees will discover not only who they really are, but also what they really wanted to do with their lives — and should have done a long time ago. Whatever the path, it's like "finding the answer to the question: 'What do you want to be when you grow up?' " says Ronald J. Manheimer, executive director of the North Carolina Center for Creative Retirement. "Some find it later than others."

John Berkenfield is an example of someone who found what he wanted to be when he grew up. A thirty-year veteran of IBM at the time, Berkenfield started his retirement career when the company offered him a generous separation package. On July 1, 1989, he left IBM to work as Director of the El Rancho de Las Golondrinas Museum near Santa Fe, New Mexico. Although 200 people applied for the job, Berkenfield ended up with it. Apparently, most people didn't want the job after they learned about the low pay and few benefits.

> Do not let what you cannot do interfere with what you can do.
>
> — John Wooden

To Berkenfield, the nature of the job, and the fact that he would be doing something completely different, meant a lot more than the financial benefits. Having always had an interest in the arts, Berkenfield thought that the new job was a nice match. He had developed an intense interest in the arts in the late 1950s and

> Accomplishment of purpose is better than making a profit.
>
> — Nigerian proverb

early 1960s when he lived in New York's Greenwich Village.

"My parents retired to Florida," Mr. Berkenfield told *Wall Street Journal* reporter Glenn Ruffenauch in 1998. "My father fished; he grew old. His growth as a thinking man stopped. I have no intention of growing old. I've probably got thirty years left. And I intend to be active, involved, and intellectually challenged as long as I can." Berkenfield also advised retirees who want to keep working: "Spend your time learning and doing something very different from what you've done in your past life. This way, you have a better chance of remaining intellectually stimulated."

As John Berkenfield has indicated, it's important to separate the meaning of a job from its normal trappings. Disassociate yourself from how much money the job will pay, disassociate yourself from the status and prestige you can attain, and disassociate yourself from what others think about the job. You — and only you — have to decide what's meaningful to you in a retirement career. In other words, what will make you jump out of bed in the morning on the days you are going to be working?

Your true calling will surface when you are ready for it. Paradoxically, some retirees find their true life's calling just when life appears to be going downhill. It could be part-time volunteer

> We are not in a position in which we have nothing to work with. We already have capacities, talents, direction, missions, callings.
>
> — Abraham Maslow

work for a charity, or an assignment with a special-interest group, that becomes a full-time mission. It could also be a neglected hobby that turns into a full-time passion — even an extremely profitable business. Here are some other jobs and careers that retirees have discovered as their true calling:

- ➤ Start a service business that helps people have a better work/life balance.
- ➤ Teach individuals to reach their full potentials.
- ➤ Open a nonprofit wildlife reserve and share it with others.
- ➤ Start a pirate radio station devoted to a specific cause.
- ➤ Buy a basketball team and run it as an avocation.
- ➤ Start and operate a humorous and exciting

website for retirees.
- ➤ Promote a cause such as environmentalism that benefits all of society.
- ➤ Create a health product that enhances people's lives for the long term.
- ➤ Invent something useful.
- ➤ Help homeless people live better lives.
- ➤ Preach the gospel of one's church to people in a foreign land.

Summing up, a true calling can fulfill your inner needs more than money or other activities ever can. Working part-time at something you enjoy allows you to stay busily and happily involved in life while still enjoying the benefits of retirement. Being productive well into your later years will enhance your self-esteem plus give you intellectual stimulation and social interaction. It is also a way to enrich the lives of others while enriching your own at the same time.

> It's time to take a look at my failures and stop calling them successes. Now I can start working at something that can use me best.
> — Nina Simone

Above all, your true calling will help you become much more than you have ever been. "There comes a special moment in everyone's life, a moment for which that person was born," proclaimed Winston Churchill. "That special opportunity, when he seizes it, will fulfill his mission — a mission for which he is uniquely qualified. In that moment, he finds his greatness. It is his finest hour."

Work at Something That Is Not So Much a Job, but a Fun Thing to Do

Some retirees will have a difficult time pursuing their true calling in a job, but still would like some type of work to enhance their retirement years. After all, it's not easy for everyone to discover their true calling. Even if they do discover it, some retirees may not be ready to pursue it. Moreover, it's not always possible to find the right job in which one can pursue a special purpose. In the event that you yourself are unable to merge work with a passion or personal mission, there is still no reason to take any job just to keep busy.

Perhaps you need a ready-made structure, a ready-made purpose, and a ready-made community that a workplace provides. Be clear, however, that working at a lousy job just to give you structure, purpose, and community is not the best way to live. There is so much more to life than a boring job. As we shall see in chapter 3, the elements of structure, purpose, and community can be created on your own if you set your mind to it. Alternatively, you can get yourself an enjoyable job that provides these three important elements.

By an enjoyable job, I am referring to what some retirees call a "fun job." For example, Cliff and Babette Marten of Des Moines, Iowa, get their kicks in retirement by driving vehicles across Iowa, across the midWest, and even clear across the United States. They get a chance to drive many types of automobiles — including Cadillacs and Lexuses — and they get paid for it. "About every drive is a different situation," Cliff Marten, seventy-seven, told the *Des Moines Register*.

> Man needs, for his happiness, not only the enjoyment of this or that, but hope and enterprise and change.
>
> — Bertrand Russell

For a fee, the Martens drive new and used cars for Betts Cadillac, a Des Moines auto dealership. The couple is in a pool of fifteen to twenty drivers who drive cars to dealerships in other states or to private individuals who have purchased a car from Betts. The drivers are paid by the hour and reimbursed for expenses such as food, tolls, and lodging.

On out-of-state deliveries, Cliff Marten will drive the car to be delivered and Babette will follow in another car that will later be used to bring them back home. The Martens have driven from Iowa to Florida, California, Michigan, and Connecticut, and passed through many states in between. They sometimes get the opportunity to visit family or friends along the way. "We get paid to have fun," declared Babette Marten, seventy years old at the time.

Bob Laabs also got himself a fun job after he "retired." A former high-school principal, Laabs took a job as a historic interpreter in his hometown of Williamsburg, Virginia, a popular tourist center. Today he gives tours of the buildings in Williamsburg and lectures tourists on the events of 1774—1776. "It's not so much a job, but a fun thing to do," admitted Laabs, sixty at the time. "I like history, I like people, and this is a melding of both of these things."

Although the extra money Laabs makes allows him to live in more financial comfort than if he weren't working, this isn't his main point of working in retirement. "You've got to retire to something, not from something," Laabs advises people about to retire. "Don't just get away — do something that enhances your lifestyle."

All things considered, if you are going to work in retirement, the nature of the work should be much more important than the money you can make at it.

> Am I retired already? It's possible. I'm having way too much fun for this [job] to be work.
>
> — Robin Fowler

Should it be the case that you need a reasonable income from your retirement career, careful thought and preparation will be needed to find part-time work that is both enjoyable and profitable. On the other hand, if you have a good retirement income without a job, even one that pays the minimum wage should be taken in the event that it provides you with satisfaction and enjoyment.

Here again, as in a job that represents a true calling, look for a job where the normal concerns don't apply. A fun job is one in which we don't have to worry about achievement factors such as status, power, financial rewards, and advancement opportunities. Equally important, a fun job is hard to differentiate from leisure; it's an opportunity to work at something for the personal satisfaction of doing it well and having loads of fun at the same time. At its best, a fun job is something that you would happily work at — or play at — for no pay.

> Patrick, I know you retired from your former CEO position with $2 million in your portfolio. What in the world are you doing driving cab?

> After I retired I discovered that regardless of how much I dislike any type of work, I still find work much more fun than fun itself.

While pursuing a fun job, we should do the right thing for ourselves, regardless of what others may think of the job. It's okay to take a job that has less status than the one we had in our primary careers. A good example of a person who did just this is Dick Remy, a can-company supervisor before he retired at the age of fifty. For the first five years Remy worked part-time as a consultant. Regardless of the fact that being a consultant gave him a measure of status, Remy didn't find his retirement job much fun. Eventually he did something about it. "I decided to see what was out there," stated Remy.

As it turned out, Remy's fun job ended up being a truck driver, a job some retirees may have dreamed of doing as a kid, but never got around to pursuing due to the job's perceived lower status in society. This didn't stop Remy. He was first trained as a truck driver by Kreilkamp Trucking Inc. of Allenton, Wisconsin, before the company hired him. Now he spends up to forty hours a week behind the wheel of an eighteen-wheeler that he has nicknamed "Sweet Pea." Remy declares, "This is a great job for me because it keeps me moving — I'm happiest when I'm on the go."

> We only do well the things we like doing.
>
> — Colette

Particularly if you have a nice retirement nest egg, you too can easily make the transition from "I have to work" to "I want to work for the fun of it." Getting the right fun job will allow you to work at something you like, at your own time, at your own pace. The beauty is that you don't have to get a job for the whole year and you can work as much, or as little, as you want. You can experiment with various short-term (a week or a month) or part-time positions (one or two days a week).

Following are several other fun jobs that will appeal to certain retirees and that you may want to consider:

- Become a busker or street entertainer.
- Become a guide for a local tourist attraction.
- Work on a golf course and learn more about the game from the experts.
- Work as a travel agent to learn more about other countries and get some good deals on travel.
- Become a Zen monk — like singer Leonard Cohen did — by joining a monastery where you can drink tea in silence, meditate, chant, study, shovel snow, scrub floors, and cook.
- Engage your musical abilities by joining a band that plays on a cruise ship.
- Join the inn crowd by opening a bed & breakfast place.
- Get work as an extra with a studio doing a film or a TV documentary in your area.
- Expose yourself in the name of art and get paid for it. Model in the nude for a painting, drawing, or photography class.
- Become a roadie with a traveling rock band such as the Rolling Stones.

- Take off for the winter on a two-month-long trip to Las Vegas and work as a blackjack dealer in one of the casinos.
- Drive a tourist bus based in Banff in the Canadian Rockies.
- Offer your public-speaking abilities to conventions in major cities in exchange for travel expenses, food, and lodging.

Especially if your career work was nothing more than labor and drudgery, a fun job may bring you a measure of enjoyment and satisfaction that you didn't think was possible. Indeed, getting a fun job after you retire from your primary career gives you the best of both worlds. Having enjoyable work while also having more leisure time is a great way to enjoy life. You can have a freer lifestyle because of the increased leisure time, and still enjoy the many positives of having a job.

> It is not real work unless you would rather be doing something else.
>
> — J. M. Barrie

Best of all, retirement is your opportunity to try out many different lines of work just for the adventure of it. If you find a job that really turns you on, you may want to stick with it for the longer term. The most fascinating aspect of a fun job is that it may actually end up being your true calling in life. As metaphysical author Louise Hay concluded, "New careers can start at any age, especially when you do it for the fun of it."

Reclaiming Your Creative Spirit Will Put Joyful Purpose into Your Retirement Life

And the first rude sketch that the world had seen
was joy to his mighty heart,
Till the Devil whispered behind the leaves
"It's pretty, but is it Art?"
— Rudyard Kipling

A chief source of happiness for retirees, whether they continue to work part-time or fully retire, is an artistic pursuit. Because they gain their freedom, and have more leisure time available than ever in their adult lives, many retirees reclaim their creative spirit after leaving their full-time careers. In the process they are fortunate enough to discover an artistic pursuit that engages their essence and their soul.

Once you retire, you too can reclaim your creative spirit and find an artistic pursuit that will ignite your inner fire. Your artistic pursuit — whether it's painting pictures, writing poetry, or making pottery — will rekindle a part of you that has been suppressed for years by the structure of a job and the routine of daily life. Not only can it make you feel more alive, an artistic pursuit can constitute the primary reason for your being.

At sixty-seven, my friend Hendrik Bres has been a full-time artist for almost two decades. After working as a pressman for many years, he took early retirement at the age of fifty to pursue what he felt he was destined to be. Like most artists, he hasn't become rich and famous yet. His reward is being what he always wanted to be. Moreover, he gets great satisfaction from the fact that his works are now represented in numerous private and public collections in Canada and the Netherlands.

Perhaps you are already retired and saying to yourself, "I would like to do something artistic, but I'm not creative." Nonsense! You were born creative, as was every human being. You have to rediscover your creativity. Reclaiming your creative spirit will put the joyful purpose into your retirement life that you are yearning for.

> To love what you do and feel that it matters — how could anything be more fun?
> — Katharine Graham

Everyone has the deep-seated desire to produce something artistic. In everyone there is a creative person wanting to break out and make a difference in this world. And everyone has the creative ability to be artistic. "Every child is an artist," Pablo Picasso proclaimed. "The problem is how to remain an artist once he grows up."

The majority of adults don't get halfway to reaching their full creative potential due to self-imposed limitations. Sadly, many people have suppressed both their desire and their ability to be creative for so long that they think they are naturally uncreative and inartistic. You may be one of them. Yet to deny your creativity is to lie to the world and, worse, to lie to yourself. In fact, it's harder to suppress your creativity than to use it.

Clearly, being creatively satisfied doesn't have anything to do with attaining success in the traditional sense of the word. All too often, people think they can buy creative fulfillment if they are in a position to buy the richest of artistic pleasures. Not so! Buying the most expensive Rembrandt or Monet won't give people a fraction of the fulfillment that completing one of their own works will give them.

We all have hopes and dreams of achieving something creative, regardless of our age. Retirement is the time to revisit old fantasies and make time for something wild you have always wanted to do. Remember, however, that irrespective of how fantastic your retirement dreams are, they are ten times worse than mediocre when you don't do anything with them. As is to be expected, what you don't get around to doing will never succeed.

To aim for the ideal retirement lifestyle requires that you know what you want out of retirement. Let there be no doubt about the importance of being focused. Few people give any thought to what they are doing and why. It's all too easy to get lost in frivolous pursuits, people, and various other distractions. Only by concentrating on the things that matter can you make your retirement dreams come true.

> When all is said and done, monotony may after all be the best condition for creation.
> — Margaret Sackville

Developing your ability for self-expression will open up your world to new and exciting experiences. This holds true particularly if in your past you have often imagined yourself as a writer, musician, sculptor, or painter. If you have never tried being one, what is holding you back? Now is the time to start painting those landscapes or writing those novels. Otherwise you may never achieve fulfillment in what are supposed to be the best years of your life.

By becoming actively and passionately involved in an artistic endeavor, you make the jump to living a truly creative life. The key is to find something that will stretch your natural talents more. Have at least one continuing artistic project on which you work a bit each and every day. It can be a book, a painting, a sculpture, stained glass, a quilt, or anything else that challenges your creativity.

Without exception, there is no such thing as creative satisfaction without some sort of challenge, effort, and risk involved. This being the case, a great way to challenge yourself is to tackle a creative pursuit for which you have always thought you have no talent. Chances are you will surprise yourself. In five or ten years you may wind up as a well-known artist after having convinced yourself that you couldn't even paint your kitchen door another color.

Although you may attain it eventually, your main goal shouldn't be to become a famous painter or a wealthy sculptor. Your main motivation, instead, should be the enjoyment, wonder, and satisfaction that come from being creative. In this regard, well-known author Julia Cameron tells us, "Creativity lies not in the done but in the doing." Speaking of Julia Cameron, I strongly urge that you read her book *The Artist's Way*. It will help you conquer many of the psychological barriers to being artistic that so many individuals experience.

> He is very rich and he is very poor. Money cannot buy him creative fulfillment.
>
> — Julia Cameron

To get in touch with your creative inclinations, it's best to spend some time thinking about your natural creative talent and about new artistic activities that you can pursue. To be a certain type of artist, study what others have done in this field. Learn from the great masters and you just may become one yourself. "He who can copy can do," advised Leonardo da Vinci, a master in his own right.

Luckily, you don't have to rely solely on yourself to help develop your creative ability. Besides reading books, you can explore the options available at universities, community colleges, and private organizations. For example, the Cummings Centre in Montreal has an art department that offers courses whereby one can develop one's artistic talent from scratch. Other educational institutions have everything from creative-writing seminars to painting classes to sculpting courses complete with exhibitions.

Being an artist will give you the overriding purpose that so many people lack in retirement. Indeed, a creative pursuit can give you a sense of satisfaction, fulfillment, and happiness that many people don't experience anytime during forty years of working at a primary career. Not only will you be doing what you love, you may actually do well at it. This will give you a sense of self-respect, which in itself goes a long way towards getting the respect of others.

A new artistic pursuit will ensure you are constantly growing and learning. It can lead to important breakthroughs in other areas of your life, such as having better relationships with your friends and family. Moreover, a new artistic pursuit can be thought-provoking, challenging, and amusing. Last, but not least, your health can benefit as you develop your creativity. An artistic pursuit will help you relax and reduce stress in your life. When you get totally engrossed in a passionate activity, such as painting a picture, you will clear your mind of needless worries and other mind chatter that has absolutely no benefit to your well-being.

It's never too late to pursue a lifelong dream of being an artist — whether it's a painter, a musician, or a sculptor. Regardless of how old you are, you can pursue it with vigor. If you need an education that will coincide with your reaching your creative calling, then get it. An excuse that arises is: "But I am fifty-nine and I will be sixty-three when I get there." In four years, you are going to be sixty-three anyway. If you don't do what you have to, you will be sixty-three and just as dissatisfied as you are today (or more dissatisfied).

Tens of thousands of individuals in their late fifties and beyond exhibit great zest, vigor, and enthusiasm while getting a formal education to better prepare themselves for their artistic pursuits. La Salle, Quebec, resident Brian Foran, for example, first developed an interest in music when he purchased a guitar and learned how to play it in the late 1960s. It was also at this time that he first dreamed of being a professional musician. Approximately a decade later, a friend convinced Foran to sing along with a group in a Legion Hall. At this point he discovered his musical passion — singing bass in a choir. He would wait for many years before he could fully dedicate himself to this passion.

I always wanted to be a painter but I haven't been blessed with the right-brain tilt that you artists have.

In the summer of 2002, Foran retired from his job as a manager at the Canadian Textile Bureau in Montreal. Retirement gave him the opportunity to pursue his lifelong dream to study music at a university and become a topnotch musician. "I never had music lessons as a kid. I never even went to a school that taught music," Foran, sixty-four, told a *Montreal Gazette* reporter. "Music wasn't the thing to do at the time for someone like me. But I could never get this dream out of my system."

After auditioning along with a number of other applicants — most were half his age or younger — Foran was accepted for one of the limited number of openings in the Integrative Music Studies program at Concordia University in Montreal. He will be sixty-seven by the time he graduates with a Bachelor of Fine Arts in 2005. This, however, doesn't faze him. "Nobody has told me that I'm nuts going back to school," confessed Foran, "but even if they

> I see no reason for calling my work poetry except that there is no other category in which to put it.
>
> — Marianne Moore

had, I wouldn't frankly care. My biggest regret would have been to give up on the dream."

Foran isn't concerned that he will be too old to use his music education after he graduates. "Time is on my side," he observed. "Basses and baritones — unlike tenors — get better with age. We can barrel on until we die."

Perhaps, like Brian Foran, you too have a lifelong dream, a dream beyond all other dreams to become a creative force in this world. With enthusiasm as your driving force, you too can strike a higher level of personal growth than you have ever achieved before. "Whatever you can do, or dream you can, begin it," declared Johann Wolfgang von Goethe. "Boldness has genius, power, and magic in it."

Everything and everybody in this world — including you — retains their true essence only by being put to their best use. Pursuing your creative calling means you no longer have to hold back on the contributions you were meant to give to this world. Your creative purpose in life will contribute to making the world a better place for humanity.

As important as it may be, however, your creative purpose shouldn't be something that you pursue with anxiety and desperation. There, instead, should be a joyfulness to your actions, a sense of serenity and peace with the world as you contribute to it and change it for the better.

By indulging yourself in challenging and satisfying artistic pursuits, you don't have to accept the low standards by which many people rate whether their retirement is a success. You have the ability and the creative talent to transcend these standards and retire happy, wild, and free. In doing so, you will help transform the world in some little way and experience great satisfaction from having done so.

> Art is an absolute mistress; she will not be coquetted with or slighted; she requires the most entire self-devotion, and she repays with grand triumphs.
>
> — Charlotte Cushman

The great thing about being an artist is that this is something you can pursue for the rest of your life. Picasso continued to create masterpieces well into his later years. He not only painted, but also worked in various media, creating lithographs, ceramic pieces, sculptures, and engravings.

In short, an artistic pursuit will likely

turn out to be an extraordinary challenge; it can be a challenge above all other challenges that will keep you vibrant and enthusiastic in your later years. In this regard, Picasso insisted, "We artists are indestructible; even in a prison, or in a concentration camp, I would be almighty in my own world of art, even if I had to paint my pictures with my wet tongue on the dusty floor of my cell."

> A primitive artist is an amateur whose work sells.
>
> — Grandma Moses

Not Writing a Book Can Be More Difficult than Writing One

Like many people, you may have always wanted to be a writer. Deep down there has always been something about the Starbucks cappuccino-and-laptop-computer crowd that appealed to you. If you have thought intuitively for a long time that you should have been a writer, you should give it some serious consideration. Indeed, if deep down you have always wanted to write a book, not writing one can be more difficult than writing it.

Perhaps in response to a best-selling book on the *New York Times* top ten, you have declared to yourself or others, "I could have written a book better than this one." Yes, you possibly could have. So, why don't you? This also applies to any other person's creative accomplishment that you are capable of duplicating or surpassing. If you have always wanted to achieve in a certain area, you are selling yourself short by sitting back and talking about it.

I have decided to devote a bit of space to what it takes to write a book simply because there are so many people who would like to do so. Writing a book can be the principal expression for your mind and creative talent. Many options and opportunities await you if you look for them. Whether it's writing a novel, a self-help book, or a travel guide, you must choose the genre that will give you the most interesting challenge and satisfaction.

To be sure, not everything about writing a book is easy. Richard Bach, author of best-selling *Jonathan Livingston Seagull*, admitted that it was tough for him to write his next best-seller, *Illusions*. Ernest Hemingway confessed, "I read my own books sometimes to cheer me when it is hard to write and then I remember that it was always difficult and how nearly impossible it was sometimes." Joseph Heller, author of *Catch-22*, summed it up very well when he stated that all great writers have difficulty writing.

No doubt some people are born with more talent than others. This superior talent gives them greater potential to excel at certain things, including becoming an accomplished author. Writing a book is largely dependent upon commitment and perseverance, however.

Take me, for example. I know my limitations as a writer. My writing abilities will never approach those of George Bernard Shaw or of any other Nobel Prize winner. Indeed, giving me the Nobel Prize in literature would spark one of the biggest controversies ever in the world's literary community.

On the other hand, I won't allow my limitations to stop me from writing the books I am capable of writing. What I realized some time ago is that I can't write a book on the same level as William Faulkner, but I can write a book by me. Surprisingly, by the time I realized how bad of a writer I really was, I was too successful to quit. To deal with my bad writing, I decided to write more books and try to improve in the process.

A week doesn't pass by in which I don't meet someone much smarter and literately more capable than I am who desperately wants to write a book but hasn't gotten around to it. Notwithstanding my having failed a first-year university English course three times in a row, I know that I can accomplish more as a writer than millions of people who have three times my ability. I realize that most talented people who want to write are too afraid of failure or too distracted with life's frivolities to attempt a book.

Above all, my writing accomplishments are the result of my agreement with myself to write a minimum of three hours a day. I try to write four pages during this time. These pages don't have to be masterpieces. Sometimes, they contain some pretty pathetic writing, but at least I have four pages to work with. Even if I break my agreement to write three hours a day, and write for only fifteen minutes, I am still closer to completing a book than people who talk for ten hours about writing one, but never spend a minute on it.

> Only passions, great passions, can elevate the soul to great things.
> — Denis Diderot

According to *Writer's Digest* magazine, 81 percent of Americans think they should write a book, but only 2 percent have completed a manuscript. Do doubt most people cop out by saying that they can't write. Others say that they don't have enough time. Still others think that no one would be interested in what they have to say. These are excuses, far from being good reasons. If people are too lazy to write, at least they should admit it, and take responsibility for their own laziness.

Many retirees from all walks of life are achieving their dreams of writing and publishing memoirs, novels, nonfiction books, short stories, and poetry through creative writing classes offered at various institutions. Michael A. Smith, the author of six published novels, teaches beginning and advanced creative writing courses offered through the Adult and Community Education Program of the School District of Flagler County in Florida. One of his classes is specifically directed at retirees. In 2002, at the storefront facility in the Palm Harbor Shopping Village, Flagler County retirees from all walks of life were achieving their dreams.

I still haven't made the New York Times *best-seller list.*

Try writing a book first!

Wilma Shulman was concentrating on poetry and short stories. Catherine Morsink, author of a published textbook for special needs students, was completing a self-help book titled *Spend Low, Live High* for publication with Writers Club Press. Lorraine Thornton was writing her memoirs, with a focus on the importance of tolerance within her extended family. Harriet Dietrich was writing a novel that examined personal interactions and conflicts within a retirement community. Dietrich also had intentions of developing a newspaper column on the same subject.

It's never too late and you are never too old to write a book. At the prime age of ninety-eight, Jessie Lee Brown Foveaux, a great-great-grandmother and an unschooled and unskilled writer, turned a memoir she wrote in a writing class for senior citizens into a book. Then she sold it for a small fortune.

In an auction Warner Books paid $1 million to publish *Any Given Day*. The book contract allowed Miss Foveaux to fly on an airplane for the first time, take limousines, stay at fancy hotels, appear on talk shows, and be written about in newspapers. Somewhat humble about her success, Miss Foveaux contended, "I imagine I'll be like everyone else who ever got into a mess like this."

You too can take a course on writing books but it's not necessary for many people. Indeed, most famous writers never took a creative writing course. Again, as Nike advises, "Just Do It!" Put another way, just start writing. Conversely, you may have noticed that it takes an eternity to complete something you aren't working on.

There is no question that being an author offers one of the few opportunities to make a great deal of money in a short period of

> Anybody can write a three-volume novel. It merely requires a complete ignorance of both life and literature.
>
> —Oscar Wilde

time. There are far greater payoffs, however — adventure, personal satisfaction, and acknowledgment from readers. Most accomplished writers profess that the biggest reward isn't financial. It's the thrill of sharing their views of the world with others, and having others tell them that they experienced pleasure — even spiritual fulfillment — from reading their books.

You can also share in these benefits if you are prepared to do all the difficult things that are necessary to write a book and make it a best-seller. If you can't find a publisher once you have written a book, publish it on your own if you believe in it. Many books that went on to be best-sellers were self-published. But don't equate success with producing a best-seller. If your book is enjoyed by one person other than yourself, it's a success — anything over and above this is a bonus.

Writing is something you can do well late into retired life. As long as you can think and punch a keyboard, you can keep writing until you are eighty or ninety. All told, if you have always had stories you wanted to tell, retirement is the stage in your life in which to do it. Time is plentiful and the investment is minimal — a laptop computer is preferable, but you can get by with a pen and paper. The beauty is that you, as a retiree, can write anytime the fancy hits — whether it's six in the morning or eleven at night.

There is at least one other benefit from writing that I haven't yet mentioned. Sixty-nine-year-old Dan Montague, retired tourist director and now part-time writer, told a newspaper reporter, "I think it [writing] helps you get along with your wife. My wife said, 'Thank God you've got that writing; get in there [and] quit bothering me.' "

Summing up, you will put more life into your life with creative writing. Write a novel, write a poem, write a play, write a short story, or write an opera. Whatever you have wanted to write, start today. Even write an unauthorized autobiography, but make sure

> When one has no particular talent for anything, one takes to the pen.
>
> —Honoré de Balzac

you write. Writing is simply putting your knowledge and ideas into words on paper and then trying to arrange them in publishable form, whether it's for a book, newspaper, magazine, or a website. Above all, writing is one of the best ways to express yourself to the world.

3

So Many Worlds, So Much to Do!

To Be Bored Is to Retire from Life

'Tis easy to resign a toilsome place,
But not to manage leisure with a grace;
Absence of occupation is not rest,
A mind quite vacant is a mind distress'd.
— William Cowper, *Retirement*

Making the most out of retirement entails taking advantage of increased freedom to establish a lifestyle that is adventurous, exciting, and rewarding. The good news is that the time available for extracurricular activities expands greatly when the long hours previously taken up with full-time employment cease. The bad news is that this often leads to boredom. At best, bored retirees feel lost. At worst, they develop emotional conflicts and problems, including excessive drinking, overeating, and serious depression.

Most people looking forward to retirement feel that they will find plenty of things to keep them occupied. Yet the sudden change from work to retirement can be unnerving. Once they actually retire, many individuals find that they don't have nearly as much to keep them occupied as they had anticipated. Regardless of whether or not they had a good work/life balance in their careers, a life of total leisure can be the greatest challenge people have to face in their adult lives.

> In this country . . . men seem to live for action as long as they can and sink into apathy when they retire.
> — Charles Adams

Weird as it may seem, the inability to conquer boredom in their personal lives is why many people shun retirement and continue to work at the most boring jobs imaginable. British-born American writer and critic W. H. Auden remarked, "A tremendous number of people in America work very hard at something that bores them. Even a rich man thinks he has to go down to the office every day. Not because he likes it but because he can't think of anything else to do."

> Half of our life is spent trying to find something to do with the time we have rushed through life trying to save.
> — Will Rogers

No doubt there will always be people who display impressive talent in the work world, but aspire no higher. They have no inclination to develop themselves as more rounded human beings by getting immersed in the world of leisure. These people will probably want to work at their boring jobs until they drop dead, or can no longer work due to ill health.

Many individuals, however, muster enough courage to leave their boring and unfulfilling jobs for a life of leisure. Alas, some find that an abundance of leisure that retirement brings doesn't translate into an abundance of happiness. These retirees, after six months of total leisure, have become so bored that they would do practically anything to be back working. Indeed, one study showed that approximately a quarter of all North American retirees are unhappy because they would rather be working. Almost a third of retirees return to work sooner or later; most do so within a year of retiring.

People who cherish and can handle freedom undoubtedly do well at retirement and are seldom bored. The capacity to grow and the ability to choose are indispensable for handling the free time that retirement affords. Unfortunately, not all retirees — even well-educated and highly intelligent ones — are able to handle freedom and avoid boredom. How well-educated and highly intelligent individuals can excel in the workplace, and yet fail at retirement so miserably, is one of the sadder aspects of human existence.

On the other hand, how millions of individuals covering the full spectrum of education, intelligence, and income levels can be happy in retirement is one of the positive aspects of human existence. Sara Rix of the AARP (American Association of Retired Persons) points out that millions of retirees are highly active and not bored in the least. Indeed, many have no desire to go back to work — not even part-time.

"Many older people spend a lot of time surfing the net. They're traveling," declares Rix. "They're engaged in sports, they're mountain climbing, they're playing tennis, they've got recreational vehicles and they're traveling around the country, and they continue to interact a great deal with their grandchildren."

Again, retirement can be extremely fulfilling and rewarding or it can be extremely boring and disappointing. Richard Bach offered an important warning: "In order to live free and happily, you must sacrifice boredom. It is not always an easy sacrifice." Particularly if you have wasted the first part of your adult life on boring work, you certainly don't want to be like so many individuals who waste the second part of their adult lives on a boring retirement.

I may be a genius to design this funky bicycle. But God only knows if I am creative enough to enjoy a life of total leisure like Socrates and Plato advocated.

If you have been forced into retirement by ill health or the inability to get suitable employment after being forced out of your long-time career, you don't have the luxury of part-time work to help alleviate boredom. Nevertheless, instead of looking at retirement as an unavoidable, boring stage in life, you must make it a positive and rewarding experience. Whatever it takes, you want to avoid being one of the many retirees who spend their last years in utter boredom.

Although boredom in itself doesn't appear to be a serious problem, it's at the root of many psychological afflictions that retirees experience. Surprisingly, boredom can actually be more of a problem than poor physical health. David Evans, a professor of clinical psychology at the University of Western Ontario in London, and Terry Lynn Gall, a professor in the Faculty of Human Sciences at Saint Paul University in Ottawa, found that although health plays a role in the good quality of life, just as important, if not more, are the mental pressures of coping after leaving the workforce. They concluded that symptoms associated with boredom, such as being unhappy, depressed, or lonely, can be more bothersome on a daily basis for retirees than physical symptoms.

For good measure, you can add an early death sentence to the list of serious symptoms that accompany boredom — even for those bored retirees who are still alive. In the eighteenth century, English statesman Lord Chesterfield lamented about his own and his friend's dilemma after the two had retired. "Lord Tyrawley and I have been dead these two years," remarked Chesterfield, "but we don't choose to have it known."

Given that life offers us so much in the way of interesting pursuits, to be bored is to retire from life. When you retire, you want your life to be more than just something to do when you aren't sleeping. Whether you avoid boredom and depression will be determined by the nature of your leisure activities. You must not commit the grave mistake of making the couch, the fridge, and the TV your three best friends. This trio not only contributes to boredom big time; it also contributes to poor mental and physical health.

> And when I get real, real bored, I like to drive downtown and get a great parking spot, then sit in my car and count how many people ask me if I'm leaving.
>
> — Steven Wright

For your retirement to be the best time of your life, you must be able to dream on your own, plan on your own, make decisions on your own, and take action on your own. What's right for others is not necessarily right for you. Just being busy, however, is not enough to avoid boredom. Even a favorite leisurely pursuit — whether it's fishing all day on a favorite lake or painting masterpieces in Paris — can lead to boredom if one spends too much time on it.

Regardless of how much you want to immerse yourself in your major purpose or your most passionate pursuit in life, you should still learn how to enjoy other leisure activities. In the event that you are semiretired, it's wise to avoid being overly goal-oriented or judging yourself totally on work-related and materialistic accomplishments. The quality of each and every one of your retirement days should be evaluated, at least in part, by how much you relaxed, laughed, and played while immersed in activities other than your part-time job.

Another key to conquering boredom is not to ever actually commit yourself to retirement in the traditional sense of the word; the term should not be taken literally. Retirement should be a reorientation of living. We should call the disengagement from a full-time career "self-actualization" or "self-realization," rather than "retirement." Either term signifies that we are soaring to new heights, both outwardly and inwardly, when we leave full-time employment behind.

For individuals who have their psychological act together, even a traditional retirement — one without part-time work or a major passionate pursuit — doesn't have to be boring. On the contrary. Many people find traditional retirement much more exciting and stimulating than being in the workforce. Take, for example, Betty Sullivan, one of several Miami Beach retirees featured in filmmaker Marian Marzynski's PBS documentary *My Retirement Dreams*. Unlike many individuals, Sullivan, sixty-nine at the time, didn't find traditional retirement a major disappointment in her life.

> The cure for boredom is curiosity. There is no cure for curiosity.
>
> — Ellen Parr

Before Sullivan retired, she was an administrator in the Department of Animal Pathology at the University of Miami for seventeen years. Prior to this, she and her husband owned an appliance and sewing machine store in Amherst, Massachusetts. For Sullivan, retirement was liberation from years of tedious responsibilities associated with work and family.

"Before I left," Sullivan disclosed, "some of my co-workers had warned and joked about the perils of retirement: boredom, imaginary health problems, lack of purpose, and possible depression. None of these things has happened to me. Why? I exchanged a grueling nine-to-five routine for a well-earned casual and carefree lifestyle."

Betty Sullivan retired happy, wild, and free. Like other self-actualized retirees — including Ian Hammond and Robert Radford mentioned in chapter 1 — Sullivan found that retirement is at least as exciting and interesting as her work life was. "Do I miss the challenge of the workplace that had once been so much a part of my persona? Heavens, no," she told an interviewer.

"My days are filled with healthy activities — swimming, working out at the gym, shopping, bicycling, taking classes such as writing, art, and yoga," Sullivan added. "In the evenings there are movies, concerts, dining and dancing. Soon, I may do a little traveling. And you know what? If I don't feel like doing anything at all except lounge around my apartment, I'll do that too."

Betty Sullivan has emphasized that there are many ways to avoid boredom once you retire. You can do more of the things that you were doing too little and less of the things that you were doing too much. Particularly if you worked in a boring and unfulfilling job, the thing that you were doing too much of was work. Now, you can utilize the time freed from work and devote it to such things as spiritual fulfillment, quality family time, creative pursuits, and fulfilling leisure activities.

All things considered, your retirement reward should be a life that is at least as exciting and interesting as your work life was. In fact, with creative and constructive use of your time, you can be happier than you ever were in the workplace, regardless of how much satisfaction your work provided. Retirement turns out the biggest nothing of all time to many people simply because they refuse to put in the effort to conquer boredom.

> Is not life a hundred times too short for us to bore ourselves?
>
> — Friedrich Nietzsche

The word "boredom" should not even be part of your vocabulary. As Jules Renard commented, "Being bored is an insult to oneself." You as a creative individual have the ability to pursue interesting activities. Creative expression is the natural inclination of life. Keep reminding yourself that retirement can be a series of adventures and wonderful discoveries because deep down you are a creative person and not a boring one.

Plant Your Get-a-Life Tree and Watch It Grow and Grow

Notwithstanding the fact that many retirees don't know what to do with their time, the world of retirement is overflowing with opportunity. Retirees can experience many different events, things, people, and places. Indeed, the incredible variety of opportunities available to retirees offers endless possibilities for enjoyment and satisfaction.

Whether you are already retired or soon-to-be retired, now is the time to plant your Get-a-Life Tree in order that you have a busy and fulfilling retirement. I first introduced the concept of a Get-a-Life Tree in my previous book *The Joy of Not Working* as a Leisure Tree. I am compelled, however, to change the name to a Get-a-Life Tree. A happy retirement is not necessarily based on leisure activities alone. The Get-a-Life Tree is a variation of what is commonly known as a mind map, spoke diagram, thought web, or clustering diagram.

The Get-a-Life Tree is simple, but powerful. It is a creative approach that allows us to generate a substantial number of choices of activities that we may want to pursue after we check out of the workplace for good. Because our memories are not as good as we think they are, it is important to write all our ideas down before we select those activities that we are going to pursue. If you are like most people, you normally use a list to record ideas. A list is better than nothing, but it may limit the number of ideas you generate. The Get-a-Life Tree is more effective in this regard.

A Get-a-Life Tree is started at the center of a blank page by recording the goal, theme, or objective. In figure 3-1 on the next page, "Options for My Retirement" appears in the center of the page. Branches or lines are drawn from the center towards the boundary of the page. On these branches are printed any principal ideas that relate to the objective of the tree. Principal ideas are recorded on separate branches near the center of the page.

Three important principal ideas should be used to generate retirement activities that you may want to pursue:

1. Activities that turn you on now

2. Activities that turned you on in the past (but you have stopped doing)

3. New activities you have thought of doing (but haven't done yet)

On secondary branches from the primary ones, you should add the various activities relating to the category. As indicated in figure 3-1, for the primary idea, "New activities I have thought of doing," you can add "Working as an Actor," "Volunteering for Charities," and "Night Classes." You can add more branches off the secondary ones to record a third level of ideas; for example, for the general activity "Night Classes" there are specific classes: "Zen," "Wine Tasting," "Writing Fiction," and "Business Courses." You could even add a fourth level; for example, "Marketing" and "Accounting" (not shown) from the "Business Courses" branch.

> Millions long for immortality who don't know what to do on a rainy Sunday afternoon.
> — Susan Ertz

Now is the time to plant your own Get-a-Life Tree, using figure 3-1 as a guide. Utilizing the first three primary categories, make sure you generate a total of at least fifty things that you truly like to do now, have liked doing in the past, or have thought about but never gotten around to doing. Record every idea, no matter how frivolous it seems. Don't judge your ideas here. You must get at

Figure 3-1. The Get-a-Life Tree

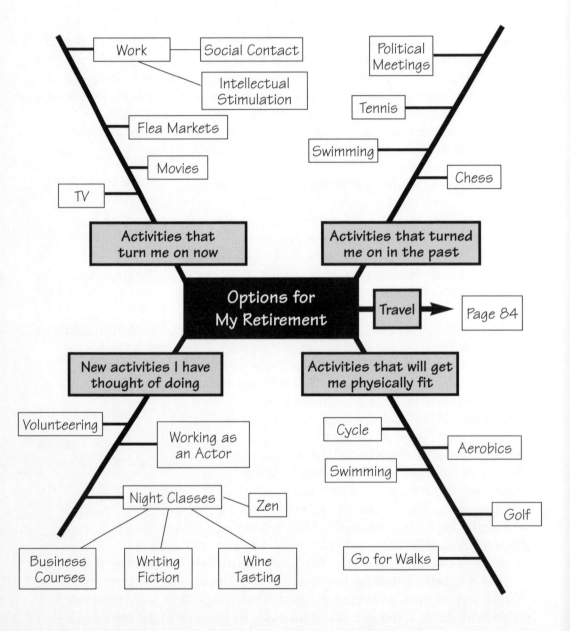

least fifty even if it takes you two days; forty-nine won't do!

Other principal ideas can be added if you have special categories of activities you want to actively pursue. For example, you may be very interested in getting fit and traveling in your retirement days. Then, as in figure 3-1, you can record the principal ideas, "Activities that will get me physically fit" on one primary branch, and "Travel" on another primary branch. Note that if you run out of room, the Get-a-Life Tree can be expanded to another page, as this one has been for travel.

It's fine for the same idea to appear in more than one category. In fact, if this happens, you've identified a leisure activity that may be a priority in your life. In figure 3-1, "Swimming" appears in the categories "Activities that turned me on in the past," "Activities that will get me physically fit," and "Travel." If this was your actual Get-a-Life Tree, swimming would have to be one of the first activities that you pursue immediately.

> The basic ingredient in my definition of retirement is action. The things I have planned for that time of my life continue to grow.
> — Brooky Brown

Let's look at the benefits of using the Get-a-Life Tree as an idea-generating tool: First, it is compact — many ideas can be listed on one page. If needed, the Get-a-Life Tree can be expanded to additional pages. Second, your activity ideas are assigned to categories and thus are easier to group. Moreover, you can expand on your existing ideas to generate many new ideas.

Still another advantage of the Get-a-Life Tree is that it can be used as a long-term tool. After setting it aside for a while, you can come back and generate a batch of fresh ideas. In fact, you should update it on a regular basis to ensure that you can choose from an endless number of retirement activities.

Color and images make for a more creative Get-a-Life Tree, and at the same time enhance our ability to remember what's on it. The images used in the enhanced Get-a-Life Tree on the next page make it a lot more interesting and useful than a conventional list.

After you expand your Get-a-Life Tree to five or six pages, you are in a position to choose from a vast number of different retirement activities. If you have any zest for living, you should be able to record enough activities to keep you busy not just for five years, but for five lifetimes.

Finding the right set of activities for a full life is a personal matter. But it's easy to overlook many possible activities. To help you add to those you have already placed in your Get-a-Life Tree, I have included over 300 activities on pages 85 to 91. Rate each

Figure 3-2. Enhanced Get-a-Life Tree

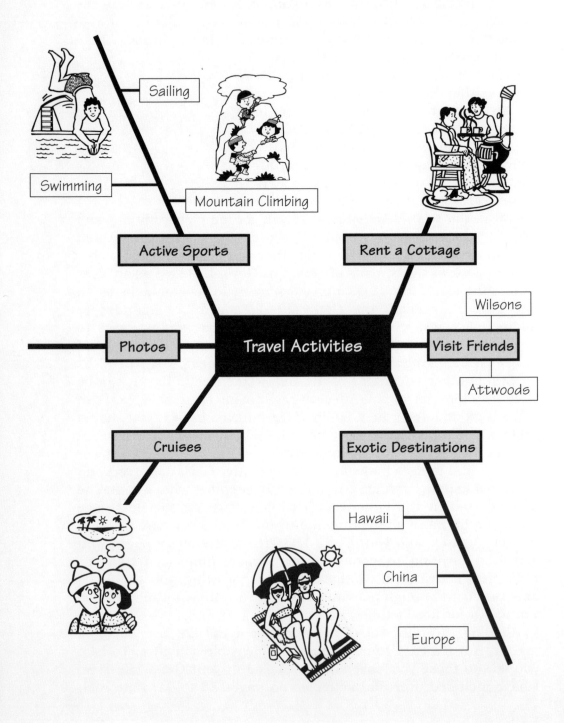

activity according to whether it:

1. Turns you on now

2. Has turned you on in the past

3. Is a new activity that you would consider doing

4. Does not interest you at all

Obviously, activities in categories 1, 2, and 3 interest you and belong on your Get-a-Life Tree. As you add these activities to your Get-a-Life Tree, they may trigger new ideas that you will also want to put on the tree. In no time, your Get-a-Life Tree should have enough activities to keep you busy for a long time.

Activities for Your Get-a-Life Tree

Spend a lot more time with your grandchildren

Climb the mountain you have always wanted to climb

Take up golf for the first time

Go to a baseball game on a Wednesday afternoon

Play tennis again

Go to Mardi Gras in New Orleans

Teach English as a second language

Phone an old boyfriend or girlfriend just for the fun of it

Walk barefoot through a mountain stream

Type your name in an Internet search engine and see what comes up

Skip rocks on the water

Start a new business for enjoyment, not for the money

Attempt a form of writing, such as a song or a poem, that you have never tried before

Join a club such as the Lions or Kinsmen

Go on a cruise to the Caribbean

Record the history of your home town

Treat yourself to a massage

Learn to be a child again

Play the guitar that has been in the closet for twenty-six years

Write the novel that you tell everyone you are capable of writing — now is the time to walk the talk

Paint a self-portrait — if it

doesn't turn out well, you can always blame the subject

Teach children of low-income parents to read

Write your autobiography

Play an instrument

Learn to play an instrument

Walk

Run

Volunteer

Choose a person who you have been angry with and write a letter of forgiveness

Join a discussion group

Sit on the beach and contemplate the ocean

Choose someone famous in your hometown who you admire and would like to have dinner with — ask this person to dinner

Write a letter to yourself listing the goals you expect to accomplish within the next five years — seal it and open it in five years

Learn to play the piano

Become a movie critic

Surprise a good friend

Prepare a meal for yourself

Learn how to cook

Create a new recipe

Visit present friends

Visit old friends

Try to meet new friends

Go hiking

Write letters to celebrities

Take a survey

Sleep

Meditate

Drive around in the city

Drive in the country

Count the items in this list to see if there are really over 300

Read books

Listen to the radio

Watch television

Listen to the stereo

Travel

Go to the movies

Make a movie

Learn computing

Write a computer program

Paint your house

Golf

Fish

Walk through a jungle

Go camping

Climb a mountain

Become involved in politics

Attend a poetry reading

Write your own poem about your experience of a poetry reading

Take part in a poetry reading

Start an underground newspaper

Have a heart-to-heart conversation with a friend in which there is no planned ending time — let it end when it ends

Research your ancestors

Create a drawing of your family tree

Write a book about how your ancestors have affected your life

Become a connoisseur of inexpensive restaurants

Have a latté while reading the newspaper in the outside patio of a coffee bar on a weekday morning

Ride a bicycle

Ride a motorcycle

Invite friends to your home

Invent a new board game

Go to the library

Play with children

Appear on a talk show

Offer to work for nothing

Play billiards

Dance alone for relaxation

Dance with someone else

Take dancing lessons

Restore an old car

Restore a piece of furniture

Renovate your house

Clean your house

Telephone old friends

Write a book

Write in your diary

Create a new cartoon

Write someone's biography

Make a dress, hat, or other apparel

Try to create an interesting wardrobe for only fifty dollars

Start a collection of ...

Pan for gold

Sunbathe

Swim

Have sex

Go to church

Dive in the water

Go scuba diving

Go snorkeling

Get a pilot's license

Take up photography

Develop a photo album

Find out what a rebus is and create ten of your own

Find out what was happening the day you were born

Have a garage sale

Rearrange your living-room furniture

Take up acting

Write a play

Fly a kite

Learn to run backward

Learn to impersonate someone famous

Plant a garden

Ride a horse

Pick some flowers

Write poetry

Write a letter to a friend

Attempt a record for running backward

Learn how to sing

Write a song

Memorize a poem

Join an encounter group

Learn famous quotations

Memorize a song

Gaze at the stars

Truly experience a sunset

Watch the moon

Learn about new religions

Build a house

Design a unique house

Go live in another country

Go sailing

Play hockey

Build a boat

Watch interesting court cases at the courthouse

Learn more about the stock market

Invent a better mousetrap

Start a new club

Window shop

Learn how to repair your car

Throw a dinner party for a variety of people

See how many strangers will say hello to you

Dance in the rain

Do a rain dance to make it rain

Adopt a new identity and try to live the whole day with it

Approach a stranger on the street and ask him/her to tell you their life story

Take a walk through the rough part of town just for the fun of it

Go to the library and leaf through old magazines to remind you what life was like in your teens

Reminisce about your favorite childhood pastimes — then choose one to relive today

Take up wood working

Write a hand-written letter to an old friend

Have a long conversation with a child to see what you can learn

Research the Green Tortoise bus tours on the Internet and choose one for your next out-of-town trip

Photograph nature while enjoying the outdoors

Shop for clothes

Watch people in public

Roller skate

Play cards

Telephone a talk show to voice your opinion

Have a candlelight dinner with someone

Join a club to improve your public speaking

Join a wine-tasting club to learn about wine

Go back to university or college to get a degree

Take up skydiving

Learn all about health and fitness

Pick fruit in an orchard

Visit local tourist sights

Take up a new hobby

Create your own palindrome

Help fight pollution

Go to a flea market

Take a catnap

Go to garage sales

Help an environmental group preserve a rain forest

Use the Internet to search for former classmates

Test your memory by seeing if you can name all your school teachers from grade school to senior high

Prepare a collage of all the things you want to do in retirement

Create your own file of jokes and graffiti and see if you can get it published

Start a pirate radio station

Record a CD

Sponsor a foster child in Haiti

Go visit your foster child in Haiti

Start your own personal web page with your favorite quotations and other things that others may find interesting

Choose somewhere exotic in Europe or elsewhere that you would like to visit — then take a part-time job to earn the extra money so that you can go

Climb a tree

Go to horse races with ten dollars

Ride public transit for fun

Start a newsletter

Write a letter to a pen pal in another country

Walk in the wilderness

Do crossword puzzles

Start and operate a bed and breakfast

Build a swimming pool

Daydream

Attend a sports event

Travel to old haunts

Go white-water rafting

Go up in a hot-air balloon

Be a big sister/brother

Go to your favorite restaurant

Try a new restaurant

Go to a tennis ranch to improve your tennis

Teach your dog new tricks

Learn a new trick to show your dog

Attend live theater

Attend the symphony

Go to a retreat to relax

Truly communicate with someone special today

Enter your favorite recipe in a contest

Play with your pet

Train your mind to be creative

Run for political office

Visit a zoo

Make your own wine

Kick the television habit

Raise your vocabulary

Learn how to read financial statements

Learn how to judge

personalities better

Improve your personality

End the evening by reflecting on your day

Start a new charity

Study clouds

Make a list of all the successes in your life

Play a prank on a friend

Dream up new pranks

Take twice as much time as usual to eat

Go bird-watching

Create a new comic strip

Try doing nothing

Visit a museum

Join a new club

Go play bingo

Check this list to see whether any activities are repeated

Start a new country

Skip rope

Start an argument

Watch someone work

Lie on a beach

Wash and polish your car

Start a hobby farm

Help fight crime

Learn about solar energy

Write a book on leisure

Learn how to hypnotize yourself

Have your palm read

Do a jigsaw puzzle

Visit a craft show

Learn a magic act

Cook a lousy meal for

someone not to enjoy

Learn to speak French, Spanish, or any other language

Care for someone ill

Be a philosopher

Be nasty to politicians

Write down five of your greatest faults or weaknesses and then choose one to overcome over the next year

Compile a to-do list for the rest of your life

Write a fairy tale

Truly enjoy the atmosphere of the present season by looking out of your front window for a few minutes

Organize a protest group for your political pet peeve

Compile a not-to-do list for the rest of your life

Take stock of all the material things you don't want or need; sell these and use the money to throw a big party for your friends

Visit a cemetery and find the most interesting epitaph

Also look for the funniest epitaph

Imagine what your epitaph will say

Teach a lifelong hobby to others at a night school

Research a certain era of your country's history that keenly interests you

Trade homes for a month with a friend who lives in

another city or country

Put something out-of-the-ordinary in your will so that your heirs will have to earn their money in a fun way

Invent a new service, product, gadget, or the like

Choose a town within fifty miles of your home and spend the afternoon there

Go to a park and sit in silence for thirty minutes to absorb the sounds of nature

Celebrate your adventurous spirit by ...

Reconnect with a hobby from your youth

Expand this list to 500 activities to outdo me

You Don't Have to Watch One Minute of TV When You Retire — and Perhaps You Shouldn't

Perhaps you are already retired and have joined the group of unfulfilled individuals who spend most of their time watching TV and the rest of their time contemplating why life is so weird, stale, and boring. Not to worry; there's medication available to help you conquer boredom. Well, not really. There is good news, however: You can do something about the problem.

To conquer boredom, you must get to the source. Be clear that there is only one source. If you still don't get it, perhaps these words of Dylan Thomas may be of some help: "Something is boring me; I think it is me."

When you have had as much as you can take of yourself, you will finally realize that you are

I didn't think that anything could ever be as boring as the government paper-pushing job that I was in for thirty-five years. Well, my first year of retirement is giving the job a good run for its money.

Early Retirement Day #337

the source of your boredom. Watching a lot of television is a choice you make and not a great way to spend the bulk of your retirement years. If you are not yet retired and spend most of your leisure time in front of the TV set, this is certainly not good training for leading an active retirement.

"What's wrong with watching television?" you may vehemently ask in defense of one of your best friends. There is nothing wrong with watching an hour or two a day. And there are a lot of reasons that you shouldn't watch more than that.

The biggest reason is that the boredom experienced in retirement can be a form of prolonged suicide for those who end up watching TV most of the time. If you are going to do nothing but watch television, putting yourself out of your misery may be the better way to retire. You may as well dig a hole, climb in it, and pull the dirt over yourself.

> Television has proved that people will look at anything rather than each other.
>
> — Ann Landers

As a matter of fact you don't have to watch one minute of TV when you retire — and perhaps you shouldn't. Granted, it would be a little too extreme for me to suggest that no one should watch any TV. Even so, given the detrimental aspects of TV, we should try to minimize our time with it whether we are retired or not. People who easily get addicted to things will do themselves a big favor by getting rid of their TV set and replacing their TV habit with one or more healthier addictions, such as golf or painting.

The probability of having a happy and successful retirement is inversely proportional to how much television an individual watches. Watching TV is an activity that yields low satisfaction for most people. Although a large number of people admit they watch too much television, they continue to do so because it is an easy form of entertainment to access. More satisfying activities take more motivation and creativity — requiring effort that many people aren't willing to expend.

TV watching, like most activities, is harmless in moderation; most retired people are not moderate in their viewing, however. Research indicates that today's full-time North American retiree watches an average of twenty-six hours of TV a week. That's almost four hours a day. Remember, many active full-time retirees have a hard time fitting in four hours of TV in a complete spring and summer. What's more, some don't even own a TV. And if the average is almost four hours a day, that means many retirees are watching TV eight or more hours a day.

Retiring happy, wild, and free is about fulfillment and there is nothing very fulfilling about watching eight or more hours of television a day while vegetating on the couch. TV is low involvement, not only physically, but mentally as well. Highly evolved individuals don't call it an "idiot box" for nothing.

> It [television] is a medium of entertainment which permits millions of people to listen to the same joke at the same time, and yet remain lonesome.
>
> — T. S. Eliot

TV substitutes for time that would normally be spent in personal encounters with real human beings. As we shall see later, intimate human encounters can add immensely to retirees' happiness. David Campbell and other members of a Harvard research team recently reported that television viewing has a corrosive effect on social and public life. People who adopt TV as their primary form of entertainment are significantly less likely to attend dinner parties, visit friends, entertain at home, go on picnics, give blood, and send greeting cards.

Moreover, these same researchers discovered that chronic TV viewing corresponds with the "jerk-type personality." Being somewhat deficient in character, chronic TV viewers are more likely to give you the finger in traffic than occasional viewers. The researchers did not comment on whether the jerk-type personality is just prone to watching way too much TV or that their jerk-type behavior is actually caused by their TV habit.

Regardless of whether you are actually a jerk or not, creative and constructive use of your time will leave little need to watch TV. After he had been retired for four years, Hammond Stith, sixty-one at the time, concluded that there are seven constructive things that retirees can do with their time. "You can work and you can play and you can sleep. You can improve your mind or you can improve your health. You can work in civic activities or educational activities, or you can work in some spiritual area for the church. As far as I know, there's nothing else you can do . . . And my retirement has been great. It's better than anything I ever expected it to be."

Take note that Stith did not mention watching television as one of the seven constructive things you can do with your time. At best, most television provides superficial entertainment with nothing of depth. This tends to wither the mind instead of stimulating it. After we finish watching television, we seldom feel educated or enlightened. Instead, in the extreme case, we may feel empty and dejected.

Summing up, television fills the void for those retirees who don't have a major purpose or other interesting activities to pursue. Television will do very little to conquer boredom, however. What will cure retirees of boredom is their getting off the couch and branching out in new directions. In his book *The Four Agreements*, Don Miguel Ruiz states, "Action is about living fully. Inaction is the way we deny life. Inaction is sitting in front of the television every day for years because you are afraid to be alive and to take the risk of expressing what you are."

An Ounce of Action Is Worth a Ton of Sitting Around

So many worlds, so much to do,
So little done, such things to be.
— Alfred, Lord Tennyson

For most of us, a happy retirement won't be attained by freedom from duty and responsibility, leading to a life filled with nothing but passive leisure and pleasure. Undoubtedly, if you have read this book this far, you don't want to end like up the average North American, looking for as much recreation, entertainment, and cheap thrills as you can get at the expense of doing something that is challenging and exciting.

> Any idiot can face a crisis — it's day to day living that wears you out.
> — Anton Chekhov

The vast majority of North American workers spend their leisure time watching a lot of TV, or doing other activities that provide little personal satisfaction. The less physical and thought-provoking the leisure activity, the more attractive it is. These activities, however, are poor preparation for a retirement that is happy, wild, and free. Only by being physically, intellectually, and creatively challenged can individuals find satisfaction and fulfillment in their leisure activities.

A recent poll indicated that over 50 percent of retired people felt less useful after retirement than before. It doesn't have to be this way for you. The key is to avoid spending all your time on activities that add little to your sense of self-worth.

Being genuinely active is essential to a retirement that is

happy, wild, and free. Indeed, an ounce of action is worth a ton of sitting around. When Willie Sutton was asked why he robbed banks, he answered, "Because that's where the money is." Similarly, if you want challenge and adventure in your retirement life, you will have to go where the action is.

Being genuinely active is more than getting out of bed every morning, making yourself a big breakfast, and then watching TV for most of the day. It's also more than skimming newspapers and listening to radio talk shows. Being genuinely active transcends being involved in only passive activities that do little or nothing to stimulate any part of you.

For many retirees, who have a difficult time filling their days, gambling becomes an appealing activity, simply because it's easy to do. A United States federal government study found that the percentage of sixty-five-and-over Americans who recently gambled jumped from 20 percent in 1974 to 50 percent by the start of the new century, a surge unmatched by any other age group. Loneliness, boredom, and a craving for excitement are usually cited by experts as the factors fueling the huge increase in senior gambling.

Sadly, gambling is an activity that often creates more serious problems for retirees than the ones it's supposed to solve. Gambling addiction has led to many retirees losing a good portion, or all, of their retirement savings. The embarrassment, loss of self-esteem, and depression that accompany the loss of great amounts of money have made it difficult for some retirees to live with themselves. Be clear that this expensive activity is best left to those with too much money to burn and nothing better to do. The best part of a casino, after all, is the outside of it.

Instead of fewer problems, I have lots of new ones since I gave up my career, such as not knowing what to do with my time.

I just read somewhere that if you view your problems closely enough, you will recognize yourself as the major source of every one of them.

The next time you are in Las Vegas, pay attention to the faces of the gamblers in the casinos. You won't see many happy faces simply because gambling is a passive activity. There is no real sense of accomplishment even if the gambler manages to come out on the winning side. Luck will have determined whether the gambler wins and not skill, talent, or perseverance.

Gambling, like watching TV, is nothing more than mindless entertainment, something that can't be very satisfying. Poet, singer, and songwriter Leonard Cohen once told a British reporter, "We can be destroyed just as easily by mindless frivolity as we can by obsessive depression." For this reason, you must be deliberate with your leisure pursuits.

> Nothing is more terrible than activity without insight.
>
> — Thomas Carlyle

In retirement, as in any stage of life, you will find that it's hard feeling active when you aren't being active. The argument can be made that one is always active as long as one is alive. However, it's a matter of degree; passive activities don't make us feel alive. Too many people choose activities that involve them primarily on a superficial level, both mentally and physically. These activities, such as watching soap operas on TV, leave them feeling empty and unfulfilled.

On the other hand, meaningful activities involve some measure of effort. At the same time these activities provide physical, mental, and spiritual stimulation. There are even more intangible rewards such as a sense of satisfaction and accomplishment.

Recently a group of psychologists separated happiness into two types: feel-good happiness and value-based happiness. Watching a hockey game on TV — a type of feel-good happiness — is, unfortunately, ruled by the law of diminishing returns. With time — sometimes in minutes, rarely in more than a matter of hours — the satisfaction from the activity decreases until it reaches zero.

Value-based happiness, on the other hand, comes from meaningful activities that serve some higher purpose than just plain pleasure. Ultimately, value-based happiness stems from attaining a sense of satisfaction. And that satisfaction is attained from fulfilling some deeper purpose in tune with our values. The activities contributing to value-based happiness are not normally ruled by the law of diminishing returns. If they are, the time to reach zero satisfaction is normally a lot longer than for activities that provide pleasure-based happiness.

For some people, the nature of their leisure activities must change when they retire. They may have been able to get away with passive leisure activities while they were employed. Not only may their jobs have provided them with physical activity, they provided them with challenges, accomplishment, and satisfaction. With the loss of their jobs, they will need to indulge in leisure activities that bring them these same benefits. They will need activities that challenge their mental as well as their physical abilities.

In order that the participant experience satisfaction, leisure activities should be creative, challenging, and constructive. It follows that this leaves out watching TV and gambling. Retirement can be so much more satisfying with activities such as gardening, tennis, mountain biking, hiking, painting pictures, climbing mountains, traveling to out-of-the-way places, playing an instrument, taking a Spanish course, starting a part-time business, and volunteering.

> Rest is a good thing, but boredom is its brother.
> — Voltaire

The Academy of Leisure Sciences, a group of academics who study time use, have determined that we get the most satisfaction from leisure activities that are harder and more challenging. It's best for us to put our time into activities requiring high levels of physical and intellectual energy. A leisure pursuit will be truly satisfying if it meets all or most of the following eight criteria:

1. You have a genuine interest in it.

2. It is challenging.

3. There is some sense of accomplishment associated with completing only a portion of it.

4. It has many aspects to it so that it doesn't become boring.

5. It helps you develop some skill.

6. You can get so immersed in it that you lose the sense of time.

7. It provides you with a sense of self-development.

8. It doesn't cost too much.

Based on the above criteria, we can group leisure pursuits into passive activities and active ones. Following are ten examples for each category:

Passive Activities
- Watching TV and videos

- Drinking beer
- Going for a drive
- Junking out on food
- Gambling
- Napping
- Watching spectator sports
- Shopping
- Talking about yesterday's news
- Goofing off in shopping malls

Active Activities

- Writing a book
- Hiking
- Cross-country skiing
- Auditing fun courses at a university or college
- Attending plays, concerts, and movies
- Taking piano lessons
- Tracing your family tree
- Drawing cartoons
- Creating stained-glass windows
- Helping solve the world's problems

Without exception, there is no such thing as personal satisfaction without some sort of challenge and effort involved. Such being the case, the degree to which you have a fulfilling retirement will be inversely proportional to how much you indulge in passive activities and how much you avoid active ones. Generally speaking, passive activities are those that retirees indulge in for pure pleasure without much effort on their part.

> When you start having a good time, you're supposed to be somewhere else.
>
> — Unknown wise person

Passive activities seldom, if ever, give us the mental highs that will banish boredom. These activities are typified by no real challenge, no overriding purpose, low arousal, monotony, and lack of novelty. Although these predictable and safe activities provide security and safety along with pleasure, we get little or no long-term satisfaction and self-fulfillment from them.

Contrary to popular belief, individuals will not achieve enduring happiness from pleasure alone. In fact, if life was all pleasure and nothing else, there would be no happiness. In *Henry IV, Part I*, William Shakespeare wrote, "If all the year were playing holidays, to sport would be as tedious as to work." Moreover, Josh Billings warned us, "Don't mistake pleasure for happiness. They are a different breed of dog." Indeed, total pleasure and comfort can become detrimental to our well-being.

There is nothing wrong with regularly indulging in pleasurable activities that, for example, involve rest and relaxation. I am a strong advocate of a daily afternoon nap, given that napping has been proven to enhance our health. Nonetheless, I am not impressed by anyone who tries to make a marathon out of this activity. The rewards will be fleeting at best. If our passive activities aren't complemented by active ones, we won't experience the degree of happiness we are looking for in our retirement years.

> Many men die at twenty-five and aren't buried until they are seventy-five.
> — Benjamin Franklin

Study happy retirees and no doubt you will notice active individuals undertaking challenging pursuits that provide a good measure of satisfaction. When retiree Frank Kaiser is asked by his friends why he and his wife take hot-air balloon rides, fly motorless gliders, and skydive, he answers, "I suppose part of it is that we don't want to become like so many old farts, sitting around, dead, and not knowing it."

In designing a happy and successful retirement, you must find out what makes you tick. What sort of interests and active activities would make your life much more challenging and well worth living? Perhaps accomplishment is important to you. You can achieve this in many ways. For example, training yourself to run five miles every day when you are sixty years old may be challenging and difficult considering that the majority of sixty-year-old retirees have a hard time running twenty feet. Achieving this is sure to leave you feeling good about yourself.

It is worthwhile to develop a bank of retirement activities and options that are worth pursuing in case you get bored with your original choices. This is where the Get-a-Life Tree can play a big role. A wide variety of activities — both physical and mental — will go a long way towards conquering boredom. Best of all, you won't have to watch television — or pretend to enjoy watching it with others — ever again!

Take the time to discover the types of leisure activities that you can be passionate about. Start by making a list of your favorite college courses, cities, countries, resorts, sports, games, exercise, songs, artists, authors, and artistic pursuits. Incorporate these in as many active leisure activities as you can. These activities will contribute to personal growth, higher self-esteem, less stress, improved health, excitement and adventure, more satisfaction, more happiness, and an overall higher quality of life.

Now is a good time to return to Ian Hammond from Scotland, who was mentioned earlier in this book. Note that in his resignation letter quoted on page 6, Ian had planned a variety of activities for his retirement. Moreover, all of his activities fell in the active category versus the passive category. Given that Ian pursues these activities, do you think he gets bored?

In August 2002, I sent Ian a letter and a copy of my book *The Lazy Person's Guide to Success* (as a bribe) to find out what he was up to. I was also curious about how old he was, given that he had not mentioned this in his earlier letters. Here is Ian's response:

Dear Ernie,

Thank you for your letter and a copy of your latest book. I hope to return the compliment one day, because I still intend to write my travelogue, starting next year. It will be fairly easy reading, detailing my bike journeys (one country per chapter), with humor, historical snippets, and descriptions of

> The time you enjoy wasting is not wasted time.
>
> — Laurence J. Peter

landscapes, but also with some autobiographical content and a few opinions of life philosophy. I want to write it for myself (the best reason!) and maybe self-publish it with my own paintings or illustrations. Of course, I have never written a book before and have no idea how to do it, so it will be fun. As you say in your books, the process is more important than the result.

Since I last wrote I have been too busy to write my book, in spite of not working. I biked Chile for 2001/2002. Chile was a superb choice and exceeded all my expectations (each destination does, but this was exceptional). The landscape was incredibly varied, like a 'super New Zealand'. But the real reason was the warmth and generosity of the people, which I have never experienced anywhere else. The Chile chapter will be a long one! This summer I went round several islands of our west coast here, the Hebrides.

Apart from travelling, I've learned Spanish so that I've almost fluent (this meant I got more out of my South American trip than being an observer). Next year I'd like to start some Portuguese because I refuse to go there until I can speak it! This year has also seen me try painting in oils as I've been doing watercolours since retiring and wanted to branch out a bit. Also a lot of classical guitar (still terrible) and chess (won a tournament).

On the personal side, I did a 'grand tour' of various family members scattered around England (some of whom I hadn't seen for a decade), much perusing over photo albums, country walks, meals out, and reminiscing. And in spite of being away for a few months each year, I see my immediate family more than when I was working. I think if I ever return to the workforce it will be in some sort of semi-voluntary capacity overseas.

> People can be divided into three groups: those who make things happen, those who watch things happen, and those who wonder what happened.
>
> — John Newbern

My immediate plan is to continue biking. Next month I hope to go to West Africa (there are cheap charters to Gambia) and head east, possibly as far as Arabia but more realistically to Timbuktu in an out-and-back loop south of the Sahara, through Senegal, and Mali. More chapters for the book . . .

Best wishes and success for your next one,

Ian (age 40)

Undoubtedly, provided Ian keeps at least half as active as he is now, he will avoid ending up one of the older retirees who spend their last years bored, lonely, and depressed. To repeat, a variety of activities is essential to avoid boredom and its detrimental effects. Moreover, at least some of these activities should be challenging, meaningful, and satisfying — much like those that Ian has pursued.

Researchers at the University of Southern California confirm that variety is the spice of life. They found that individuals who regularly do new things, such as going to places they have never been or playing a new game, are happier and have a greater sense of well-being than people who keep doing the same old things. The researchers concluded that people with many interests live not only happiest, but longest, too.

On one hand, a great deal of leisure time in retirement can mean idleness, uselessness, and boredom. On the other hand, this leisure time can lead to excitement, adventure, and fulfillment. The way to move from the former to the latter is to indulge in a variety of activities with most of them in the active category.

In short, retirement life is a game of action. Happy people are the players. Unhappy people are the spectators. Which would you like to be?

Create New Structures and Routines with Your Leisure

As mentioned earlier, being without a job can be detrimental to many retirees' well-being and self-esteem. Retirement stress can result from the lack of predictability, lack of control, and lack of social contact. Indeed, after they have left their careers for good, some retirees are so lost that they have been known to start missing jobs that they hated and colleagues who used to drive them berserk.

> Most of the time I don't have much fun. The rest of the time I don't have any fun at all.
>
> — Woody Allen

Even the lowest ranking job is better to some people than a life of total leisure. "Sometimes people's rituals keep them held together, and it gives them a sense of who they are — their job title, their role, whatever it is," proclaims Beverly Hills psychologist Kathleen Mijas. "When it's just you, then you have to get in touch with what's there, and that could be empty or scary or overwhelming."

Most retirees who wind up unhappy without a job don't tell the truth about the workplaces they long for. After they leave a job, these retirees don't necessarily miss the work that they hated or the obnoxious colleagues with whom they used to work. They, in fact, miss more important things that the job brought with it.

A job provides us with many rewards; these include self-worth, status, achievement, recognition, room for growth, power, and money. Upon leaving the job, these rewards are lost. Leisure in retirement will be satisfying only if it can provide most of the rewards that we find important. All our needs, which were previously satisfied at the workplace, will now have to be met in different ways.

In preparing for a successful retirement, it's valuable to figure out what work has meant to you. What intangible or non-financial aspects of work have given you meaning and satisfaction? These may include friendship, challenge, accomplishment, purpose, and power. It is possible for you to implement all these elements into many leisure activities.

University of Michigan researchers concluded that the most contented retirees had made the most effort to replace the relationships and activities they lost upon leaving work. Often all it took was volunteering for charity. "The important thing is to reach out and grab what you like," advised one of the researchers.

To design the best possible retirement, figure out the types of interests and leisure activities that can bring you the same types of benefits and rewards that work brings you. Napping and watching TV certainly won't provide these benefits, but volunteering or running your own non-profit organization may. Pursuing satisfying and productive interests will ensure that your retirement life has as many rewards and as much meaning as your work life has.

There are three important human needs that most jobs inadvertently fill. The needs are structure, a sense of community, and purpose. Even if we work at a job that is low status or undesirable, the job generally provides us with the means for satisfying all these three needs.

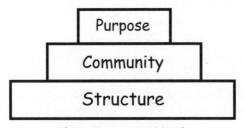

Three Important Needs

For some people, giving up the structure, community, and purpose that come from their job is much more difficult than they initially expected. A switch from a rigid work schedule to an unstructured lifestyle jolts many retirees. According to researchers, this transition can seriously affect one in five individuals, leaving them in a state of mild to severe depression.

> I'm trying to arrange my life so I don't even have to be present.
> — Graffiti

A full life requires at least some structure, sense of community, and purpose. In a traditional retirement, all these needs have to be met through our own initiative. We have already discussed how we can put more purpose in our lives with a true calling, a fun job, a creative pursuit, and constructive leisure activities. In chapter 6, we will discuss how to put more friendship and community into our retirement lives. Here, though, we will discuss the importance of erecting new structures and routines.

Initially, the loss of ready-made structures and routines sounds great: no need to get up early in the morning, no need to rush breakfast, no meetings to attend on time, and no commuting in rush-hour traffic. In other words, the clock no longer rules us. The problem is that most of us, no matter how creative, like at least some structure and routine in our lives. Being creatures of habit, we get addicted to structure. There is a great deal of comfort from the routines, and, of course, we all like comfort.

> Habit is habit, and not to be flung out of the window by any man, but coaxed downstairs a step at a time
>
> — Mark Twain

Losing structure and routine can create much havoc, especially for very rigid and highly structured people. Time must be filled to pass the days, but empty time can end up being the rule instead of the exception. Empty time results in boredom and joyless living. Rigid people may even withdraw from society and lead a life of desperation because they refuse to adjust to an existence in which they have the personal freedom to do what they want. In extreme cases, mental and physical capabilities rapidly deteriorate.

If you are independently minded and self-motivated, the loss of structure will be a blessing rather than a curse. Retirement is the time to enjoy your freedom and to create your own new routines. The task of setting routines and structure will be much easier if you have created some driving purpose in your life.

Structure can be established in many ways. For example, after I semi-retired many years ago, I had to create my own routines to replace those provided by the organizations where I had worked. Exercising twice a day to keep fit puts routine and structure in my days. I do stretch exercises for about fifty minutes soon after I get up. Later in the afternoon, I exercise for up to one-and-a-half hours with a combination of cycling, running, walking, and playing tennis. Besides all the other great benefits I get from exercising, I create over two hours of routine every day.

I also put more structure in my days with activities such as regularly visiting coffee bars to have coffee, chatting with the regulars, and reading three different newspapers. Setting regular time slots to write this book, as well as ten others, has provided me with even more structure. I have established routines because I realize that a moderate amount of structure is

> There is no pleasure in having nothing to do; the fun is having lots to do and not doing it.
>
> — John W. Raper

necessary for my well-being. In his book, *Ageless Body, Timeless Mind*, Deepak Chopra emphasizes the importance of daily routines for retarding the aging process.

Below are a few other ways to put routine and structure into your retirement life that will assist you in adjusting to retirement life and help you age better.

- Take courses at your local college or university.
- Have an artistic pursuit that you indulge in for three to four hours a day.
- Take a one-hour walk every morning and evening.
- Join the boards of charities that meet regularly.
- Involve yourself in a team sport that you can do on a regular basis.
- Start a part-time business or work as a volunteer.

If you have developed as a person, your interests should be so varied that the lack of routine and structure won't be a problem. One of your most powerful inner resources is your own creativity. The big advantage of being creative is you get to design your routines and schedule around your leisure time, your friendships, and your relationships with the world. This ensures a lifestyle that is truly your own.

Early to Bed and Early to Rise Makes a Person Dull, Boring, and Despised

Shortly after having started writing this book, I was halfway through my afternoon run when I decided that I was enjoying it more than usual. This was the first warm and sunny day in a long time; thus, I decided to depart from my routine and run an extra fifteen minutes over my normal forty-five minutes. I did so by extending my run into a new neighborhood.

Here I encountered two little girls walking on the sidewalk towards me. One was about five years old and the other one was about three-and-a-half. They both had some toys with them and seemed to be enjoying themselves even more than I was enjoying myself. As I passed by the smiling little girls, I said, "Hello," and they both responded by saying, "Hi."

I continued on my merry way, but about five seconds later, I heard, "Why are you running?" I looked back and was surprised to see the three-and-a-half-year-old running in an attempt to catch up to me. I responded with, "Because I like it!"

A few seconds later, I looked back again and saw that this little toddler, with a big smile and rosy red cheeks, was still running full tilt trying to catch up to me. Again, she yelled, "Why are you running?" I replied, "Because I want to," but the little girl ignored this. Eventually, after running about half a block, she gave up. I was totally blown away how the little girl decided, at the spur of the moment, to leave her friend and run after me in an attempt to find out why I was running.

At this point you may be thinking, "What does this story have to do with retirement?" Actually, nothing; I just kind of like the story. Seriously, this story has a lot to do with the importance of being spontaneous for avoiding boredom in our retirement years.

After encountering these two little girls, I thought about how much more adults would enjoy life if they could at least once or twice a week be as spontaneous as children. I also realized that if I had not been spontaneous myself, by running for an extra fifteen minutes, I wouldn't have had the wonderful experience of having this three-and-half-year-old girl remind me how to enjoy life more.

Unfortunately, many retirees have resigned themselves to a life of acceptable — and even respectable — routine and mediocrity. They actually believe the words of Benjamin Franklin: "Early to bed and early to rise, makes a man healthy, wealthy, and wise." I agree with Benjamin Franklin on a lot of things, but this is one case where I must make an exception. Based upon my observations, Franklin's words should be modified to: "Always early to bed and early to rise makes a person dull, boring, and despised." (Okay, I am overdoing it with the "despised.")

> Dawn comes no sooner for the early riser.
>
> — Spanish proverb

The fact is, people who always go to bed early and rise early thrive on routine and rigidity. They end up going to the same old places, associating with the same people, taking the same route home, listening to the same radio stations, and watching the same sitcoms on TV. No wonder they get bored. Trying something new would do wonders for their psyches.

Routine is good to a certain degree; we all need some routine in our daily lives. Too much routine, however, can be detrimental to our well-being. Routines can eventually turn into deep ruts. Doing the same things every day with the same people who think the same thoughts is no way to enhance our retirement and outlook on life.

Breaking away from your routine may take some effort, particularly if you are a rigid person. "Improvisation is too good to leave to chance," said Paul Simon paradoxically. Put another way, spontaneity is too important to be left to your whims. To put more excitement in your life, you must make the decision to be more spontaneous. I don't mean that you should plan to be spontaneous at 7:00 P.M. tomorrow. Only an accountant with no intention of retiring until he is ninety would try something that silly.

> For the happiest life, days should be rigorously planned, nights left open to chance.
> — Mignon McLaughlin

Today, you can plan to be more spontaneous by giving yourself permission to do something impulsive in the future. Then, tomorrow or after tomorrow, commit yourself to doing something interesting and out of the ordinary the moment that the thought of doing something out of the ordinary strikes. Spurn any reasons for not doing it. Instead of having your rational mind reject the idea as silly, be unreasonable and go with it.

Wondrous things happen with surprising frequency when we learn how to be more spontaneous. Some of the most fascinating things in this world are things that we don't go looking for. Thus, allow more chance into your life. The more chance you allow, the more interesting your world will become.

The ability to be spontaneous goes hand in hand with the ability to be different. The ability to be different has two aspects to it. The first is the ability to be different from the way we have always been. The second is the ability to be different from the way others are. The fact that most retirees are "early to bed and early to rise" doesn't mean that you have to be the same.

The quality of your retirement life will vary directly with the quality of your choices. You determine your happiness and well-being by making the right choices, and not adopting the choices of society or others who may have an influence on you. Right choices are ones that go against the grain. The best choices always appear to be the most off-the-wall ones to others.

Perhaps, if it weren't for television, you — like many other retirees — wouldn't have any nightlife at all. Then it's time to get out of the house and do something about it. You must put more effort into adding novelty to your life instead of doing the same old things. Constantly challenge your inhibitions about trying new activities or going to new and different places. Meeting new people and exploring new things should be a regular activity and not something you do once every ten years.

The biggest problem I have with full-time retirement is that I never get a day off.

The unknown and unexpected can add immensely to your experience of life. Be sure to seek out new people, new places, and new points of view. Talk to the young and the old, the sailors and the painters, and the waiters and the writers. Communicate with them, express yourself to them, and listen carefully, particularly if they have a different viewpoint from your own.

Retirement, more than any other stage in your adult life, allows you great opportunity to get away from routines. Take advantage of this. Have at least one or two hours of unstructured time every day to do something unplanned and different. Also, vary what you do on weekends. Notice how your life is enriched.

Retiree Betty Sullivan, first mentioned on page 79, had this to say about the freedom from routines that retirement life provides: "It's midnight. I suppose I should go to bed. But why? I'm not tired. No matter how late I go to bed, I can sleep as long as I want in the morning. I'm no longer bound by time schedules. To this day, after five years of not getting up in the morning to go to work, the smile is still on my face."

4

Take Special Care of Yourself — Because No One Else Will!

You Too Can Exercise Your Right to a Healthy and Happy Retirement

Joy and Temperance and Repose.
Slam the door on the doctor's nose.
— Henry Wadsworth Longfellow, *The Best Medicines*

In most Western nations today, the plethora of ever-evolving laws can overwhelm us. Luckily, there is still no law that says we can live only to a certain age or at a certain level of health and happiness. Many retirees take advantage of this; they live much longer and healthier and happier than others. Millions of others, unfortunately, allow their health to slide through sheer neglect. Given that health is an important element of happiness, these retirees set themselves up for an unhappy retirement.

Although some retirees with poor physical health, but great mental health, can still experience a good measure of happiness, it doesn't come easily. Staying physically and mentally active is the easiest way to retire happy, wild, and

> Health is my expected heaven.
> — John Keats

free. The degree to which we maintain our mental and physical fitness, before and after retirement, will largely determine how fulfilling our retirement years will turn out.

Of course, if you aren't retired yet, adopting a healthy lifestyle is something you should have done long ago. This improves your chances of reaching retirement and enhances your ability to enjoy retirement once you get there. In the event that you are less healthy than you should be, you should put a lot more time and energy into improving your health than increasing the size of your retirement portfolio. Retiring rich, but unhealthy, won't do you much good. Without good health you can never be truly rich.

> People who don't know how to keep themselves healthy ought to have the decency to get themselves buried, and not waste time about it.
>
> — Henrik Ibsen

Perhaps you know several people in their seventies and beyond who are in excellent mental and physical condition. They are living life with more vigor and joy than most people in midlife. They play tennis or hockey, run, walk, hike, dance, communicate, and debate with the same amount of energy that they had in their thirties or forties.

On the other hand, you undoubtedly know many people only in their forties or fifties who appear lazy, tired, and unenthusiastic. For them, getting out of bed in the morning, twisting a bottle cap, or turning on the TV set is a major project. Not only is their physical well-being significantly compromised by midlife, but their mental well-being is far from what it used to be. They are negative, complain a lot, and never seem to learn anything new. To add to their woes, their spiritual health leaves a lot to be desired.

The $64,000 question is: What measure of physical, mental, and spiritual fitness would you like to have in your retirement years? Undoubtedly, like everyone else, you want to wind up among the active people with an incredible joie de vivre. Now the million-dollar question is: What are you doing about it today? This question applies whether you are presently in your late thirties and working at a full-time job or in your sixties and fully retired.

Paradoxically, many working people who say they look forward to an active and healthy retirement are setting themselves up for the opposite. By working too much, many workers are subjecting their bodies to excessive stress that can lead to many ailments, including cancer. Others are also eating too much, watching too much TV, and exercising too little. Still others keep on smoking cigarettes despite all the evidence that smoking dramatically increases the risk of serious health problems such as cancer, heart disease, and emphysema.

If you are still working full-time, it behooves you to do everything within your power to maintain good health now so that you still have it when you retire. More than anything else, poor health will limit you; it will put a lot of stress on your retirement. In fact, poor health can disrupt the plans that both partners have for their retirement years. Studies show that when one partner's health is poor, both partners have a much more difficult adjustment to retirement.

Even if you retire early, the first decade of retirement will probably be the most fulfilling. After that, health problems can multiply, especially if you don't take care of yourself. Aging brings enough new aches and pains without your having to add to these with an unhealthy diet and a lack of exercise. Feeling good about yourself at midlife and beyond is an important aspect of overall well-being.

> Happiness? That's nothing more than health and a poor memory.
>
> — Albert Schweitzer

Maintaining great health is also important so that you don't have to become dependent on others. Not being able to drive a car or walk to the shopping mall will mean that you will have to ask someone else to drive you wherever you want to go. This can have a serious effect on your self-esteem and sense of freedom.

In the event that you still have great health, it is a mistake to take it for granted. Great health is often not appreciated until it's lost — sometimes for good. For certain, there are no quick fixes for regaining your health once you lose it.

Some people are able to stay healthy for a fairly long time without having to exercise, eat healthy foods, or stop smoking. They think that they are invincible, and that those health nuts are wasting their time and money on exercise and good nutrition. One day, much to their surprise, they realize that their health is far from what it used to be. They also realize that they could have done a lot more to prevent their health from deteriorating.

Unfortunately, the majority of people in Western nations are unwilling to do as much as they can to ensure that they don't wind up experiencing poor health. Researchers have concluded that slothfulness increases the risk of many chronic diseases including colon cancer, breast cancer, heart disease, stroke, and diabetes. Moreover, the United States government's health department estimates that about 300,000 Americans die prematurely each year because of physical inactivity and poor diet, a number second only to smoking, which kills about 400,000.

"The trick to staying young is not getting old," says Dr. Roland Klatz, co-author of *Stopping the Clock*, and co-founder of the American Academy of Anti-Aging Medicine. "By the time you need

All those health nuts who eat nutritious foods and exercise regularly are going to feel really stupid when they die of nothing.

some high-tech surgery," he adds, "it's a little late. Prevention is much better for you."

Generally speaking, retirement allows you more opportunity to spend time on your health. With a lot more spare time available to you, why not devote a good portion of it to being healthy? Indeed, you may want to make health the focus of your day with all activities centered on maintaining good health.

At sixty, retiree Peter Heegaard had this to say: "A big difference when you retire is that you move health to the top of your priority list. When you are a full-time chief executive, you are always sacrificing vacation time, downtime, or exercise time because there's always another meeting or another place to go. This time in my life keeping my health is my first priority, family is second, and then come all those other things."

You too can exercise your right to retire healthier and happier. Keep in mind that health goes beyond the physical. Without excellent mental and spiritual health, you can't claim to be healthy, regardless of your physical condition. In this regard, the Constitution of the World Health Organization states, "Health is a state of complete physical, mental, and social well-being, and not merely the absence of disease or infirmity."

The key to aging well is to stay active in constructive leisure activities. Indulging in nothing but passive activities contributes to physical and mental deterioration. For this reason, you should plan your activities based on how much they will contribute to your physical, mental, and spiritual health. Studies show that university or fitness courses, writing, community involvement, volunteering, and entertaining are the common pastimes of active and happy retirees.

Many excuses can be given for not putting in the effort to indulge in constructive leisure activities that can slow down the aging process. One excuse regularly given is that you can't fight genetics. To be sure, hereditary plays a part, but the aspects of aging that are genetically based are much less prominent than people make them out to be.

The real story, as noted in the groundbreaking study on *Successful Aging* sponsored by the John D. and Catherine T. MacArthur Foundation, is that only 30 percent of how we age can be attributed to genes. The remaining 70 percent is determined by our lifestyle choices.

Put another way, successful aging is overwhelmingly in our control. We can influence our environment — regulating factors such as diet, exercise, pollutants, health habits, and smoking — to prolong our lives. Notwithstanding that genes play some role, "Most of us who take good care of ourselves probably can get into the eighties," concludes Thomas Perls, director of the New England Centenarian Study at Harvard Medical School.

Clearly, if you think that life is too much fun to leave at an early age, the onus is on you to ensure that you don't. For a health-filled retirement, you must take special care of yourself — because no one else will. The key is to take charge of your health and stay engaged in life so that you use, rather than lose, your physical and mental capabilities.

Let Harold Fisher of the Detroit suburb of Harper Woods be an inspiration to you. In 2001, Fisher, one hundred years old at the time, was still designing religious buildings for six to eight hours a day. The work was helping keep Fisher's mind in great shape. This,

> He who has health has hope, and he who has hope has everything.
>
> — Saudi Arabian proverb

however, was not enough activity for Fisher. He realized that his type of work was not adequate for a healthy body. To keep his century-old body in shape, he was lifting weights and walking about a mile three days a week. "My body is hard as a rock," he claimed. "Two of my sons are doctors and they tell me that I'll live to be 110."

Like Harold Fisher, you will have to put the time and effort into maintaining your health even when you reach one hundred. More than anyone else, you are responsible for your health. Neither your doctors nor your hospital nor your health insurance policy can do one hundredth as much for your health as you can. It comes back to maintenance and prevention. Your three best doctors will always be wholesome food, exercise, and a positive attitude.

Obesity Is Really Widespread
— Avoid It If You Can

Health is the greatest gift.
Our body is precious.
It is our vehicle for awakening.
Treat it with care.
— Buddha

"Obesity is really widespread," concluded Joseph O. Kern II. Particularly in North America, nothing is more true. The reason is that life is too good. Far too many North Americans are overweight due to laziness and their habit of eating two to three times as much food as their bodies require.

> Some people are born to fatness. Others have to get there.
> — Les Murray

According to Statistics Canada, 48 percent of Canadians are overweight, including the 13 percent who are obese (dangerously overweight). Not to be outdone by Canadians, 61 percent of Americans are overweight, including 20 percent who are obese. Even worse, researchers say that people tend to under-report their weight. Thus, these figures may be considered somewhat conservative.

The obesity problem is not confined to North America. Even in France, once thought to be a slim nation, obesity is reaching epidemic proportions. At the start of the twenty-first century, a French government report found that although the rate of obesity is still lower than in Britain and the United States, the number of obese French people had risen by 17 percent in three years to 4.2 million. In fact, the World Health Organization has declared obesity to be a worldwide epidemic. Ironically, there are now about 1.1 billion overweight people in the world, the same number as the malnourished.

Although obesity is more common than it has ever been, this is no reason for it to affect you as well. It can be avoided. Your chances for achieving a healthy retirement will be much higher if you keep yourself as slim as possible, and I'm not talking about being anorexic.

The reality is that most people put on weight as they grow older. Studies show that the average sixty-year-old woman has almost twice as much body fat as one aged twenty. Men fare not much better. To a lot of people, these studies are "proof" that they can do nothing about it and offer an excuse for gaining weight, in spite of the truth.

People do have control over their weight. Although only 10 or 20 percent of the population manage to maintain the same weight in their later years as they did in their early twenties, this, however, shows that it can be done. Moreover, blaming obesity totally on hereditary factors is an insult to those genetically predisposed to gain weight who have nevertheless lost substantial weight, and kept it off for years.

To be sure, it gets a little harder to maintain a constant weight as one ages. The first problem is that the average human's metabolism slows 5 percent every decade after the age of thirty. "So you have to decrease your food intake by that much just to stay even," states Kelly Brownell, a weight-loss researcher and professor of psychology at Yale University. This shouldn't be too hard for most North Americans since they eat way too much anyway — regardless of their age. It's a matter of being committed to remaining healthy instead of being committed to eating more than one must.

> Imprisoned in every fat man a thin one is wildly signalling to be let out.
>
> — Cyril Connolly

The second factor associated with maintaining a healthy weight as one ages is that physical activity also generally declines with age. Here again, this doesn't have to be the case. While people are working full-time, they use their time constraints as an excuse not to exercise — even if they watch three hours of TV a day.

When they retire, practically all individuals have more time for physical activity. Unfortunately, the opportunities to lead a sedentary lifestyle are too numerous and too tempting for most. They can now devote six or seven hours to watching TV, while snacking on junk food, instead of only three hours.

Many experts now agree that waistlines should not automatically expand with age. In fact, recent United States Government guidelines indicate that gaining weight with age is avoidable. Guidelines jointly issued in by the United States Department of Agriculture and the United States Department of Health and Human Services no longer make age-related weight distinctions for adults. The guidelines state that people should not gain more than ten pounds after they reach their adult height, which generally occurs by age twenty-one.

As is to be expected, some other experts take issue with these guidelines, particularly those who themselves are overweight. It's a lot easier to avoid the reality that they don't have to be overweight than to do something about it. Unfortunately, being in denial about important health issues doesn't keep people healthy.

It's easier to stay out of trouble than to get out of trouble. This is what exercise is supposed to do. Exercise by itself, however, won't prevent obesity. Along with lack of adequate exercise, the two primary reasons for obesity are overeating and eating the wrong foods. In the early 1600s, George Herbert concluded, "Gluttony kills more than the sword." Things haven't changed much over the years.

A healthy diet is critical for preventing obesity and slowing the aging process. The first factor of a healthy diet is the quality of food. Robert Ringer, in his book *Getting What You Want*, mentions how a friend stated that the greatest killer of human beings is not war, but fast-food outlets. Plenty of fruits and vegetables and little fat will go a long way towards great health and maintaining the same weight that you were in your twenties.

> Thou seest I have more flesh than another man, and therefore more frailty.
>
> — William Shakespeare

The second element of a healthy diet is the size of servings. With the explosion of portion sizes in North America, it's easy to fall into the trap of believing that it's normal to overeat. A survey published in the *American Journal of Public Health* found that restaurant plates are larger than they were years ago. Even cup holders in cars and trucks have been getting bigger to account for the bigger soft drinks served by fast-food outlets.

Interestingly, nutritionists tell us that a normal portion of meat — whether it's three ounces of lamb, chicken, or beef — is roughly the size of a deck of cards. A serving of cheese is one ounce, the size of a thumb tip. And one serving of pasta is the size of a tennis ball.

If you presently have a weight problem, you can borrow a technique from the elders on the Japanese island of Okinawa. Certain researchers consider these elders the healthiest and slimmest on Earth. The elders practice a habit called *hara hachi bu*. This means: "Stop eating when you are 80 percent full." Consequently, these Japanese elders take in 10 to 40 percent fewer calories than Americans.

If you still have a weight problem after practicing *hara hachi bu*, try giving your problem away. Two days a week go on a fast and donate the money allocated for food to some of the many charities that help starving people in Third World countries. Not only will you end up thinner, you will have contributed to the health of people a lot less fortunate than yourself. Both of these results will make you feel good about yourself. Of course, how you feel about yourself is just as important to your overall well-being as your general physical health.

> He had had much experience of physicians, and said, "The only way to keep your health is to eat what you don't want, drink what you don't like, and do what you'd druther not."
>
> — Mark Twain

If You Don't Take Care of Your Body, Where Do You Intend to Live?

> *Better to hunt in fields, for health unbought,*
> *Than fee the doctor for a nauseous draught.*
> *The wise, for cure, on exercise depend:*
> *God never made his work for man to mend.*
> — John Dryden

A graffiti writer asked us, "If you don't take care of your body, where do you intend to live?" Well, I don't have an answer to this question. Do you? I suspect that you don't either.

Oddly, most people take better care of their cars and houses than they do of their own bodies. The most exercise they get is exercising their excuses for not doing it. Indeed, about two-thirds of North Americans are physically inactive and at great risk to themselves. As indicated previously, physical inactivity leads to tens of thousands of premature deaths.

Exercise is the art of being active and being active is the key to good health. Fitness legend Jack LaLanne, who at eighty-one was still going strong with his exercise program, claimed that it's crucial for good health. "If you don't exercise on a regular basis," warned LaLanne, "it's like going to bed with a rattlesnake; it's going to get you."

You have probably read about the benefits of regular physical exercise more than once. It's worthwhile, nonetheless, to mention them again, since all of us have a tendency to forget what is good for us. Various research studies conclude that exercise helps us lose weight, experience less anxiety, conquer depression, reduce the urge to eat, and sleep better. It also decreases the risk of colon cancer, breast cancer, heart disease, strokes, high blood pressure, prostate problems, and diabetes.

In the long term, physical activity contributes to robust health, long life, physical attractiveness, and happiness. Dr. Roy Shephard in his article "Exercise and Aging" (featured in the May 2002 issue of *Geriatrics Magazine*) claims that retirees who regularly indulge in moderate exercise can expect to avoid institutional health care for ten to twenty years longer than people who don't exercise.

> Health is the vital principle of bliss.
> And exercise, of health.
> — James Thomson

It's always easy to find an excuse for not exercising. Yet knowing that you have to exercise regularly for good health, and still not doing it, can cause you to feel lousy and disgusted with yourself. This is a big energy drain that can further negatively affect your health.

Exercise is not the only factor that affects the quality of retirement that one experiences, but it is one of the most important ones. You should be doing something physical, if not every day, at least every other day. Even moderate amounts of rigorous exercise can improve your health substantially.

Whether you are in your early forties or considerably older, you may think that you are getting too old to exercise vigorously. Think again! Many retirees in their sixties and beyond start a regular exercise program after having been physically inactive for decades.

For example, when she turned sixty-four, Rhoda Williams suffered from high blood pressure. To add to her difficulties, she felt "fat and lonely." Despite not having been to an exercise class in thirty years, she forced herself to join a fitness program for adults over fifty at Ottawa's Carleton University.

After just a few months of exercising in the pool and gym, Williams' blood pressure dropped fifty points; moreover, she lost four inches from her waistline. There was more good news: She learned how to swim for the first time and made some much-needed new friends. "I thoroughly enjoyed it," she told an *Ottawa Citizen* reporter. "I discovered that you don't have to wear yourself out to get into a fit condition. Now I'm more agile and toned."

All things considered, the benefits of regular exercise are overwhelming. If you haven't exercised in a long time, these benefits should be reason enough for you to stop reading right now and head for the gym. If your excuse is that you never find time for exercise, it might be wise to place these words by Edward Stanley somewhere where you can see them every day: "Those who think they have not time for bodily exercise will sooner or later have to find time for illness."

There are many other excuses that you can use to avoid exercise. Excuses are just that — excuses and nothing else. Being an adult, you should have noticed by now that making excuses is always an exercise in tedium with no results to show for it.

Richard Simmons, America's eccentric — but wise — fitness guru, told *USA TODAY*, "For twenty-four years, I've been telling people, 'Please exercise, I beg you to exercise.' They have the time to see a movie. They have the time to go shopping. They have the time to go out and eat. But they buy a piece of exercise equipment and it ends up in the closet."

Archie, I just don't get it. How is watching Richard Simmons exercise with all those young women going to increase your metabolism and get you fit and trim?

The important point about exercising is getting out there and doing it. The times that you don't feel like exercising are the times you need it most. Motivation is the key. You must consciously force yourself to overcome any excuses.

The first ten minutes of any physical activity is always the hardest. More often than not, I must force myself to go running or cycling. Once I am out there, I feel great. When I am finished, I am always grateful that I went. In fact, I wonder whose voice it was inside my head that was trying to persuade me not to exercise.

If for some reason you can't partake in vigorous exercise such as running or aerobics, then commit yourself to something less strenuous. Just taking a brisk thirty-minute walk every day is helpful. The key to losing weight and keeping it off is to put as much activity into your daily life as possible, says British obesity expert Dr. Susan Jebb. She has these tips:

- ➤ Stand rather than sit, whenever you can.
- ➤ Hide all your remote controls.
- ➤ Always use the stairs rather than an elevator or escalator.
- ➤ Walk as much as possible throughout the day.

➤ Try to find time for proper exercise, but regard it as icing on the cake.

> Never hurry. Take plenty of exercise. Always be cheerful. Take all the sleep you need. You may expect to be well.
>
> — James Freeman Clark

The fact is that retirement allows you the time for exercise that you may not have had when you were working full-time. According to a recent survey conducted by Trimark Investment Management, 45 percent of retired Canadians said they increased their level of physical activity after they left the workforce. You can do the same.

All told, it's important to build a lot of physical activity into your daily routine. When you don't have enough time for your hour of exercise, at least spend twenty or thirty minutes. You will still feel a lot better than if you don't do any.

The Shortcut to Being Truly Fit and Trim Is Long-Term Rigorous Action

In his later years, nineteenth century Italian composer Gioacchino Antonio Rossini loved to work in bed. He had become so lazy, according to some rumors, that if he dropped a sheet of music, he would rewrite the whole page rather than get out of bed and pick it up. Undoubtedly, many North Americans today would give Rossini a good run for his money. Even though they would like to be fit and trim, laziness is their forte.

If you want to be fit and trim throughout your life, you are going to have to work at it and work at the right things. It's wise to eat healthy foods, but this must be done in moderation. No matter how well you eat, exercise is required for fitness. Not only is exercise required, it is vigorous exercise that makes the difference.

To be sure, everyone wants to be fit and trim; unfortunately, not very many people want to pay the price. With so many benefits to be reaped from regular exercise, it's a mystery to health professionals why more people aren't physically active. The correlation between healthy people and regular physical exercise is irrefutable, yet less than 10 percent of American adults exercise vigorously at least three times a week.

As *USA TODAY* reported, "Despite years of study and millions of dollars spent, despite evidence that physical activity is a key to robust health, long life, and good looks, despite all we know about cholesterol and heart disease and diabetes and obesity, the fact remains — we are a nation of sloths!"

Apparently, even people whom we expect to be fit aren't. A study by the Ontario Heart and Stroke Foundation found that the image of baby boomers as an exercise-crazed generation is a myth. Surprisingly, baby boomers are less fit than their parents were at the same age. The obvious reason is that they are looking for a shortcut.

As it turns out, the shortcut to being truly fit and trim is long-term vigorous action. French journalist Pierre Joseph Proudhon proclaimed, "The chief condition on which, life, health and vigor depend, is action. It is by action that an organism develops its faculties, increases its energy, and attains the fulfillment of its destiny."

> The only athletic sport I ever mastered was backgammon.
> — Douglas Jerrod

You aren't going to get fit by casually riding a bicycle at five miles an hour or going for a fifteen-minute walk while window shopping. A Harvard University study found that only vigorous activity sustained for longer periods will get you fit. The study, which linked vigorous exercise to longevity, indicated that playing a standard round of golf couldn't be considered a vigorous workout. Similarly, gardening for a half hour is better than nothing; this won't get you fit, however. The physical benefit is just that — a little better than nothing!

In the same vein, a British research study, reported in the May 2002 edition of the *Journal of Epidemiology and Community Health*, found that brisk walking is a much healthier option and a better way to keep fit and lose weight than mopping floors, dusting, and cleaning windows, particularly for older women between the ages of sixty and seventy-nine. Women in the survey who walked vigorously for two-and-a-half hours a week or did an equal amount of gardening were less likely to be obese and had a lower resting heart rate, which is a sign of physical fitness. "Older women need to be doing more physical activity. Housework probably does not cut the mustard," proclaimed Dr. Shah Ebrahim, an epidemiologist and expert on aging at the University of Bristol, in southwestern England.

Notwithstanding this study, even brisk walking may be insufficient exercise if you want to live a long life. Regular brisk walking might keep you limber and make you feel better, but it is unlikely to stave off an early death from heart disease, according to a 2003 research study by Queen's University Belfast. The researchers concluded that regular exercise has profound benefits on health, but that only vigorous exercise — such as jogging, hiking, stair climbing, swimming, racquet sports, and heavy digging — seems to make any difference to the risk of premature death from heart disease.

> Be careful when reading health books; you may die of a misprint.
>
> — Mark Twain

Resist being like most baby boomers who are inclined to choose those activities that require the least effort. A recent newspaper article indicated that the baby boomers were going for more "relaxed exercise." If ever a term came close to being an oxymoron, without actually becoming one, "relaxed exercise" is it. No one is going to get truly fit with relaxed exercise. Watching TV is the ultimate in relaxed exercise.

There are 168 hours in every week. A rule of thumb is that you should devote at least five hours to rigorous physical exercise. For optimal exercise, the American College of Sports Medicine recommends twenty to sixty minutes of continuous aerobic exercise — running, brisk walking, swimming, or dancing will do — three or more times a week.

The guidelines also recommend weight training twice a week. Lifting weights helps to improve balance and posture and to keep muscles and bones strong. You may suspect that not only are you too old to indulge in aerobic exercise, you are also too old to take weight training. Happily, this isn't true.

Adventurous gerontologists at Tufts University put a group of the frailest residents they could find in a nursing home on a weight-training program. No doubt most people would suspect that this led to a few deaths. On the contrary, these seniors did very well. Their wasted muscles were rejuvenated by 300 percent, their coordination came back, and their balance greatly improved. In short, they were all able to lead active lives again. Incidentally, the youngest member of the group was eighty-seven, while the oldest was ninety-six.

No question — exercising vigorously on a regular basis is not easy. But living in poor physical condition sometime in the future will be much more difficult to contend with than spending an hour or two a day running, walking, cycling, or swimming. Being overweight and unfit will interfere with your ability to enjoy many great pleasures in life. It's tough to enjoy or be good at many leisure activities, such as baseball, tennis, hockey, golf, travel, and sex when you are overweight.

Being serious about getting fit and losing weight means choosing those activities that require the most effort. Reject any thoughts that you can coast for a week or two. You must do something physical every day, or at least every second day. Make no exceptions during your vacations. Sitting around the pool, and having drinks brought to you all day, won't keep you fit and trim.

Don't look around for someone to blame if you have gotten terribly out of shape. It's your fault for letting yourself go,

Swimming in this channel can get you in pretty good physical shape in no time flat.

no matter how many excuses you can fabricate. I have designated the weight and fitness level that I am comfortable with and have worked hard to maintain myself at this level for many years. Your duty is to do the same if you want to feel good about yourself.

A fit and trim body commands the respect of others. More important, it commands self-respect. No doubt, if you are overweight and out of shape, creating weight loss and attaining fitness won't happen overnight. You must invest the time and energy in strenuous exercise. The return on your investment, however, is well worth it. You will be the person with a spring in your step while other people your age show their age, or look considerably older than they really are.

An Active Walk in Nature Is the Best Medicine for Many of Your Ailments

Depending on how you handle and reduce the normal stress of daily life, you can end up a bright light, a flickering one, or a complete burnout. Often we don't pay enough attention to how daily stress can interfere with our health and contribute to illness. When we find ourselves feeling a little down, it's best to rejuvenate our spirits by reconnecting with nature. Proper exercise in the open air and sunshine is among the greatest gifts you can give your body.

Some days you may be so stressed that you think you have a nervous breakdown coming on. Instead of seeing a psychologist, head for the closest park, seashore, or forest. An active walk in nature is the best medicine for many of your ailments. Walking outdoors will do more to relieve your stress, and revitalize you, than prescription drugs, six Miller's, two hours of TV, a big meal, or a visit to your therapist.

> Give me health and a day, and I will make the pomp of emperors ridiculous.
>
> — Ralph Waldo Emerson

Given that strenuous exercise will not only reduce your stress, but will also prevent you from getting stressed out in the first place, you shouldn't wait until you get to that super-stressed-out state before you take a walk. Attacking your stress early on, before it gets out of hand, is much more effective in the long term. Start noticing your stress early on before it starts affecting you in any significant way. That is the time to relax both your body and your mind by heading outdoors for a walk.

Taking part in nature's big picture with exercise will not only make you feel better, you will value life more. We keep forgetting about the many benefits nature has to offer. The more humans have removed themselves from nature, the more alienated from the world they have become. If you are an in-tune person, you will find walking through a park or the woods much more relaxing and satisfying than spending time in a room full of gadgets, trinkets, and other trappings of modern society.

What comes through nature costs little or nothing. Instead of thinking you have to join a fitness club, get into the habit of using the outdoors as your personal gymnasium. Being outside the house or office is in itself a great remedy for stress. The sounds, smells, and rhythms of nature compel us to slow down and relax.

There are other reasons why you should take the opportunity to be outside of your apartment or house as much as possible. A recent newspaper article cited a research study that indicated there are many more pollutants in the average house than outside. Thus, even walking on a busy street filled with polluting automobiles is healthier than being physically inactive inside your house or apartment.

Obviously, millions of retirees know about the benefits of walking outdoors and are taking advantage of it. According to a survey conducted by American Sports Data Inc., fitness walking that is performed at least one hundred days a year is the most popular exercise among older Americans. Indeed, 20.2 percent of the fifty-five-plus age group indulged in fitness walking in 2000 as compared to only 15.9 percent in 1987.

"As people age, they worry more about their health and their ability to maintain independence," states Mark Fenton, author of a book on walking and editor at large of *Walking* magazine. "Even if you haven't been a jock your whole life, walking is something you can do easily. It is beneficial even if you don't start until your fifties or sixties or even seventies."

For a healthier you, try to walk at least an hour outside each day. Walking has not only highly significant physical rewards, but also highly significant psychological benefits. Because it has tranquilizing powers, it is one of the best ways to relieve stress.

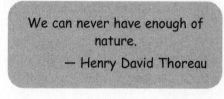

We can never have enough of nature.

— Henry David Thoreau

Researchers confirm that walking is a great way to calm our troubles. As with any other vigorous exercise, a brisk walk will prompt your body to produce endorphins. These are chemical compounds that reduce pain and stress as they enter the brain. Endorphins are said to enhance memory and judgment as well. Walking quickly also produces increased levels of serotonin, an important brain neurotransmitter that increases feelings of well-being while reducing mild depression and anxiety.

The benefits of going for a walk go well beyond the merely physical. Walking is a great way to jump-start the brain and generate fresh thoughts in the process. On your daily walks, you can create world-class ideas for your artistic projects or part-time business that may change the course of humanity when you put these ideas into action.

Given that walking is as beneficial for the mind and soul as it is for the body, there is no reason not to walk at least a mile or two a day. Take your walks in nature, instead of city streets, if at all possible. Of course, not only is walking in nature beneficial for your mind, body, and soul; it is just plain fun.

Your Mind Needs a Good Run Too

At books, or work, or healthy play,
Let all my years be passed;
That I may give for every day
A good account at last.
— Isaac Watts

Rigorous physical exercise will help keep your body in great shape. Equally important is rigorous mental exercise to keep your mind in great shape. Your mind, as much as your body, regularly needs a good run, too, if you want it to serve you well in your retirement years. Of course, in addition to keeping your brain in shape for the future, mental exercise will keep you from getting bored in the present.

> Old minds are like old horses; you must exercise them if you wish to keep them in working order.
> — John Quincy Adams

At least as much mental involvement as you had in your work life should be your goal. Your brain will lose its capability to respond to new challenges and learn new things in the future if you don't give it the exercise it needs today. Results of recent studies, such as the extensive research project sponsored by the MacArthur Foundation, indicate that keeping the brain active, engaged, and constantly learning help to prolong its health and ability to function properly.

Intellectual challenges will not only keep your mind in shape, they, in fact, can help get it in better shape than it's ever been. Over time, our physical fitness will gradually decline, no matter how much effort we put into being fit. But our minds can continue to grow and become gradually more fit with time.

Tony Buzan, author of *The Mind Map Book* and an expert on the human brain, feels that people's memories can actually get better in the years beyond their forties and fifties if they simply take the time to utilize and expand their brains. Sure, statistically, people are less likely to exercise their brains and increase their powers of recall as they get older. Buzan attributes this more to sociological than physiological reasons, however.

It's not uncommon for people to say, "I'm having a senior moment," as soon as they forget something. This draws the ire of Buzan. In Buzan's opinion, this leads to forgetful people in their forties unnecessarily fretting that they are suffering from dementia when, in fact, they are just being normal.

"The more you learn," declares Buzan, "the sharper your memory becomes over time." To be sure, there is no reason why you can't master a new language or learn the complete history of the Italian Navy in your sixties or seventies. What it takes is the desire and motivation to make it happen.

If your brain isn't challenged to learn new things for a prolonged period of time, it will lose its ability to discern and assimilate new information. The biggest cause of brain neglect, no doubt, has to be laziness. Spending your entire retirement life watching TV — physical and mental laziness at its best — isn't going to keep your mind in shape.

Heed the words of someone who should know. Bette Midler may appear on TV, but, in her fifties, the singer-actress maintains a strict TV ban at home, not only for her daughter, but for herself as well. "I won't allow it," she recently told the *TV Guide*. "I made a pact with myself a long time ago. Never watch anything stupider than you. It's helped me a lot."

> In a disordered mind, as in a disordered body, soundness of health is impossible.
> — Marcus Tullius Cicero

Several research studies support the conclusion that mental capacity tends to deteriorate when the brain is not exercised over an extended time frame. One such study was conducted by University of Kentucky professor David Snowden on nuns with the School of Sisters of Notre Dame. The Minnesota order of 678 nuns allowed Snowden and his assistants to intensively investigate their writing, diet, lifestyle, and even their brains when they died.

Snowden concluded that nuns who were mentally challenged well into their old age, by learning new things and teaching these things to others, lived longer than nuns who didn't continue to challenge their brains. What's more, the more educated nuns were less prone to get brain ailments such as Alzheimer's disease. This is in accordance with other research that has shown people with high levels of intelligence and education tend to have lower rates of Alzheimer's disease and age-related mental decline.

Activity through challenging activities and intent observation helps to keep the mind in shape. Lawrence Katz, a professor of neurobiology at Duke University in Durham, North Carolina, advocates that people do routine activities in novel ways, which use all five senses. Even small things done in novel ways are a big help, especially if you don't have the inclination to learn to play violin or speak a new language.

Scientists theorize that brain-stimulating activities strengthen the information-processing ability of the brain while at the same time offsetting age-related declines in brainpower. The key is to be involved in unfamiliar areas and activities. Katz, co-author of *Keep Your Brain Alive*, advises, "The goal is to activate the brain's own biochemical pathways and to bring new pathways online that can help to strengthen or preserve brain circuits." Here are some of Katz's suggested activities:

> ➤ Take a new route to your best friend's house.
> ➤ Choose your clothing based on sense of touch rather than sight.
> ➤ Read a book upside down.
> ➤ If you are right-handed, brush your teeth with your left hand.

In case you want to keep a mental edge over people your age, playing bridge may be the best way to do it. Addicts say that it is very stimulating to play it well. Bridge demands superior concentration, memory, and stamina. This is evident by the fact that certain corporations encourage employees to play bridge, expecting the employees to develop sharper minds and to contribute to better corporate performance. "It's a very challenging card game in that you never learn it completely," states Matthew Greenways, manager of the Edmonton Bridge Club in Edmonton, Alberta. "No one ever really masters the game."

> True enjoyment comes from activity of the mind and exercise of the body; the two are ever united.
>
> — Wilhelm von Humboldt

Surprisingly, playing bridge may also enhance your physical health. Marian Diamond, University of California at Berkeley professor of integrative biology, found that members of a bridge club in Orinda, California, not only had sharper minds than non-bridge players, they also had higher levels of the white blood cells that seek out viruses and other body invaders. Keep in mind that playing bridge is also a great way to meet new people and enhance your social life. There are now more than 4,200 bridge clubs in North America.

Given that bridge can keep people's minds alert while they are in the workforce, it's probably even more beneficial to retired people who don't have the regular challenges that a workplace provides. Researchers at Chicago's Rush Alzheimer's Disease Center say that brain-stimulating activities such as playing bridge and doing crossword puzzles can reduce the risk of developing Alzheimer's disease by almost half. Even information-processing activities such as reading newspapers are beneficial. People who routinely participate in stimulating mental activities suffer far less cognitive decline than those who do not.

There are many other ways to keep your brain in tiptop shape — things as basic as reading, engaging in active discussions, experimenting with mind games, and playing chess. Exploring new places, learning new things, and meeting new people with fresh perspectives also play an important role in stimulating the mind — as well as helping you experience more joy and satisfaction in retirement.

Why do you spend so much time on self-development?

My mind is important to me. It's where I spend most of my time.

The goal is to keep your mind busy. Explore new fields of learning, particularly new intellectual pursuits instead of new manual skills. Your curiosity can be the force that gets you involved in something totally different from what you are used to.

As an accountant you may have wondered what makes a computer work. Now is the time to find out. Similarly, as a nurse you may have been interested in different religions, but never had the time to explore them due to your heavy workload. Why not pursue a degree in theology at the local university or college?

Nothing keeps your mind in shape as much as learning. Whether it's absorbing new knowledge or acquiring a new skill, learning enhances your mental ability. The fact that you aren't paid to think anymore doesn't mean you have to stop thinking. In fact, retirement may be the time to do some real thinking instead of the uncreative thinking that is required in most workplaces. These intellectual challenges will do you a great deal of good.

> A sound mind in a sound body, is a short, but full description of a happy state in this World: he that has these two, has little more to wish for; and he that wants either of them, will be little the better for anything else.
>
> — John Locke

> One of your most powerful inner resources is your own creativity. Be willing to try on something new and play the game full-out.
>
> — Marcia Wieder

Being an active learner throughout your retirement years will not only help you conquer boredom, it will also keep your brain in great shape. Being involved in new and unfamiliar areas of life is key. Things that are intellectually stimulating will keep your brain active and prolong its ability to serve you well in your retirement.

To sum up, research conducted by the MacArthur Foundation concluded that people who are continually active and engaged in life lead longer and healthier lives. Being both physically and mentally active improves memory, learning ability, and physical and mental well-being. Thus, health should always be an important consideration when you plan your retirement activities. Choose your activities based on how much they will contribute to your physical, mental, and spiritual health and your retirement will be enhanced immeasurably.

5

Learning Is
for Life

Commit Yourself to Being a Lifelong Learner and Your Life Will Never Be without Purpose

The love of learning, the sequestered nooks,
And all the sweet serenity of books.
— Henry Wadsworth Longfellow

As a matter of course, the most important elements of a successful retirement are good physical and mental health, spiritual fulfillment, great relationships with family and friends, and a variety of interesting things to do. Committing yourself to being a lifelong learner will go a long way toward making your world enthralling until the day you die. What's more, when you commit yourself to being an ageless learner, your life will never be without purpose. Having an important purpose, to be sure, can be a savior in retirement.

> Real education should educate us out of self into something far finer; into a selflessness which links us with all humanity.
>
> — Nancy Astor

Regardless of how old you are, there's always something intriguing to learn and the opportunity to do so. In Western nations today there are more opportunities than ever for retirees to keep learning. Indeed, many retirees, regardless of how old they are, go to extremes to continue learning.

A case in point is ninety-year-old Milton Landowne. Every morning, Landowne rides a shuttle bus along with several other

131

retirees to attend courses at Lasell College in Newton, Massachusetts. Landowne must take 450 course-hours per year whether he likes it or not. Like the undergraduates at the college, he must also write papers and take quizzes, but unlike the undergraduates, he doesn't have to take the final exams.

Landowne is a resident of Lasell Village, the retirement facility built by Lasell College for its faculty and alumni. There are nearly seventy colleges and universities in the United States with similar retirement facilities and twenty-five more have plans to construct their own. People moving into Lasell Village must sign an agreement that they will complete a full course load each year until they are deemed medically unable to do so. The retirees are permitted to take some fitness classes and one or two independent correspondence courses.

The heavy course load hasn't fazed Landowne. In his second year at the college, he enrolled in a Web-design class even though he knew nothing about computers and suspected the course material might be too tough for him. After he passed the final project with flying colors, he decided to enroll in more computer classes in the next semester. "I never want to stop learning," Landowne told a *Newsweek* reporter in 2002.

Become a College Drop-In and Stay More Engaged in Life

Likely, not all retirees who want to keep learning and broaden their scope of the world will go to the same extremes as Milton Landowne. Fortunately, there are alternatives. One of the best ways for any retiree to become more engaged in life is to become a "college drop-in."

> The brighter you are, the more you have to learn.
> — Don Herold

Even retirees who have previously earned degrees take college courses for the satisfaction and enjoyment of it. Indeed, for some retired individuals, educational stimulation becomes not just a nice thing to do, but an essential one for their well-being. "Again and again I hear retirees saying, 'I want to learn, to be engaged.' " divulges Ronald Manheimer, director of the North Carolina Center for Creative Retirement in Asheville.

Lifelong learning becomes a pursuit for those individuals who realize that they are not retiring from life — just from a job. Many instructors who teach in these programs say that they learn as much from the students as the students learn from them. "I enjoy the people the most," insisted an instructor with the Creative Retirement Institute at Edmonds Community College. "They come because they want to learn. They bring a whole lifetime of experiences."

> The length of your education is less important than its breadth, and the length of your life is less important than its depth.
>
> — Marilyn Vos Savant

Some retirees prefer to enroll full time at a college or university to receive a degree, whether to qualify for a job or become better educated. According to United States Department of Education statistics, well over 500,000 seniors are enrolled nationally in colleges and universities. These students take regular classes on the main campus and share the classroom with a variety of other students, many of whom are the age of their children and grandchildren.

The majority of retirees, however, enroll in programs that offer non-degree courses. The students in these programs are required to pay a one-time fee for each course and meet for sessions rather than for an entire semester. Although academic substance is important to the students, the courses they take are keyed to their interest in the subject, and not tied to any desire to improve their earning power.

Many retirees enroll in programs like the one offered by the North Carolina Center for Creative Retirement, a part of a network of well over 200 Learning in Retirement Institutes across the United States and Canada. These academic programs, normally sponsored by a local college or university, are essentially grassroots universities that offer non-credit courses for retired people. The students vary from retired professionals who already have several academic degrees to high-school dropouts who never went to college.

"The Learning in Retirement program provides an opportunity for retirement-age individuals to take part in courses and activities that empower them to be continual learners," asserts Ronald Zaccari, president of Valdosta State University in Georgia. At the Learning in Retirement program at Valdosta State University, participants have their choice of over thirty classes each term, including Introduction to Computers, Digital Photography, Beginning Quilting, Spanish for Fun, Intermediate Bridge, and Line Dancing. At the end of each term, students vote on which courses they would like to have offered next semester.

As most retirees realize sooner or later, learning is for life. No doubt you will want to keep learning and growing throughout your retirement years. To help you do this, the Learning in Retirement Institutes provide a formal setting with open discussions and topnotch information as priorities. You have the opportunity to learn practically anything imaginable in these programs. Check out your community newspapers or the Internet to see if a Learning in Retirement Institute exists in your area.

Take a Joy Course for Personal Growth, Self-Development, and Lifelong Learning

If there is no Learning in Retirement Institute available in your hometown, there are other avenues for you to learn in a formal setting. You can actually enroll in courses designed for degree-seeking students and not have to actually complete a degree. Many universities in Canada and the United States have a policy that permits retirees to audit courses for a nominal fee, as long as the classes aren't fully enrolled.

Didn't you tell me that you were going to enroll in a course on self-esteem?

I didn't think that they would accept me.

Elizabeth Maidstone, a retiree in Vancouver, B.C., labeled these courses "joy courses." She has audited political science, German, and English. Auditing a course makes it a joy course simply because the student gets to learn enjoyable material without the stress and pressure of writing exams. What's more, auditors of college and university courses don't have to prepare assignments or write papers.

Auditors are not seeking a degree; more importantly, they are sitting in on classes because they are seeking to learn something new. As retiree Gladys Holland of Nanuet, New York, remarked, "Even if you learn just one thing, it's more than you knew before."

Kenneth Gang, eighty, and his wife Fay, seventy-seven, of Rye Brook, New York, have been auditing courses at New York's Purchase College for several years. Kennett, a retired neurosurgeon, and Fay, a retired teacher, actually had a total of five college degrees between them when they started auditing courses. Instead of adding to their degrees, auditing provides the Gangs with personal growth, self-development, and lifelong learning.

Kenneth and Faye Gang can be found somewhere on the Purchase campus three or four times a week, for several hours each time. "We finished college many, many years ago, but we won't quit," Kenneth told *The Journal News*. Faye added, "We just finished a course on the Middle East, and it was fantastic. We got such a view on what is going on there. It's all about learning."

Work on a University Degree and Experience a Sense of Belonging with Younger People

Going back to college for further education can give retired people a sense of accomplishment and pride, not to mention other valuable benefits. This happened to June Whitman. After five years of study, Whitman graduated with honors from Fordham University's Lincoln Center. "I worked hard, but I absolutely loved it," Whitman told Marilyn Gardner of *The Christian Science Monitor*.

In the late 1940s, Whitman dropped out of Wellesley College in her sophomore year to get married and raise children. Almost fifty years later, she enrolled at New York's Fordham University. She first entered the university's College at Sixty Program, which serves people fifty and over. After completing a few courses, she transferred into a regular degree program at Fordham University's Lincoln Center campus.

> You may be a redneck if . . . you have spent more on your pickup truck than on your education.
>
> — Jeff Foxworthy

Not only did Whitman eventually get great satisfaction from earning a degree, she felt truly engaged in life while taking the courses. Moreover, she experienced a sense of belonging with the younger students. "Aside from the learning, being with all the young people made the classes more interesting," she claimed. "I just received the sweetest letter from a student about how much our friendship meant to her."

It's More Fun to Be Wired than Not

At one time Mildred Evans of Tampa Bay, Florida, experienced fear whenever she encountered a computer. "I didn't want to touch it," Evans admitted. "I thought I'd break something." What's more, Evans didn't see much use for computers in her personal life.

> Education is the best provision for old age.
>
> — Aristotle

This all changed by mid-2002. Evans, sixty-three at the time, had just graduated from an eight-week computer course through The Florida Kinship Center at the University of South Florida. "It's a whole new world," Evans told a *Tampa Bay Tribune* reporter. "I never thought there'd be this much to learn, just by hitting a few keys."

Evans now even owns her own computer. She bought it not only for herself, but also for her fourteen-year-old grandson, whom she is raising. Although Evans graduated from a computer course designed for people raising their grandchildren or other young relatives, she now applies her computer knowledge, including going on the Internet, to many aspects of her own life.

To be sure, retirees enhance their lives considerably when they learn how to use a computer and the Internet. Unfortunately, only about a quarter of retiree households were online in 2002 according to the AOL Roper Starch Study of Online Seniors Fifty-Five & Over. Based on the experiences of "wired retirees" such as Mildred Evans, many of the three-quarters that were not "wired" could benefit immensely if they were.

According to the AOL Roper Starch Study, active online senior Americans are averaging more than twenty hours a week on the Internet. An overwhelming number of wired seniors — 93 percent — feel that the Internet has improved their lives overall. Moreover, 63 percent say the Internet has brought their families closer together.

The good news is that even though they knew nothing about computers before they retired, tens of thousands of retirees have learned how to use the Internet to enhance their retirement years. Today, many groups across the United States and Canada give courses to seniors on how to use the computer as a communication and learning tool. For example, SeniorNet (telephone 1-800-747-6848), a San Francisco based nonprofit organization, currently has about 20,000 members. To make its courses affordable, SeniorNet recruits seniors to help other seniors use computers.

Many community colleges and universities also have courses on how to use a computer and the Internet. Typical of these is the "Seniors Internet" course offered by the Continuing Education Department at the University of Calgary. In Montreal, the McGill Institute for Learning in Retirement is a good place for seniors to start learning about computers and the Internet. Courses are usually taught by experts in the field and require a small registration fee.

> Education is learning what you didn't even know you didn't know.
>
> — Daniel Boorstin

Perhaps you are a retiree who has resisted learning how to use computers and the Internet. You may not be aware that there are many ways in which you can use the Internet to make your retirement years easier and happier. Following is a list of a few of them. This list may even give you a few new ideas if you have been wired for some time.

- Communicate with friends and relatives, including grandchildren.
- Find out about bargains on new or used cars.
- Plan your next travel adventure.
- Explore new business opportunities.
- Help other retirees start a new business.
- Research material for a new book.
- Start a website to sell your artwork or crafts.
- Learn how to stay healthy in your later years.
- Find out how to deal with insomnia.
- Find a job through a Seniors Job Bank.
- Check out which books are available at the library and put them on reserve if they are.
- Discover how to better cope with an ailment such as arthritis or Parkinson's disease.
- Get in contact with former classmates.
- Make new friends on chat lines.
- Watch downtown New York on a live camera.
- Shop for convenience and hard-to-get items.
- Do your banking.
- Meet singles of the opposite sex in the personals.
- Arrange to meet a travel partner.
- Invest in the stock market.
- Check out reviews of books at www.amazon.com and other websites.

- Take part in auction sales on www.ebay.com.
- Send bad jokes to your friends.
- Check out retirement communities.
- Take part in a discussion forum on politics.
- Check out your daily horoscope.
- Keep up-to-date on sports scores.
- Identify public benefits for which you qualify on government websites.
- Indulge in ego-surfing. Type your name into a search engine and see if you can find something about yourself on other websites.

If you still aren't convinced about the value of the Internet, here is a bit of information that may persuade you to start embracing computers: Once someone — usually a friend, a son or daughter, or a grandchild — convinces seniors to sit at the computer and log on for the first time, they become among the most enthusiastic users of the Internet, according to a study by The Pew Internet & American Life Project.

Susannah Fox, the project's research director, reported, "These seniors, once they realize the vast amount of information available for them, they love it." The Pew Project found that almost 70 percent of seniors able to use the Internet do so on a typical day. This compares with 56 percent for all users. The most popular Internet activities for seniors include using e-mail to keep in contact with others, reading the latest news reports, researching health concerns, and checking on the weather.

> It's what you learn after you know it all that counts.
>
> — John Wooden

Discover Elderhostel If You Want to Discover the World

"When I retired at sixty and started complaining about not having enough to do with my brainpower, my wife told me 'use it or lose it,' " revealed Dennis Thompson, sixty-three, of Connecticut. "So, we started looking at local adult education course catalogs and attending public lectures at the local college. I began volunteering as an ombudsman for nursing home residents. And, we discovered Elderhostel."

Thompson, a retired lawyer, and his wife Brandy, a former school nurse, include at least two Elderhostel programs in their vacation plans every year. "Last summer, we stayed in Connecticut and enjoyed a week studying at a local historical seaport museum," Thompson recently told a reporter, "then we went to New York to learn about medieval church music and life in a monastery. This year, we're being even more adventuresome and going to British Columbia to learn about the geology and wildflowers of the Canadian Rockies."

You may want to check out Elderhostel yourself if you want to discover the world like never before. This is the world's largest educational and travel organization for adults fifty-five and over. Each year Elderhostel draws more than 300,000 students at 1,900 sites worldwide. The learning adventures can last from several nights to several weeks and include daily lectures, field trips, and activities along with accommodations and meals.

Does Elderhostel have anything to add to my liberal education? I already know the arts of feather balancing, paper-airplane making, pen bouncing, creative beer-can crushing, and generating false symptoms of physical self-abuse.

From the organization's website: "Elderhostel is a not-for-profit organization dedicated to providing extraordinary learning adventures for people fifty-five and over. From New Hampshire to New Zealand, South Africa to South Dakota, Elderhostel offers you a world of educational opportunities — at exceptional values."

Socializing and meeting new people is a big part of the Elderhostel experience. Happy hours, bridge games, and tourist outings facilitate the creation of new friends. "There are lots of interesting people there, too," says Dennis Thompson. "You meet folks from all kinds of backgrounds, and you enjoy the experience together. The friendships are part of the package."

Above all, Elderhostel enables retirees to keep active and stay engaged in life. They get to travel, meet others, and learn about everything from photography to marine life at universities, colleges, and other educational institutions in many parts of the world. The list of courses covers practically any subject imaginable — computer science, history, architecture, literature, poetry, engineering, creative writing, drama, film, dance, and mathematics.

Most courses in Canada and the United States are a week long and cost about $350. The cost covers room, board, tuition and some extracurricular activities. Travel costs are not included. Participants must make their own travel arrangements to the campuses of their choice. Elderhostelers experience campus life staying in a dormitory and eating in campus facilities. They attend lectures and participate in discussions with anywhere from twenty to forty other students.

> It is impossible to withhold education from the receptive mind, as it is impossible to force it upon the unreasoning.
>
> — Agnes Repplier

For those who despise exams and studying, the great news is that Elderhostel's not-for-credit courses involve no exams, grades, or homework. Moreover, no prerequisite studies of the topics are required. This means you can have a Ph.D. or a grade-nine education and still enroll in any course you desire.

Retirees wanting to experience more exotic destinations can enroll in Elderhostel's international program. Two- or three-week stays at colleges and campuses can be arranged in several countries such as Australia, New Zealand, Britain, and Italy. The courses in the international program are usually related to the particular country's culture, history, economy, and politics.

Prices are much higher for the international program but they cover practically all incidental costs including round-trip airfare, room and board, transfers within the country, and limited accident, sickness, and baggage insurance. Typically, a two-week sojourn to Europe can cost $3000 or more. International programs require that the participants are in good health because these involve a fair amount of walking, baggage carrying, and travel by train, bus, or ferry.

Besides its national and international travel programs, Elderhostel also sponsors the Institutes for Learning in Retirement mentioned earlier. Members of the respective Institutes, however, determine the curriculum of their programs. (For more information on Elderhostel, write to 11 Avenue de Lafayette, Boston, MA, 02111; call 1-877-426-8056 toll-free; or visit www.elderhostel.org on the Internet.)

Whether it's through Elderhostel or other avenues of education, learning throughout your life will give you a sense of well-being, help you think better, and enhance your longevity. Keep learning to broaden your scope of the world and you keep your mind sharp — and yourself young — regardless of how old you get. "Anyone who stops learning is old," advised Henry Ford, "whether at twenty or eighty. Anyone who keeps learning stays young. The greatest thing in life is to keep your mind young."

6

Your Wealth Is Where Your Friends Are

Above All, Friends Make Life Complete

From quiet homes and first beginning,
Out to the undiscovered ends,
There's nothing worth the wear of winning,
But laughter and the love of friends.
— Hilaire Belloc

You may not miss much from your workplace after you retire; what you are likely to miss most, however, are the people you work with. It doesn't necessarily have to be specific people that you miss, but people in general. Social interaction, even when somewhat superficial, makes life more enjoyable for most of us

In chapter 3 we discussed "sense of community" as one of the three important human needs that the modern-day workplace provides. Not only is there social contact during work hours, there may be many company-sponsored social events. These include sporting events (bowling night, softball, and bridge), picnics, pub nights, parties (birthday, Christmas, and retirement), and even casino nights.

As a matter of course, the only companionship and socializing many people get while pursuing their careers is at the workplace. In fact, over the years some workers become totally reliant on the company for social intercourse, so much so that they eventually lose the skills necessary to develop new friendships away from the

> Good friends, good books and a sleepy conscience: This is the ideal life.
>
> — Mark Twain

workplace. Upon retirement, these ex-workers become social misfits. They no longer have the corporate social haven that provided them with familiarity, security, and community.

New retirees have to replace the sense of community that the company provided them with some other means of social contact. The degree to which these retirees establish social interaction outside the workplace will depend upon whether they are married, whether they have children and grandchildren, and whether they rely on siblings for social support. To feel part of a community, individuals must optimize different ways of being involved with and enjoying family, friends, and acquaintances.

A study (titled *It's My Turn Now*) conducted by the Simon Fraser Gerontology Research Centre in Burnaby, B.C., found that the happiest seniors tend to be those who are experiencing community involvement. They belong to an active community of peers found in such places as churches, clubs, or housing communities. Study director Veronica Doyle concluded, "It isn't how often you see your kids — it's how many places in the world you are a somebody."

For most retirees, making and maintaining great friendships are keys to creating a new sense of community that translates into social, emotional, and physical well-being. Several research studies conclude that people who have intimate relationships with others live happier, healthier, and longer. On the other hand, lonely people who have few or no friends stand a greater chance of becoming ill and dying an early death.

Titus Maccius Plautus, the Roman playwright whose works influenced Shakespeare and Molière, proclaimed, "Your wealth is where your friends are." Put another way, the more people who truly care whether you get up in the morning, the richer you will feel. You will find this particularly true when you retire. Regardless of how much wealth you have acquired, you cannot expect to have a great retirement if you do not have great friends. To be sure, the worst poverty is to be without any friends.

> If I don't have friends, then I ain't nothing.
> — Billie Holiday

Former United States president Jimmy Carter had this to say about the elements of successful retirement: "There are two basic secrets to successful aging: One is staying active in doing things that we find to be interesting. And the other one is having an intimate relationship with other human beings, so we don't just become a vegetable sitting in front of a flickering TV screen and depending on other people to do things for us that we are fully capable of doing ourselves."

As is to be expected, yearning for close friends can take on a greater sense of urgency when people retire. Modern working life makes our individual lives busier and more fragmented to a point where many people neglect to devote time to making close friends while they are working. Retirement provides much personal time to devote to friends, but for some people retirement also detracts from the number of friends they end up having.

This is one of the challenges of taking early retirement. Although you may be in a mental and financial position to retire at thirty-five, that doesn't mean any of your friends are. There is the danger that you may have a lot of time for interesting activities, but no one to pursue them with. Of course, you can always make new friends, but it may be a little difficult to find like-minded people in your age group.

It is most helpful to develop a broad-based network while still employed. Developing a number of relationships outside the workplace will ensure that you have a wide circle of acquaintances to associate with when you retire. For example, getting to know your neighbors, parents of your children's friends, or people with whom you attend religious services and social or athletic clubs will be a great help.

Surprisingly, a sense of community can have more of an impact on the quality of your retirement than good health and finances. Canadian researchers David Evans and Terry Lynn Gall concluded that the need to interact with others, the need to feel wanted, and the need to have a sense of belonging have more of an impact on retirement life because their impact is more immediate compared to health and financial concerns, which tend to set in over time.

> If you want an accounting of your worth, count your friends.
>
> — Merry Browne

Another interesting study conducted by the Psychology Department at the University of Michigan confirms that social and emotional support — much more than money — can create the difference between a happy and an unhappy retirement. The researchers started off by surveying one hundred soon-to-be retirees about their satisfaction and happiness levels. At a follow-up inquiry, they surveyed these same people four years after the commencement of their retirement.

Sadly, for a sizeable portion of the sample in the survey, the retirement years weren't all that rosy. Thirty-four said they were less satisfied after retirement, while twenty-five thought that their lives had improved. The remainder said that their satisfaction and happiness levels were about the same.

The University of Michigan researchers found that solid social support was the dominant factor in determining whether retirees were happy and satisfied four years after leaving the workforce. The people who were most pleased with their retirement years had sixteen friends or good acquaintances that they could rely on compared with the fewer than ten that were typical of the unsatisfied retirees. Tony Antonucci, one of the researchers, asserted, "While friendship can't replace things like health and money, it can help you manage the stresses associated with an illness or a financial difficulty, for instance."

> The best time to make friends is before you need them.
>
> — Ethel Barrymore

To be sure, your best support during troubled times will always be a dear friend. According to an old Greek proverb, "It is better in times of need to have a friend rather than money." Perhaps you have noticed that attention and kindness from a true friend will warm your heart a lot more when you are sick than receiving $1,000 from a distant or crabby relative.

At this point it is worth remembering that friendship isn't important only when you are ill. Without great friends, a journey to a foreign land can be much less adventurous; a million dollars will not have as much use; Christmas will be a lousy day; the most important of your accomplishments may appear worthless; and life itself will not even come close to being as precious and fulfilling.

Unfortunately, many retirees, men more so than women, don't have many solid friendships to fall back on once they quit working. They can wind up severely lonely, bored, and dejected, mainly because they hadn't taken the time to develop real friends during their working lives. Moreover, they have lost the skills to cultivate real friendships. Another reason that many retirees don't have solid friendships once they retire is that they have neglected former good friends in favor of their careers.

Happy retirees not only have a number of quality friendships when they retire, they are good at making new friends after retirement. A key consideration is how we find new friends when we no longer have the workplace to rely on. Needless to say, like-minded people are drawn to each other much more often than people who have little or nothing in common. New friendships can come from family

> Friends are like fiddle strings, they must not be screwed too tight.
>
> — English proverb

members, previous classmates, ex-colleagues, and neighbors. Of course, new acquaintances are also a good source of new friends.

All things considered, happiness is one of the cheapest things in the world when we secure a good part of it through friendship. As with all true happiness, there is little monetary cost. There is a significant cost, nonetheless: the time and effort we must invest creating and maintaining our friendships.

Portland resident Lenny Dee told an *Utne Reader* reporter, "I have always thought you could invest your energies in making money or making friends. And they achieve much the same ends — security, new experiences, personal options, travel, and so forth. I have always found it more fulfilling to make friends."

> Friends are the sunshine of life.
>
> — John Hay

Above all, friends make life complete. Have you ever noticed that when you have dinner at a restaurant with a good friend, a terrible meal will end up tasting a lot better? Good friends will also make a long journey seem a lot shorter. Indeed, even ten minutes in the company of a good friend will make any extremely difficult and depressing day worth living.

Two or Three Real Friends Are Worth More than a Hundred Superficial Ones

To retire happy, wild, and free, virtually every one of us needs friends with whom we can interact personally, philosophically, and spiritually. We don't necessarily need many friends, but we need a few close ones. Indeed, even two or three close friends are worth more than a hundred superficial ones.

True friendship will not be experienced with the casual acquaintances that retirees encounter from time to time. Moreover, retirees should not count on true friendship from former colleagues. Generally speaking, what are known as "work friends" are acquaintances with whom people spend a lot of time — and nothing much more. In some cases, what is commonly called friendship in workplaces is merely association among individuals who don't know what true friendship is. This is particularly true for workaholics who have no interpersonal contact outside of where they are employed.

If you are still fully engaged in your career and have no friends outside your workplace, now is the time to make some true friends. The fellow worker with whom you share a perverse interest in the weather and the fortunes of the New York Yankees is not likely to maintain any sort of relationship with you once you retire. Even if he or she wanted to, why bother? There is a lot more to friendship than talking about unpredictable things and superficial events.

> I have friends in overalls whose friendship I would not swap for the favor of the kings of the world.
>
> — Thomas Edison

There is also a lot more to friendship than just talking about work. "Do not keep company with people who speak of careers," advises Roger Rosenblatt. "Not only are such people uninteresting in themselves; they also have no interest in anything interesting. Keep company with people who are interested in the world outside themselves. The one who never asks you what you are working on; who never inquires as to the success of your latest project; who never uses the word career as a noun — he is your friend."

The nearer you are to retirement, the more important it is that the majority of your friends not be associated with your job. As a matter of course, you need at least two or three friends who are close to you and with whom you can relate on a deeper level. These should be individuals whose company you enjoy and with whom you share a number of interests unrelated to your career. They should care about you deeply enough to want to spend a lot of time with you once you retire.

Assuming that you are married, regardless of how intimate you are with your partner, you still require close friends — not your spouse's friends, but your own. They aren't real friends if your spouse has chosen them. Relying on your spouse's friends for companionship is not anywhere as fulfilling as having your own friends.

Moreover, the older you get, the greater the chance that your spouse will die. This applies particularly to women, who tend to outlive their husbands. In the event that this happens to you, your own true friends can be counted on for support and continued companionship. In contrast, your spouse's friends are likely to drift away soon after your spouse dies.

The key to optimizing your happiness in retirement is to cultivate quality friendships with a few happy and interesting people. Quality is more important than quantity. Succumbing to the temptation to have as many friends as possible will hinder your overall happiness, since this depletes your time, energy, money, and creativity, resources that can be better utilized in getting what you want out of retirement. What's more, it's unlikely that you will develop many real friends if you spread yourself too thin among too many individuals.

Whom you associate with in retirement will vary from mere acquaintances to casual friends to true friends. Of course, to have a true friend is one of the highest prizes of life. And to be a true friend in return is one of the most formidable tasks of life. In this

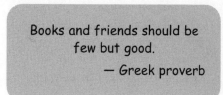

Books and friends should be few but good.

— Greek proverb

regard, always remember that friendship is a verb — and not a noun. Put another way, friendship is an active element that requires constant input for it to survive and thrive.

It's important to know the difference between acquaintances and friends. Acquaintances are like Mack trucks — cumbersome, dull, and low maintenance. They lose much of their warmth and appeal soon after you first encounter them. Friends are like Ferraris — sleek, exciting, and high maintenance. Provided you look after them, they keep their warmth and appeal forever.

Someone once said that friendship is like money — it is easier made than kept. The best way to maintain your great relationships is to ensure that the people involved want to keep you around. If you don't give friends the respect and attention they would like, they will find it elsewhere.

Remember: The best way to destroy relationships with substance is to take them for granted. If you still haven't retired, it's all too easy to neglect good friends while you pursue fame and fortune. It's also all too easy to neglect these people while you associate with people with more status and power.

If you are fortunate enough to reach a high position in this world, don't make the mistake of treating friends as mere acquaintances. This will come back to haunt you down the road — either when your friends reach a position equal to or higher than yours, or when you realize that your position in this world is not all that you imagined it to be. At this point your former friends may not even be acquaintances.

A friend is someone who sees through you and still enjoys the view

— Wilma Askinas

When you relegate friends to secondary status, you are liable to wind up with secondary friends. Placing people in the background compels them to look elsewhere for true friendship. As is to be expected, the individual who spends time with them will always be made of dearer substance than the one who doesn't.

For a friendship to succeed, it must work both ways in all respects. You must be able to trust your friends and they must be able to trust you. You must be getting something of value from them and they must be receiving something of equal value from you. You must find them pleasant to be around and they must find you just as pleasant.

> The proper office of a friend is to side with you when you are in the wrong. Nearly anybody will side with when you are in the right.
>
> — Mark Twain

People who have ulterior motives in becoming your friends should be avoided. They can cost you your time, energy, creativity, and finances. They can even cost you your health — mainly mental. Here are some signs that a person will not make a good friend:

A True Friend Is NOT:

- Someone who wants you to have exactly the same interests as they do
- Someone who wants to control you
- Someone who often relies on you for financial support
- Someone who wants to be your savior or protector
- Someone who is largely dependent on you emotionally
- Someone who agrees with you all the time or wants you to agree with them all the time
- Someone who wants you to drop your goals in favor of theirs
- Someone who wants you to eliminate other satisfying relationships with friends and family for their sake
- Someone you see only when you go for a drink at the local bar
- Someone who uses an alias from time to time.

Most important, a true friend will not desert you in times of need. The fact that you have lost your job or have come down one notch on the financial or social ladder is not a reason for your friends to disassociate themselves from you. Unfortunately, falling on hard times is when many people discover who their true friends are.

All things considered, true friends add to your happiness and seldom, if ever, subtract from it. As Alice Walker concluded, "No person is your friend (or kin) who demands your silence, or denies your right to grow and be perceived as fully blossomed as you were intended."

Try surrounding yourself with people who radiate warmth, kindness, and a fresh perspective on life in general. You are likely to wind up with at least one true friend. In my view, a true friend is someone with whom you can do something boring — and still enjoy your time with him or her. Following are a few more qualities that people cherish in a friend:

> Friends and good manners will carry you where money won't go.
> — Margaret Walker

A True Friend:

- ➤ Continues to like you whether you end up rich or poor
- ➤ Likes you despite your achievements
- ➤ Will not abuse you in any way
- ➤ Will not take advantage of you in times of weakness
- ➤ Will not desert you when you are down
- ➤ Is someone with whom you can be sincere and vulnerable
- ➤ Is a confidant who won't tell your most personal secrets to someone else
- ➤ Will defend you in your absence when someone says something nasty about you
- ➤ Will get you to laugh when you become too serious about life

Above all, a true friend reminds you of the person you would like to be. Perhaps you haven't found "the real thing" in the way of friends. If so, consider the words of Ralph Waldo Emerson: "The only way to have a friend, is to be one."

This brings up an important question: Just what kind of friend are you? Review the above list to see if you can measure up as a true friend. Not only are the above qualities ones that you should look for in a friend, these are the same qualities that you should develop and maintain if you want to attract quality friendship into your life.

You Can't Wait at Home to Be Discovered

Senescence begins
And middle age ends,
The day your descendants
Outnumber your friends.
— Ogden Nash

It's important for retirees to be good not only at keeping friends, but also at making new ones. As they get older, they tend to lose friends due to death, not to mention those who move away, or drift away to different interests. For most people, new friendships won't just happen on their own, with little effort on their part.

Although some people make friends less easily as they age, this doesn't mean that it is extremely difficult or impossible. The key is to adopt effective strategies for making new friends. Children see potential friends anywhere and everywhere they encounter other children. Indeed, they see potential friends in adults as well. In contrast, older adults see very little opportunity for friendships, regardless of the age of the people they encounter. Over time, they have become too jaded, critical, and cynical.

Moreover, some retirees become too consumed by other obligations and too caught up in nebulous pursuits, such as watching television, to add to their collection of friends. "It's not that it's hard to make friends when you're older, says Jan Yager, sociologist and author of *Friendships*, "but making friends — and finding time to maintain and nurture old friendships as well as new ones — is just one of the many concerns that occupy your time."

> The richer your friends, the more they will cost you.
> — Elizabeth Marbury

Contrary to popular belief, creating new friends is a skill older retirees can learn if they don't already have it. Creating and maintaining new friends is not easy for everyone, but it can be done by practically anyone. The most important factor is that you take action and work at it. Of course, like all skills, it takes practice before you become any good at it.

Take, for example, Gail Courney Rittgers of Alexandria, Virginia, who had to face up to the need to make friends when her husband died in 1980. "When I came back in the house after the funeral, I was seventy-seven, and I sat down at the dining room table and was alone for the first time in my life," Rittgers told a *US NEWS* reporter in 2002, "I made up my mind that I was not going to ruin the lives of my children by crying every time they called."

To deal with her new single status, Rittgers made the creation and maintenance of friends her overriding purpose. With time, she developed a close network of friends, particularly a number of individuals associated with her church. Happily, in 2002, Rittgers turned one hundred and still had several friendships to keep her life interesting.

The moral of this story is straightforward: If you want to meet new friends, you can't wait at home to be discovered. Nor are you going to meet new friends if you pursue your interests

> Friendship is a very taxing and arduous form of leisure activity.
> — Mortimer Adler

alone. If you watch TV or work on a solitary hobby all day long, you can rest assured that no new friends will come your way. Making new friends requires that you place yourself in communal and social situations where you can share yourself with others.

Where you go and don't go to meet others is important. Like-minded people are drawn to each other much more than people who have little or nothing in common. Indeed, when it comes to making friends, there's a lot to be said for bingo halls, raunchy night clubs, and seedy bars. These places attract and remove from other places a lot of people with whom you wouldn't want to associate under any circumstances.

On a slightly more serious note, given that you want to meet interesting people, you must go where interesting people hang out. Don't expect to meet many artists where Hell's Angels are known to hang out. Similarly, if discussing philosophy is important to you, you probably won't experience this with a group of customers at a Tim Hortons donut shop, who normally discuss sports, TV shows, and little else. Perhaps going to the art gallery, museum, or planetarium doesn't seem like a good place to meet others; nonetheless, you are more likely to meet a like-minded person at one of these places than at the local pub.

For some people, living in an active retirement community is a great place to meet new people and make friends. This proved to be the case for Maurice Musholt and her husband, Wayne. For the first two years of their retirement, the Musholts toured the United States in a motor home. Then they settled in Sun City Center,

My name is Howard. How do you like me so far?

So far, I think that I probably like you more than spiders and flat tires.

Florida, a community of 16,000 seniors twenty-five miles south of Tampa.

At first, Wayne was concerned whether he and his wife would be able to make new friends. "But I found it easy," he told a newspaper reporter. "We have different pockets of friends from all over. We play golf with some, eat out, or go to the performing arts with others."

What makes large retirement communities such as Sun City a great place to make new friends is the array of social activities they offer. At Sun City, groups meet for breakfast, socials, walks, water aerobics, dancing, tennis, biking, exercise classes, and horseback riding. There are genealogy, acting, ham radio, woodworking, art, ceramics and computer courses. Residents also have the opportunity to join others on trips to Tampa for concerts, museum visits, Broadway plays, and Tampa Bay Buccaneers football games.

Sun City residents can dance to live music every night, enjoy a $2 million clubhouse, and an 800-seat theater. No doubt many of the residents have been attracted to Sun City because of the 200 civic and social clubs. Another resident of Sun City, sixty-two-year-old Marcia Francis remarked, "We're out in the country but within reach of a metropolitan area. We're with people of the same age group — we party together, travel together, dine together, and solve all the problems of the world over breakfast every morning."

No doubt, retirement communities are not for all retirees. The point is that the more activities that you get immersed in outside your home, the more people you will be exposed to, and the more chance you will have to meet some new acquaintances and make friends. It's best to choose activities that you enjoy and don't make you feel out of place.

Your passionate pursuit may be an activity that lends itself to making new friends. Keep in mind that sharing common interests — such as painting pictures, collecting stamps, attending symphony performances, and writing poetry — goes a long way toward creating a bond between two people. Initially, a common interest is a good reason for acquaintances to meet before the friendship takes hold. Here are some other places and activities to consider:

Activities and Places for Making New Friends

- Personal-interest groups such as investment clubs and book-reading clubs
- Group sports such as baseball and bowling
- Aerobic classes
- Organizations that promote a social or environmental cause in which you believe
- Volunteering for a charitable organization
- Courses at colleges and universities
- Fraternal groups such as the Lions
- Church or spiritual gatherings
- Other people's parties
- Coffee bars
- Walking your dog
- Weddings
- Spectator sports
- Computer or music stores
- Art galleries, museums, and the opera
- Food markets

Meeting interesting people will depend not only on where you go, but also on how you present yourself. Taking a risk and extending yourself is one way to form a bond with someone else. The dynamics of social interaction, as well as the foundation of friendships, are based on the ability of the participants to give as well as receive.

> Love is only chatter,
> Friends are all that matter.
> — Gelett Burgess

If you want people to be friendly, show them how. You will make ten times more acquaintances in a month by being interested in people than you will in a year by trying to get people interested in you. Put another way, instead of being interesting, be interested. When you were a child, practically everyone you met had the potential to tell you something new and help you learn interesting things about the world. Refuse to be like most adults who think they know practically everything they need to know and have nothing interesting to learn from someone new.

Everyone has an interesting story to tell if you ask them for it. Being eager to learn new things is one of the best qualities you can have to help you make new acquaintances. Of course, the tangible rewards of meeting new acquaintances go far beyond the opportunity to learn something new. New acquaintances could develop into great friends.

> Your friends will know you better in the first minute you meet than your acquaintances will know you in a thousand years.
>
> — Richard Bach

Although you don't want to associate with obnoxious people, you can't be too picky when choosing new acquaintances. Don't let your mind trick you into rejecting someone who may be good for you. It's best to suspend judgment for at least a short while. This will make a world of difference regarding how fast you create new acquaintances, as well as how many you create; many of them could turn out to be great friends.

Given that even the most social of people usually don't meet more than twenty or fifty new people each year, you must give individuals a chance to show their essential qualities. No doubt there has been at least one person in your life for whom you didn't particularly care at your first encounter, but who turned out to be a great friend. People have a tendency to surprise us if we give them a chance.

In the same vein, never force or hurry a person to become your friend. Like the redwoods of California, great companionship takes time to grow. It must withstand the shocks of bad weather, many seasons, and unexpected adversity before it blossoms and matures. "We cannot tell the precise moment when friendship is formed," mused Samuel Johnson. "As in filling a vessel drop by drop, there is at last a drop which makes it run over; so in a series of kindnesses there is at last one which makes the heart run over."

In short, regular and close contact with others is a must if you want to develop new and close companionship. Take the initiative to call someone who is just a good acquaintance. More frequent meetings with a good acquaintance can result in a deeper relationship. Of course, having just one new companion can lead to others. Friends often develop in twos or threes or more. Mixing with your new-found friend's group of friends and acquaintances gives you the opportunity to develop your own circle of friends.

Whatever number of new people you choose to bring into your retirement years, the ideal is to have a variety — male and female and from all walks of life. What's more, let age play no part in your choice of companionship; try to have friends from all age groups. Particularly, try to have close relationships with individuals younger than you. They will influence you to renew your energy and have a fresh outlook on life. While older friends will help you grow old gracefully, young ones will help you think young — and stay young.

> *Wear a smile and have friends; wear a scowl and have wrinkles.*
> — George Eliot

Keep Active and Enjoy Yourself While Looking for Love

Robert Traller (his name has been changed due to the personal nature of his letter) from the state of Washington wrote to me in April 1998. His retirement, after a period of adjustment, was for the most part enjoyable and fulfilling. There was something missing, however.

Dear Mr. Zelinski:

I recently read your book, *The Joy of Not Working*. It was very interesting and informative. I especially liked the Wheel of Life and the pages pertaining to the Leisure Tree and related activities. Also, I like the quotation: Being over the hill means picking up speed!

I'm 69, single, and a retired Human Resources Manager. I used to be a "workaholic," but am adjusting to retirement.

A few years ago, my wife of 35 years passed away. It has been very difficult to find a "quality lady" who fits into my active lifestyle — dancing, golf, traveling, walking, etc.

Here's what I look for in a lady — a Christian, attractive with a pleasant personality, common interests, and 60+ years old! I have run personal ads in the Tacoma and Seattle newspapers, attended singles groups, churches, dances, tours dating services, etc., but still haven't met the right lady. My friends say the right one will "come along"!

Do you have any suggestions/comments regarding dating and relationships? I agree with you that it's better to be alone than in bad company! However, it is enjoyable to occasionally take a lady to a concert or dance.

Thank you and best regards,

Sincerely,

Robert Traller

Whether by choice or by chance, more retirees than ever before, both in numbers and as a percentage of the population, are single today. Due to separation, divorce, or death of a marriage partner, most people can expect to spend at least part of their retirement years being single. Naturally, finding a marriage partner or meaningful relationship enters the minds of many single retirees.

Happily, for millions of retirees, being single is not a problem, but a great opportunity instead. In fact, for some individuals who used to be married, being single is an opportunity to live life better than they ever did. Singlehood, in contrast to married life, allows many retirees to live happy, wild, and free.

> I think, therefore I am single.
> — Liz Winston

Twenty-six years after separating from her husband, eighty-four-year-old Elizabeth Maidstone of Vancouver, B.C., divulged that she never wanted to marry again, or even live with someone else for that matter. "I'm a bit of loner," affirmed Maidstone, "and I need lots of time to myself." Living single in her retirement years gave her the freedom to pursue what she wanted to do, without any interference from a partner. Indeed, Maidstone wasn't prepared to give up the independence that single life had brought her for anything else in the world.

For others, like Robert Traller, being single is a dilemma. Retirement would be more fulfilling if they had a meaningful relationship with a member of the opposite sex. In my reply to Traller, I consoled him with "just because you are single doesn't mean that you are alone." This was in reference to the fact that millions in today's society are single. My advice to Traller was "to keep active and enjoy yourself looking for love." In short, Traller shouldn't be anxious to meet the right person. Then, as his friends say, the right one will come along — provided it's meant to be.

The following case should provide encouragement to retirees for whom meeting someone special and forming an intimate, loving relationship is a dream. Betty Joray, a seventy-one-year-old widow and cancer survivor, wanted more companionship in her life. So the retired hospital secretary did something about it. Unlike many single retirees wanting to meet others, she didn't sit around home, waiting to be discovered. "You can sit home and feel lonesome," observed Joray, "or you can get out and be with people."

Joray also emphasized that not only is it important that people get out of the house, but that they should also remain positive and maintain a sense of humor if they want to meet interesting people. "Lighten up and don't take everything so seriously," she said. "I learned that over the years. You can do a lot of worrying, but it's not going to do any good anyway."

One of the ways Joray enhanced her social life was by enrolling in weekly dance classes at a community center in Oregon, Ohio. She ended up dancing her way to a new friend. Her positive outlook and sense of humor attracted seventy-eight-year-old Ed Linchester into her life. They have been dancing, riding bikes, and enjoying many other things together ever since.

Linchester, a widower, also emphasized the importance of a positive attitude for retirees who desire more companionship and joy in their lives. "Don't get down in the dumps. You might as well have a little fun because this is what life is. This is what we've got. Make the best of it."

As you can see from the experience of Betty Joray, the same principles apply for creating a meaningful relationship as for creating new friends. If you are looking for a relationship, and having trouble meeting other singles, the first thing that you must do is get out and meet people. My guess is that the biggest reason older people have a harder time meeting others — either for friendship or for a meaningful relationship — is simply that they don't get out of their homes enough.

> Give what you have. To someone, it may be better than you dare to think.
>
> — Henry Longfellow

Research, in fact, bears this out. Social psychologist Jerald Bachman's 2002 study at the University of Michigan's Institute for Social Research (ISR) indicates that at eighteen, 94 percent of males and 92 percent of females go out socially at least once a week. (52 percent of the men and 48 percent of the women go out three times a week.) By twenty-three to twenty-four, 35 percent of men and 24 percent of women still go out three times a week. But

We could be friends if you would face reality a little more.

Reality is a temporary illusion brought about by the absence of beer.

by the crusty old age of thirty-one to thirty-two, 73 percent of men and 64 percent of women get out once a week, while only 15 percent of men and 11 percent of women go out three times a week.

If you are like many singles who have difficulty in meeting and connecting with others, there are several ways to increase your chances. The matching industry is booming in North America. Those searching for Mr. Right or Ms. Right can use the services of health spas, singles clubs, dating services, newspaper ads, books, sports organizations, dining clubs, cruise lines, Club Med, and counselors.

The Internet provides more opportunity for finding, attracting, and maintaining a loving relationship later in life. There are several websites that strive to bring friendship and romantic encounters to their members.

One site, SeniorsMatch (www.seniorsmatch.com), claims to be "the only matching service exclusively for the over-fifty Age Group." They also claim to have thousands of members who are seeking personal contact with others. All members are over fifty years of age, with the majority being retired or soon-to-be-retired professionals.

With SeniorsMatch, you simply describe yourself and the type of person you are seeking. Then you use their computer to search their database for compatible referrals based on your tastes and preferences. You can also join in SeniorsMatch Special Events, such as vacations, cruises, weekend trips, and parties, where you can meet others.

Some people go to priests; others to poetry; I to my friends.

— Virginia Woolf

Even if you get out more often, and meet more people in the process, connecting with other singles for a meaningful relationship isn't necessarily easy. Patience is key, not only when you are meeting others, but also when you are waiting for a relationship to develop. To be sure, rarely do singles meet, or connect with, that special individual at the time that they think they will.

A relationship is going to take time, effort, and energy. Keep in mind that relationships lead to both pleasure and pain; breakups are a possibility. Relationships complicate our lives at the same time as they enrich our souls. Thomas Moore, author of *Soul Mates* states: "Relationships have a way of rubbing our nose in the slime of life — an experience we would rather forego, but one that offers an important exposure to our own depth."

Regardless of the potential complications, you may want to be in a relationship for the positive reasons of intimacy, love, support, great communication, wonderful sex — and a hundred more. If so, then you must do what is necessary to create a relationship. The next time you are feeling sorry for yourself because you haven't connected with that special person, recall that there are many retirees out there right now doing the things that are necessary to meet someone. You have to do the same.

> A man who was loved by 300 women singled me out to live with him. Why? I was the only one without a cat.
>
> — Elayne Boosler

Choose surroundings where there is no need to rush and no pressure on you to impress. Get involved in activities, such as playing tennis at a club, where there is a good deal of social interaction. This will greatly increase your chances for a relationship to develop. Studies show that almost 75 percent of meaningful relationships are initiated when there is little pressure or intention to meet a partner.

Two people learning and sharing their points of view over an extended period of time are much more likely to develop a lasting relationship than two people who meet once or twice by chance. Locations, activities, and events that allow people to meet on several occasions are most conducive for intimate relationships to develop. This is because more time is available to help them decide whether they should proceed further with a person whom they find interesting.

Volunteering with a charity or some other nonprofit organization that promotes a cause you believe in is one of the best ways to meet someone who has at least one thing in common with you. There isn't as much pressure to quickly connect with someone as with nightclubs, singles ads, or dating services. Other non-

> Plant a seed of friendship;
> reap a bouquet of happiness.
> — Lois L. Kaufman

pressure ways to meet like-minded people include joining a fraternal organization, regularly attending church or some other spiritual gathering, and becoming involved in a group activity, such as taking a course at a college.

Above all, learn to relax, enjoy yourself, and be yourself when meeting others. Most singles state that they enjoy being single most when they aren't actively or desperately seeking a dating partner. Paradoxically, many men and women reveal that their special person entered their lives when they least expected it, and when they weren't desperately searching for someone.

You Grow Most When You Are Alone

Don't you stay at home of evenings?
Don't you love a cushioned seat?
In a corner, by the fireside,
With your slippers on your feet?
— Oliver Wendell Holmes, Sr.

Regardless of how much some single retirees try to create a marital relationship, they may nonetheless wind up unsuccessful. Particularly for heterosexual women, the numbers are not in their favor. Because men tend to die at an earlier age, women over fifty are competing for a limited number of available men in their age group. Other factors, such as not being in the right place at the right time, will also contribute to thousands of single retiree's not being able to have a marital relationship for the rest of their lives.

Perhaps you have recently become single and are accepting this news with the same resignation as if you had just swallowed a live toad. Not to worry. Fortunately for you, single retirees — even those who would very much like to be in a relationship — can be just as happy as married people. In some cases, they can be happier.

Moreover, contrary to popular belief, single people can live just as long as married people. Their happiness, in fact, can contribute to their longevity. This was proven by Mary Parr, believed to be the oldest person in the United States, and the second oldest in the world. In October 2002, Parr died at the age of 113 at a retirement community in Florida. Ms. Parr, who had never wed, had often been asked about her secret for longevity. She usually answered,

"Never get married." Ms. Parr believed the headaches that a husband could have given her would have left her less content in life.

If you are a formerly married person, but recently single, you, à la Elizabeth Maidstone mentioned earlier in this chapter, can create a happy and fulfilling lifestyle that will defy explanation to other retirees — both single and married. There are many opportunities to enjoy life without a relationship. Regardless of your age, sex, financial status, or marital history, you can embrace single life and make it a satisfying experience.

The common thread uniting successful and inspirational singles is having an important purpose in life. They also have a strong sense of community, established through a number of meaningful relationships with close friends. Although these relationships aren't necessarily as intimate as typical marital relationships are made out to be, the relationships are nevertheless very important for support and companionship.

Research conducted by the Simon Fraser Gerontology Research Centre confirms that living alone can be rich, meaningful, and satisfying for retirees. Today, singlehood offers a rich mixture of options, identities, and lifestyles. The researchers found that the following factors contribute to a happy retirement for single retirees:

- Good Health
- Steady and Adequate Income
- Social Support
- Emotional Support
- Community Involvement
- Personal Hobbies
- Intellectual Pursuits

Granted, living alone doesn't come easily to some people, particularly if they have been married for some time and lost their spouse due to death or divorce. Besides having to deal with the grief of losing a spouse, they have to learn how to cope financially and socially without a spouse to help them. Nonetheless, after a few years, these same people often treasure their lifestyle. They, in fact, can value their independence and privacy just as much as people who have never married.

> In losing a husband, one loses a master who is often an obstacle to the enjoyment of many things.
>
> — Madeleine de Scudery

If you have recently become separated from a partner, effective transition to single life will require that you transform your identity, maintain high self-esteem, acquire new friends, and develop fresh interests. If you haven't exercised for years, start now. Your health will be enhanced both mentally and physically. Writing and other inner creative pursuits can be effective ways to develop your individuality. Pursue interests and activities that you have always wanted to pursue, but may not have had the opportunity to pursue in the past.

All things considered, being happily single is about freedom — freedom to sleep late, watch a soap opera, and go visit that charming member of the opposite sex at the coffee bar. Being single also affords the time and freedom to write a book, go for a ten-mile bicycle ride, and talk to a friend for two hours. All of this without being disturbed by a demanding spouse!

Although inspirational single retirees enjoy the company of close friends and other individuals, they also enjoy spending lots of time by themselves. They value their privacy, independence, and freedom much more than they would ever value having millions of dollars, if it meant having to sacrifice their solo state for it.

Kiss me and I will turn into a prince, marry you, and give you everything you want in marriage, including great companionship.

All I want is my solitude on this island. I don't even want a talking frog for a pet. So scat!

Above all the other benefits of their lifestyle, singles treasure solitude, something that is much more difficult to find in married life. Many married people have a preconception that single individuals, particularly those who spend a lot of time alone, are misfits or losers. This is not true at all. In fact, these singles are likely more well-balanced mentally than people who are always around and dependent on others. Indeed, a Hindu proverb advises us, "You grow most when you are alone."

In this regard, American poet and religious author Thomas Merton wrote, "The monk in hiding himself from the world becomes not less than himself, not less of a person, but more of a person, more truly and perfectly himself: for his personality and individuality are perfected in their true order, the spiritual, interior order, of union with God, the principle of all perfection."

This brings us to the issue of solitude as an important element for having a happy, wild, and free retirement. Because they like themselves, happy and successful retirees enjoy themselves just as much when they are alone as when they are in the company of others. This applies to all retirees — whether married or single.

By now you should know that solitude is not the same as loneliness. In this regard, Germaine Greer proclaimed, "Many a woman staring at the back of her husband's newspaper, or listening to his breathing in bed, is lonelier than any spinster in a rented room." To be sure, some of the loneliest people in the world are people who are always around other people. They are afraid to be alone because of fears of isolation, unhappiness, and negative self-assessment. Yet only by being alone a lot can they conquer loneliness.

As the Hindu proverb implies, solitude is necessary for self-discovery. Making space in your life for some solitude every day should be your goal if you want to achieve self-understanding, self-acceptance, and an individual identity. "If I had to give anyone advice," declared well-known author Rita Mae Brown, "it would be to live at least one year of your life completely alone — whoever you are. If you can't do it, you're in trouble."

> Only a person who can live with himself can enjoy the gift of leisure.
>
> — Henry Greber

In my view, Ms. Brown may be a little extreme, but her point is well made. It is only after you can establish a meaningful relationship with yourself that you can build strong, healthy, and lasting relationships with other people. And the only way to establish a meaningful relationship with yourself is to spend a lot of time by yourself.

Being alone forces you to confront yourself. In the process, you make peace with yourself. If there is a key rule for getting the most out of being alone, it is that sooner or later you must learn how to enjoy your own company. Put another way, you must learn to truly like yourself. Lots of quality solitary time will lead to self-acceptance, and eventually self-love.

Silence is golden. Make it one of your hobbies. Get away from

> Friendship with oneself is all important because without it one cannot be friends with anyone else.
>
> — Eleanor Roosevelt

the crowd and avoid noisy environments as much as possible. Take a break every day to visit yourself when you can have at least a few quiet moments away from others to treasure and enjoy. The idea is to spend a sufficient amount of time in solitude completely undisturbed by other human beings, television, radio, or the telephone.

You will find that being alone allows you to experience the world and yourself in a way not available when you are with other people. When you master the art of solitude, you master yourself — and life in general. Best of all, you no longer have to experience loneliness.

George Washington was right. It is better to be alone than in bad company!

Summing up, creating great friends and learning how to enjoy yourself while alone are two of the most precious gifts you can give yourself. You gain wealth that many millionaire retirees don't have. With these two priceless gifts, along with your health, you become the sole author of your retirement story. It will turn out rich, indeed.

7

Travel for Fun, Adventure, and More

Take Yourself Out of Your Element and Inspire Yourself with New Insights

Henceforth I whimper no more, postpone no more, need nothing,
Done with indoor complaints, libraries, querulous criticisms,
Strong and content I travel the open road.
— Walt Whitman

At the age of sixty-one, Hammond Stith retired as president, chairman, and CEO of Stith Equipment Co. "I was looking forward to it because of some things that I wanted to do that I hadn't given enough time to," Stith remarked several years later as he reflected about his retirement. As it is for many retirees, travel was the most important leisure activity on Stith's mind when he left the world of work.

"I hadn't been to the south of France, I hadn't played golf in Scotland, I hadn't been to Ireland, I hadn't been to Hong Kong, I hadn't been to Communist China," Stith declared. "So there were places I wanted to go and see and do. So I did, and I'm still doing it."

For people such as Hammond Stith, or Ian Hammond mentioned in Chapter 1, travel is one of the great pleasures of retirement. Travel, however, need not only be done for pure pleasure; it can provide a lot of adventure. Moreover,

> The longer you stay in one place, the greater your chances of disillusionment.
>
> — Art Spander

travel can support one of your purposes or missions in retirement. Wanting to understand a nation — anything from the people to the history to the economy to the geography to the customs — is an admirable purpose indeed. Best of all, your purpose doesn't have to be cast in stone; it can vary from year to year, changing from studying famous works of art to photographing the great sights of the world to experiencing the most inspirational religious sites.

> The joy of travel is in the wandering.
>
> — Joe Robinson

Travel can enhance your retirement significantly since it provides an elevated degree of stimulation, freshness, and pleasure not encountered in your everyday routine and environment. Of course, travel is a great teacher. Regardless of where you go, you can always learn something new. Learning about the food, the cooking, and the clothing of a country, along with what retirement means to the locals, are just a few things that can broaden your knowledge of the world.

Particularly when you go abroad, travel takes you out of your element and inspires you to new insights about your life in general. It is an effective way to get yourself thinking in different ways about the world and what it means to you. Above all, travel to other countries can jolt you out of your unconsciousness about how good your life is into a deep, conscious appreciation of all the great things that you have going for yourself in retirement.

Spend All the Money That You Can on Travel If Travel Really Turns You On

Perhaps it makes sense to spend all the money that you can on travel if travel turns you on more than anything else in life. Indeed, you may even want to forget about leaving your children or grandchildren any inheritance and spend the money on as many adventurous treks as you can fit into your retired life. This is exactly what one British couple has in mind.

Adair Skevington, fifty-four, and her husband, Mike, fifty-five, caught the travel bug when they both retired. Five years later, Adair, a former chartered accountant, told an *Observer* newspaper reporter, "It makes us sound awful but, yes, we are happy to spend all the money we have saved over the years on having fun now that we have retired." The Skevingtons, who live in the central-England city of Derby, had just returned from a trip to South Africa and were about to leave on a trip around Europe.

"It really depends on how long we're able to travel, but if we go on like this, we won't be leaving our children anything," declared Adair. "My parents worked until they were sixty-five, by which time they were worn out. If we don't enjoy life now and make the most of it while we're active, we will lose the chance."

> I travel not to go anywhere, but to go. I travel for travel's sake. The great affair is to move.
> — Robert Louis Stevenson

Tips on How to Enhance Your Next Journey

If the travel bug gets the best of you in retirement, you may want to stay close to home and discover your own state or province, or you may want to venture to foreign lands. Regardless of how far you go, the degree to which your next trek turns out to be pleasurable, adventurous, and satisfying will depend on how well you plan your trip. The quality of your journey will also depend on your ability to be spontaneous and how well you are able to maintain a positive attitude throughout.

Here are a few tips on how to enhance your next journey:

- Choose your vacation destination wisely. Spending time in Billings, Montana, with friends you enjoy is much better for your health and happiness than being in Rio or New York with people you don't enjoy.
- Review your passions in life. Incorporate your greatest passion into your vacation plans.
- The key to an enjoyable journey is not to put yourself under stress and duress. Try not to schedule too many things to do.
- Have periods of free time that allow for some spontaneity.
- When going on vacation in your car, don't rush to your destination. Take your time. Add to your enjoyment by stopping to read the roadside signs about the historical points of

interest.

- Have you made plans for next year's annual trek? If you have, change your plans and be more adventurous. You will be glad you did.
- If one of your retirement dreams is relocating to another city or country, then head there and treat your vacation as an adventurous research expedition.
- When visiting towns and cities, take the extra time to check out the local cafes and diners instead of eating at the restaurants catering to the tourist trade. You will experience cheaper and better food as well as a more interesting atmosphere.

> A nomad I will remain for life, in love with distant and uncharted places.
> — Isabelle Eberhardt

- To make vacations more affordable, escape expensive hotels and meal costs by finding short-term apartment, villa, or cottage rentals. These can cost less than 50 percent of hotel room prices and be much more interesting to stay in.
- Take a vacation to a destination that has special meaning to you. Visit a place where one of your parents was born or a place where you used to live but haven't visited for a long time.
- Think about your fantasy vacation. Let your mind go wild. Imagine how you would like to spend your time. Write this down. Then do everything within your power to spend your vacation exactly as you would like. If you keep working towards this, it won't be that long before you can make your fantasy vacation come true.
- Get off the beaten path. Don't let your hang-ups interfere with trying new destinations. Journeys that entail learning new things, seeking adventure, meeting interesting people, and experiencing new cultures are the most satisfying.
- Find a pub, coffee bar, or bistro where the locals hang out. Get to know them along with their music, their stories, their laughter, and

their aspirations.
> What is the one thing you would enjoy doing on your vacation more than anything else? Then why aren't you working towards making it a reality?

Use the Internet to Make Your Travel Adventures Affordable and Enjoyable

A great way to enhance your travel adventures is to use the Internet for researching and booking trips. About 13 percent of the American population (21 million people) now routinely uses the Web to book rental cars, hotel reservations, airline tickets, and complete travel packages. The Internet is especially suited for retirees who want to comparison shop so that they can get the best deals. If you are uncomfortable booking trips on-line, you can still use a travel agent to book your chosen package.

Following are some ways that you can use the Internet to make your travel destinations more economical and enjoyable:

> *Travel is the frivolous part of serious lives, and the serious part of frivolous ones.*
> — Anne Sophie Swetchine

> Use the major travel websites (such as www.travelcity.com, www.orbitz.com, and www.priceline.com) to research all sorts of information about travel options and prices. You can view descriptions, maps, photos, and even videos about travel destinations and things to do there. You select where and when you want to go and match these to various price options.
> Use the Virtuoso website (www.virtuoso.com) to research the trips catering to the carriage trade, i.e., to people with expensive tastes who can afford to fly first class to anywhere in the world.
> Find maps for practically every city (try either www.mapblast.com or www.mapquest.com).
> Use www.spafinder.com to treat yourself to a stay at an exclusive health or beauty resort

anywhere in the world.

➤ To book a last-minute getaway, and possibly save some money in the process, contact www.site59com. At times you can book a flight that leaves for Hawaii in as little as four hours.

➤ Find a bed-and-breakfast place on several websites (view bed-and-breakfast descriptions, photos, and reviews on www.breadandbreakfast.com).

➤ Detailed research can be conducted at www.worldtravelguide.net. You can learn a lot about a particular country or region — anything from its history and its government to its climate and its accommodations.

➤ Check out when Walt Disney World or Disneyland is open, how much it costs, and how to find either at www.disney.com.

> A traveler without observation is a bird without wings.
> — Moslih Eddin Saadi

➤ Discover how much your dollars are worth in another country's currency (try www.x-rates.com).

➤ Check out weather forecasts for your travel destinations at www.weather.com and www.onlineweather.com.

➤ If you are American, you may want to ensure that you don't travel to a destination that Uncle Sam doesn't like. The U.S. Department of State maintains the website www.state.gov/travel/com. You may also want to check out www.state.gov/travel/com for information about visas, passports, and U.S. embassies.

Travel with a Difference

Active, well-seasoned senior travelers, who have "been there and done that" with more traditional travel, are now looking for more exotic travel. "There's definitely growing interest in soft-adventure travel," says Vicki Brems, vice-president of marketing for TCS Expeditions in Seattle. "So many retirees have already gone to normal places — now they want to expand their horizons."

Retirees, particularly those in better physical and financial shape than other sixty- or seventy-year-olds, look for the unusual, whether it's far off the beaten track or has some adventurous aspect to it. Essentially, they are looking forward to an experience that will enrich their lives as opposed to checking into a hotel and sitting on the beach all day.

Exotic adventures of all kinds, practically everything from waltzing in Vienna to cruising on the yacht that Jackie Onassis used to cruise on, are marketed by most travel agencies today. These treks can last anywhere from a day to several weeks. Eldertreks in Toronto offers adventure for small groups (maximum: fifteen) to less-traveled parts of the world such as Borneo and New Guinea, with activities that can include exploring temples or rice paddies, but "ending the day at a comfortable guesthouse or small hotel," says its president, Gary Murtagh.

> Adventure is worthwhile in itself.
>
> — Amelia Earhart

Another travel agency you may want to consider is 50 Plus Expeditions (1-866-318-5050 or www.50plusexpeditions.com) which specializes in adventure travel for people over fifty. According to its website it offers "active holidays and exotic vacations in East Africa (Kenya & Tanzania safari), Asia (tours to Borneo, India, Nepal, Thailand, Angkor Wat), Central and South America (Costa Rica, Venezuela, Galapagos cruises, Amazon rain forest of Ecuador, Peru), adventure cruises to Antarctica (Antarctic Peninsula) & Arctic (Greenland), Europe (Danube cycling, hiking in the Austrian Alps and England), and Canada (walking in the Rockies)."

If you are craving for the adventurous and unusual, here are some of the things other travelers have experienced and which you may want to consider for your next vacation:

- Live the outdoor life on a trek in outer Mongolia.
- Check out cave tubing (nature hiking in the jungle) in Belize.
- White-water raft the Ayung River in Bali.
- Swim across the Mississippi River.
- Climb Mount Kilimanjaro, the highest mountain in Africa, in northeast Tanzania near the Kenya border.

- ➤ Amuse yourself on a ten-day Halloween ghost tour of England.
- ➤ Take an African elephant safari.
- ➤ Experience dog sledding in Alaska.
- ➤ Fly to the Swiss Alps for a massage and a mud bath at an exclusive spa.
- ➤ Take a submarine expedition under the polar ice pack.
- ➤ Go llama trekking in the Andes Mountains of Peru or Bolivia.
- ➤ Try hacienda hopping in Ecuador.
- ➤ Hike in Uzbekistan and observe lemurs in Madagascar.
- ➤ Take up bone fishing in the Seychelles Islands.
- ➤ Indulge in a multi-sport adventure in Morocco.
- ➤ Heli-hike or heli-ski the Canadian Rockies.
- ➤ Enjoy a jungle expedition along the Amazon River.
- ➤ Scuba dive among sunken ships in the Caribbean.
- ➤ Discover California's wine country in a hot-air balloon.

> They say travel broadens the mind, but you must have the mind.
>
> — G.K. Chesterton

For more ideas on offbeat vacations and those off-the-beaten-path, such as camping in Kenya, glacier trekking in Alaska, or parasailing in the Australian Outback, check out *Travel + Life*. Published four times a year, this magazine is a must for the adventurous traveler. It showcases intriguing and inspiring travel opportunities that you may not be able to discover anywhere else.

Implement Something Unique into Your Next Trek

Perhaps you would like to go one step farther and indulge in custom travel — something designed especially for you. Have you ever considered a personal guide for Hong Kong, an English-speaking driver for Moscow, a translator for Turkey, or a private jet for Europe? Provided that you can afford it, there are people willing to help.

Virtuoso is a network of 250 independent travel agents who specialize in arranging luxurious and out-of-the-ordinary getaways for the moneyed class. The agents are polled annually about the nature of the business. One of the questions regularly asked is, "What was the most unusual active/adventure trip you scheduled for clients?" Following are some of the responses that agents gave one year. These may give you an idea or two for something unique you would like to implement into your next trek.

> I have wandered all my life, and I have traveled; the difference between the two is this — we wander for distraction, but we travel for fulfillment.
>
> — Hilaire Belloc

- ➤ California-to-Florida car and driver for client and caged bird.
- ➤ Bear watching in the Arctic Circle.
- ➤ Find the home in Shanghai where I was born fifty-five years ago.
- ➤ Arrange an on-the-road New Year's Eve Party between San Antonio and Phoenix.
- ➤ Arrange for me to work five days at the Mother Teresa Center for the Dying in Calcutta, India.
- ➤ Have me fly upside down in a RAF fighter jet.
- ➤ Submarine expedition under the Polar Ice Pack.
- ➤ Transport my loved one's ashes to the Italian Alps.
- ➤ Two side-by-side suites, please . . . he snores.
- ➤ Three days' snow skiing followed by three days' private yacht charter.
- ➤ Minimum thread-count requirement for hotel bed linens — no exceptions.

Perhaps these ideas are a little too weird for you. No problem! According to its website, Virtuoso can also help you arrange the following: "Toast the season from pewter goblets in Colonial Williamsburg. Celebrate a Dickens Christmas in London. Catch 'The Nutcracker' in Prague. Waltz in the New Year at Vienna's Hofburg Palace. Or, throw tradition to the wind and sail off to a frangipani-scented isle."

Become an Ecotourist

In Zen they say, "no matter where you go, there you are." Well, here I am in Hawaii and I know "where" I am, but I still don't know "who" I am. All I know is that I like drinking a lot of beer wherever I go.

Perhaps you love nature, enjoy travel, and want to do your part to preserve the environment. Then why not combine all three? An eco-friendly, educational experience may be what you are looking for and the ecotourism industry is there to serve you.

Don't confuse ecotourism with nature or adventure tourism. With nature travel, most tourist dollars come at the cost of irreparable damage to the environment and diminishing wildlife populations. For example, the environment in the Florida Keys has been viewed by many as a tropical paradise, but most of the tourist operators are far from eco-friendly.

Moreover, don't fall for tourism advertising that paints the operator as promoting ecotourism, when, in fact, the operator is trying to be more profitable at your expense. Martha Honey, author of *Ecotourism and Sustainable Development: Who Owns Paradise?* recently wrote in the *Boston Globe,* "Take, for instance, the increasingly common practice in hotels of giving guests the option of not having sheets and towels laundered daily. A sensible step — but hardly, as was claimed in one press release, one that will save the planet. What it is does is save the hotel some money."

Above all, ecotourism stands out due to its ethical values and principles. Oliver Hillel, tourism program coordinator for the United Nations Environment Program, declares that true ecotourism "contributes to conservation of biodiversity, sustains the well-being of local people, includes a learning experience, involves responsible action on the part of tourists, requires the lowest possible consumption of non-renewable resources, and stresses ownership by the locals."

You can learn more about ecotourism by visiting www.ecotourism.org, the site of the International Ecotourism

Society. Some of the other websites offering ecotourism products include www.worldsurface.com, www.ecoclub.com, www.transitionsabroad.com, and www.ecotourism.sk.ca.

You Don't Have to Be Rich to Spend a Month or Two in a Warmer Climate

As you may already know, my hometown is not the warmest place on the North American continent, especially in winter. For the past two years, to escape Edmonton's winter in January and February, my friend Ron Homenchuk has spent two months in Mexico. He flies to

> The world is a book, and those who do not travel, read only a page.
>
> — Saint Augustine

Mexico City and takes a six-hour bus trip north to San Miguel de Allende. He likes the warm climate, cheap accommodation, art galleries, and relaxed lifestyle.

Note that Ron is not a wealthy person. He is semi-retired at fifty-nine with no pension and no big nest egg set aside for his sixties and beyond. He works part-time as a masseur. Nevertheless, he feels prosperous enough to take an annual winter vacation.

Incidentally, the AARP (American Association of Retired Persons) designated San Miguel de Allende as one of the fifteen best places to retire outside of the United States. This is what the AARP had to say about San Miguel, which makes it a great place to visit for a month or two, even if you don't want to retire there.

Nestled in the hills of north-central Mexico, this proud city of 80,000 is dominated by its nearly fifty-year-old school of fine arts and the arty folk who come from around the world to study, create, and live the Mexican good life. A year-round contingent of gringos and their Mexican friends support exhibitions, readings, concerts, and fiestas throughout the year. The foreigners have brought English-speaking doctors and upwardly mobile housing costs, though you can still find a fixer-upper for $85,000 and a two-bedroom apartment for $200-$300 a month. The cost of living is better: A man can get a haircut for $4, and electric bills are about $20 a month.

> A traveler to distant places should make no enemies.
>
> — Nigerian proverb

Despite not being wealthy, Ron Homenchuk takes an annual winter trek to San Miguel because he believes that travel is one of the best treats on earth that we can give ourselves. Ron agrees that, "Travel stretches the imagination, opens the mind, and enlivens the spirit."

Enjoy Yourself in a Myriad of Ways at a Recreational Vehicle Retirement Resort

Once you are retired, each winter you can take your recreational vehicle down to Mesa, Arizona, and soak up the Arizona sun while you enjoy all the amenities of home away from home. Better still, by taking advantage of all the amenities that Towerpoint RV Retirement Resort has going for itself, you can pursue current interests and discover many new ones.

This is what the resort's website (www.towerpointresort.com) has to say: "Our activity program, under the direction of our full-time Activity Director, is designed to encourage personal growth and better health through mental stimulation, physical exercise, educational opportunities, spiritual enrichment, and social interaction." Indeed, the resort has a ton of activities planned for its temporary and full-time residents. Moreover, special events are planned throughout the year to add to your enjoyment of the place.

Here are fifty-one activities you can enjoy at Towerpoint:

Bowling	Mixed chorus	Men's softball
Fishing Club	Tuesday movies	Crafts
Flee market	Needlecrafts	Square/Compass Club
Garden Club	Oil painting	Squires
Genealogy	Concert band	Stained glass
Golf groups	Biking Club	Pancake breakfast
Darts	Ceramics	Stitch 'n chat
Harmonica Band	Quilt Club	Hiking Club
Horseshoes	Tennis Club	Games and cards
Exercise room	Campers Club	Watercolors class
Jam sessions	Rosary	Water exercises
Ladies' Ministries	Square dancing	Woodcarving

Pool & billiards	Wood shop	Lapidary/Silversmith
Library	Sewing for dolls	Writing family stories
Shuffleboard	Yoga	Hydrotherapy pools
Line dancing	Singles Club	Friday night cabarets
Computer Club	Casual swimming	Amigos Spanish Club

Why Travel Alone When You Don't Have To?

Single? You don't necessarily have to stay home just because friends and relatives can't go with you on a journey that you would like to make. Of course, one alternative is to go alone. If you feel lonely and uncomfortable traveling alone, however, there is an alternative.

Given that there are many other single retirees who share your aspirations of enrichment through travel, why not find someone compatible with whom you can share holiday experiences and expenses? Not only will you have someone to talk to, you can avoid the expensive "single supplement" that can almost double the cost of a trip for a single traveler.

> He who has traveled alone can tell what he likes.
>
> — Rwandan proverb

One way to find a travelling companion is to use the Travel Mates service at SeniorsMatch (www.seniorsmatch.com). All members are over fifty years of age, with the majority being retired or soon-to-be-retired professionals.

Another option is the Travel Companion Exchange (www.whytravelalone.com), an "established travel-matchmaking organization," that hooks up like-minded members of the same or opposite sex. There's no age limit with this organization.

Swap Your House for a Neat Pad in Some Faraway Paradise

You may be able to visit faraway places at a cost far less than you are normally used to paying. Many retirees save hundreds or thousands of dollars on vacation travel by booking with the Seniors

> Certainly, travel is more than the seeing of sights; it is a change that goes on, deep and permanent, in the ideas of living.
>
> — Miriam Beard

Vacation and Home Exchange (www.seniorshomeexchange.com). This exchange allows you to do a straight vacation exchange of your home with people across North America, and even with people abroad. Alternatively, you can exchange a hospitality vacation in which you visit with them and, in return, they visit with you.

The cost to register as an exchange member is only $65 in US funds for a three-year listing or $100 for Lifetime Membership. Better still, AARP members pay only $45 for a three-year membership.

There are many ways you can benefit from swapping homes through the Seniors Vacation and Home Exchange. Here are some of them:

- Boats, caravans, and motor homes may be exchanged with each other or in any combination, to provide even more exciting and adventurous vacations.
- There are no hotel or motel expenses to pay.
- You don't have to take part in any organized tours.
- Security is provided at your home by your exchange partners while you are away.
- Your pets and plants can be taken care of by your exchange partners.
- You can take longer vacations since cost is not as much of a concern.
- To eliminate the need for automobile rentals, cars can be included in an exchange agreement. In fact, 57 percent of exchanges include a car. Car exchanges provide an enormous savings on rental and insurance expenses.
- You aren't confined only to your primary residence. You can exchange second homes and even motor homes.
- Exchange partners can give you valuable information about the city's or country's local attractions, shops, and great restaurants not known to tourists.

> ➤ You can take longer vacations because your exchange partners normally have a lifestyle similar to yours and not that of people with jobs or kids. Seventy-one percent of exchanges were for two weeks or more and 25 percent of exchanges were for more than one month.
> ➤ You can make three or four vacation exchanges a year.
> ➤ Exchange members can take part in travel-related discussion forums.

You can check out other house-swapping organizations. For a $29.95 membership fee, the International Home Exchange Network (www.homexchange.com) will add you to its list of people worldwide who wish to swap houses for a temporary visit. You can also contact the Vacation Exchange Club at 1-800-638-3841.

Try a Working Vacation for a More Satisfying Traveling Experience

Another way to cut down on the expenses of living in another country is to take a working holiday. Working holidays, or "volunteer vacations," as they are sometimes called, provide people with an interesting avenue for travel and adventure. Those who have done it feel that taking a working vacation provides a more vigorous and satisfying traveling experience.

A good holiday is one spent among people whose notions of time are vaguer than yours.

— J. B. Priestley

There are now more than two dozen organizations that operate hundreds of working-vacation projects in all corners of the world. Earthwatch Institute in Maynard, Massachusetts, the largest provider of what it terms "un-vacations," today serves more than 4,000 clients a year, with 720 teams flying into fifty-one countries and twenty-three states. Its projects range from collecting medicinal plants in Kenya to measuring glacier melt in Iceland.

"People are looking for a sense of accomplishment away from the workplace," declares Mary Blue Magruder, director of public affairs at Earthwatch, "and going into a rain forest and helping researchers discover a new species. These vacations aren't a canned experience."

Locations far removed from luxury are typical destinations for volunteer travel. Weekends usually are free, and volunteers often spend the days mingling with the locals and visiting scenic or historic sites. Regardless of the focus of the programs, most volunteer vacations allow participants to blend the pleasures of travel with a higher purpose — either making the world a better place or learning more about it. Volunteers normally pay for their own transportation to and from the projects. The projects can be either humanitarian and service-oriented projects, such as helping villagers build a church, or scientific projects, such as studying whales in the Pacific Ocean. Typically, each program has a project leader or principal researcher with several support staff.

> I have found out that there ain't no surer way to find out whether you like people or hate them than to travel with them.
> — Mark Twain

The projects usually provide accommodations, training, meals, equipment, and like-minded companions. The tasks can vary from the very interesting to the boring, depending upon whether volunteers have to use a computer, a camera, a hammer, a shovel, or a wheelbarrow.

By living and working with the local people, volunteers gain unique insights into the culture of fascinating lands. A lifetime of positive memories can be gained even from a brief three-week volunteering experience. The rewards that volunteers get include gaining new insights and a deep appreciation for the people and the places they visit, not to mention the sense of being engaged in the world and making a difference. "It's a way of going on vacation, living with the locals, and doing some good for people," states seventy-one-year-old retiree Cay Wendling, from San Diego, California, who has gone on several volunteer vacations.

If you are interested in taking a working vacation, here are some of things that other volunteers have done and may be available to you:

- Help scientists study the behavior of whales in the waters of Washington's Puget Sound or off the coast of Australia.
- Care for orphans with AIDS in South Africa.
- Help build houses as a carpenter's assistant for the disadvantaged in Bolivia or Guatemala.
- Assist a principal investigator on the

Watershed Restoration Project, trying to rectify the threatened river system on the Cape Peninsula in South Africa.

➤ Help native Maoris in the Cook Islands improve their healthcare system.

➤ Help build a bridge in Africa.

➤ Teach English in a village in Costa Rica or Italy.

➤ Assist archaeologists excavating ancient settlements in Russia, the Pacific Spice Islands, or Easter Island.

➤ Work in the library at the Nave Institute, a 150-year-old school with an enrollment of 2,550 students, representing some of the poorest of the poor in the northern India province of Uttar Pradesh.

➤ Hunt for sources of water in Mongolia with a Chinese hydrologist.

➤ Care for abandoned children in a remote Romanian hospital.

➤ Spend a year in Mexico working alongside Franciscan nuns in a home for elderly women.

➤ On a working holiday to India, during free time on weekends, take train rides to see the Taj Mahal and Agra Fort, as well as other historic sites.

To be sure, volunteering for these assignments can provide many advantages and rewards. These cross-cultural assignments are opportunities to deal with different environments and people. They are also a great way to test your commitment and adaptability while living in a Third-World environment.

Mr. Scanlan, from Loudon, Tennessee, who along with his wife volunteered on a project to help native Maoris in the Cook Islands improve their healthcare system, stated, "The tourists staying at a nearby resort will never know the Maoris the way we do. We know them by name. We worked alongside them in their community. We became a part of their life."

> I have, thanks to my travels, added to my stock all the superstitions of other countries. I know them all now, and in any critical moment of my life, they all rise up in armed legions for or against me.
>
> — Sarah Bernhart

Journey Close to Home and Do the Things That an Out-of-Town Tourist Might Do

Oscar Wilde was right. The sight of Niagara Falls must be one of the earliest, if not the keenest, disappointments in American married life.

Many people believe that the farther away from home one travels, the better the journey will be. Not necessarily so. "It is not worthwhile to go around the world to count the cats in Zanzibar," advised Henry David Thoreau.

As an alternative to distant travel, you can take a journey close to home and do something interesting that you have always wanted to do, but never had time for. You can even journey in your hometown. Regardless of how long you have lived there, chances are there is a beautiful park, interesting street, fascinating neighborhood, or historic site that you haven't seen. Here are some of the things you can do in your hometown that a tourist from out of town might do:

- ➤ Spend a night in a boutique hotel.
- ➤ Head to a museum.
- ➤ Take a day trip to the edge of town.
- ➤ Eat out at a different ethnic restaurant every night for a week.
- ➤ Have an expensive latte at the coffee bar.
- ➤ Visit people you haven't visited for a long time.
- ➤ Stay over at a friend's house.
- ➤ Go to a spa to get a massage.
- ➤ Go downtown with no goal in mind and spend three to four hours exploring new sights.

Whether it's a journey to all corners of the world or an occasional trek closer to home, travel should be somewhere on your agenda in retirement life. Travel near and far will help you break the routines of everyday life that can lead to staleness and boredom. Above all, regardless of how old you are, travel will renew your sense of excitement about the world and invigorate you at the same time.

8

Relocate to Where Retirement Living Is Best

Live Somewhere Else and Do What You Have Always Wanted to Do

"Go and live somewhere else," advises John Osborne, a resident of Victoria, B.C. "Try doing what you think you've always wanted to do." Osborne, a retired psychology professor from the University of Alberta, moved to Victoria after he found retirement living left a lot to be desired in his old hometown of Edmonton, Alberta.

Perhaps, like many retirees, you too yearn for a change of scenery, new experiences, and a changed set of circumstances. Moving to a new location within your own country is one way to satisfy these yearnings. Going abroad is another option. Indeed, as many as two million American retirees currently live abroad, according to David Warner, professor of public affairs at the University of Texas at Austin.

Marketing research shows that 45 percent of American baby boomers plan to move after retirement. Most, however, want to stay close to home, perhaps within fifty miles or less of their former homes. Whether retirees want to stay within their home states, or move to

> He makes his home where the living is best.
>
> — Latin proverb

another one, living around people their age in new developments that combine the comforts of the suburbs with the benefits of a resort is important.

One reason retirees move is economic — they can stretch their retirement income a lot farther. Take, for example, Ron Sadownick and Patricia Robertson. They sold their $250,000 house in Calgary, Alberta, and used a portion of the proceeds to buy a $205,000 house in Nanaimo, B.C. Not only did they wind up with an extra $45,000 in the bank as a contingency fund, they found that moving to a warmer climate helped them save on living expenses. "We save money by not having to drive the car much or heat the house much. Energy prices are cheaper here, and wine is cheaper, too," declared Ron.

> I have just returned from Boston. It is the only thing to do if you find yourself there.
>
> — Fred Allen

There are three other main motives why retirees may move to a new location. The first is to relocate to a beautiful location and find refuge there. It can be a place formerly reserved for annual vacations somewhere close to the mountains, beside the ocean, or in a nice warm climate.

The second motivation is seeking new adventures. Some people want a place that is more interesting and exciting than their present location. It can be San Francisco, New York, or some place in another country such as a nice villa in Italy.

Wanting to be closer to a support structure is the third motivation. Some retirees may want to move to a new location, not because they are seeking adventure or a change of scenery, but because they want to be closer to their children and grandchildren.

It's important to be realistic about how beneficial the move will be. People who move to be close to natural beauty may find out the beauty doesn't last. It won't take long before the ocean and mountains become mundane things to look at. Moving closer to family doesn't always meet expectations. Younger family members may themselves move, leaving retirees alone in the place they were expecting a support system.

To be sure, to move or not to move is a decision not easily made by retired people. They must weigh the advantages of new surroundings and new experiences against the security of familiar surroundings and limited new experiences. Nevertheless, many retired individuals like John Osborne relish liberation from old routines and a chance to reinvent themselves — taking classes, making new friends, traveling to exotic destinations, and establishing new roots.

For some retirees, moving far away from home has greater rewards than staying in their own country. Betsy and John Braden moved from Atlanta, Georgia, the place where they had retired and found too boring, to a rented cottage in southwestern France. "I wouldn't want to be anywhere else. Moving abroad has been challenging and stimulating, physically, intellectually, and emotionally, and it came just as I was beginning to feel brain-dead and on a tiresome treadmill," stated Betsy, fifty-seven, to an Associated Press reporter. "It's been like returning to university life as one big adult-education course."

Retiring abroad can make economic sense, particularly if you choose a country with a low cost of living. Roseanne Knorr, author of *The Grown Up's Guide to Retiring Abroad*, asserts that American retirees living abroad tend to spend less. "You're not keeping up with the Joneses," observes Knorr, who divides her time between France and Florida. "You're not worried about the latest car. If a couple is living in a small town in France, they may only need one car, not two."

> I hate small towns because once you've seen the cannon in the park there's nothing to do.
>
> — Lenny Bruce

Perhaps you have dreamt about taking up refuge in a foreign land, typically some place where you can experience a gentler climate and more favorable tax laws. Keep in mind that an offshore retirement often means seeing children, grandchildren, and friends a lot less. This is primarily the reason so few people aspire to retiring abroad. It can be tough to handle, particularly from an emotional standpoint, and sometimes from a financial one.

If you are thinking of relocating, but don't know where, the question that arises is, "What makes a good place to retire?" You must examine your priorities: What type of climate do you want to live in? What activities do you like, and are they available in your list of possible cities or countries to relocate to? Do you care more about a low cost of living or health care? What about safety? The following checklist may provide some help.

What to Look For in a New Retirement Location

- The climate is exactly what you are looking for.
- The people are friendly — warm smiles and hometown hospitality have never gone out of style.
- Whether it's the hills, rocky outcrops, thick forests, breathtaking mountains, pristine lakes, or raging rivers, the beautiful scenery beckons you to reside there.
- Regardless of whether you intend to rent or

buy, the housing is affordable.

- There are a variety of housing options to suit your needs — from a stately house to a smart new apartment, a townhouse, or a gracious bungalow with the right-sized garden to look after.

- Many cultural amenities — such as museums, theaters, and concerts — are available either locally or in a nearby city.

- Just out your back door — either a short drive or a healthy walk from your home — you can participate in outdoor activities such as skiing, tennis, golf, fly-fishing, and hiking.

- You can depend on excellent transportation facilities, including a modern transit system.

- Neighborhoods are peaceful and the crime rate is low.

- A variety of clubs and non-profit organizations welcome your participation and talents. You can eventually be part of a community of friends with similar interests.

> I'm eighty-one now. I would have been eighty-two, but I lived a year in Winnipeg.
>
> — Red Skelton

- You can embrace new challenges at computer classes, self-development seminars, drama lessons, and poetry slams.

- The cost of living is affordable.

- The city has a variety of restaurants to fit your mood and budget. You can dine at Chinese, Korean, Italian, and Mexican establishments representing a broad range of prices.

- Whatever your religious affiliation, you can find a place of worship.

- Quality healthcare is accessible and available when you need it, including a full service healthcare facility and top-notch dental care.

- You can do research for your creative pursuits at a well-equipped and properly staffed library.

- The place is known for its year-round special events, such as lecture series, brown-bag luncheons, winter and summer festivals, fishing derbies, and golf tournaments.

- There are excellent continuing learning

    opportunities at local educational institutions.
- The residents are diverse so that you can enjoy the company of those younger and older than you.
- Taxes are low.
- Pollution is not a problem — the air and water are clean.
- The country is known for its political stability.

Above all, get to know the cities and countries you are considering. Research each place carefully. Books, magazines, newspaper articles, and websites can be a big help. For example, AARP's former magazine, *Modern Maturity* (now called *AARP The Magazine*), recently chose its top fifteen places that Americans should consider if they want to retire abroad.

If you think you've found where you want to spend your retirement, the best way to check it out thoroughly is to take a vacation there first. Go more than once or twice. Try to visit the city or country in all seasons so you can get a sense for whether you'll be happy living there full time.

In your search for Shangri-la, don't overlook the possibility that paradise may be where you are right now. There is some truth to the words of Henry Ford: "Everybody wants to be someplace he ain't. As soon as he gets there, he wants to go right back."

I am going to leave this one-horse town once it's my turn to ride the horse.

Consider Moving to a College Town

While thousands of retired people are attracted to massive retirement developments, a growing number are choosing college towns or small cities. Asheville, North Carolina, is one example. With its golf courses, first-class medicare, cultural richness, small-business community, and temperate climate, it actually attracts retirees who have tried Florida or Arizona first.

Many people enjoy the small-town charm and atmosphere of

Asheville, which is, in fact, a city of 68,000 people. Downtown has upscale restaurants, shops, coffeehouses, bookstores, galleries, and boutiques. Many painters, writers, musicians, and artisans have been drawn here because of the friendly people and climate.

George Rogers, a retired engineer for the U.S. Navy and now a part-time graphics designer, moved to Asheville with his wife from the Northern Virginia suburbs of Washington. "It's a magical place," Rogers told a *Baltimore Sun* reporter. "When we go out, whether it's to dinner, or just to hang out, or to a cultural event, it's rare that we don't see someone we know. When we lived in the D.C. area, I can count on one hand how many times that happened in twenty years."

A major attraction for retirees is Asheville's North Carolina Center for Creative Retirement, which was started in 1988 just as Asheville was beginning to attract more retirees. Each semester, between five and six hundred retired people enroll in thirty courses. They develop their own curriculum, and retirees teach the classes. Today, the program is regarded as a leader in its field and reporters with the *Washington Post*, *Wall Street Journal*, and *Baltimore Sun* regularly contact the center when writing articles about retirement.

> Though one can dine in New York, one could not dwell there.
>
> — Oscar Wilde

Asheville has regularly been cited in surveys by magazines such as *Money* and *Modern Maturity* as being one of the best places to retire in the United States. Approximately 20 percent of Asheville's residents are over sixty-five; this contributes to an eclectic mix of residents from young students to working adults to middle-aged artists to third-age retirees. "For a city its size, it's quite remarkable — the cultural richness, the small-business community," boasted Rogers.

Should you have the urge to retire to a college town somewhere in the United States, you can start by checking AARP's June 2000 issue of *Modern Maturity* magazine. The magazine rated the following places as the best college towns in which to live: Austin, Texas; Charlottesville, Virginia; Columbia, Missouri; Madison, Wisconsin; Princeton, New Jersey; Iowa City, Iowa; Bloomington, Indiana; Las Cruces, New Mexico; State College, Pennsylvania; and Ann Arbor, Michigan. You can check out the various aspects of the ratings on AARP's website (www.aarp.org).

For more information on the best retirement places in the United States, you can check out two books. *Choose a College*

Town for Retirement by Joseph Lubow covers sixty-four college and/or university towns in twenty-nine states. The other book, *Retirement Places Rated* by David Savageau, compares more than 200 top retirement areas according to costs of living, housing, climate, personal safety, services, employment opportunities, and leisure activities.

The Secret to a Really Wonderful Retired Lifestyle

In one of their occasional newsletters that they send to keep friends up to date on their adventures, Bill Myers and Valerie Ossipoff pronounced, "We believe we've discovered the secret to a really wonderful retired lifestyle. It is simply to live somewhere else. When we come home to visit we are wined and dined and treated like visiting royalty. Our friends are too classy to mention that we come home every six months or so!"

> "Home" is any four walls that enclose the right person.
> — Helen Rowland

Originally from the United States mainland, Bill and Valerie now live on a Standfast 40 sailboat named "Cirrus," which is moored in a marina in Hawaii. In their newsletter, they also humorously divulged, "Life aboard Cirrus continues to go well, we still like each other, we still don't sail enough, and we still don't have any idea 'what's next.' We stay busy with projects both on and off the boat."

Here are some of the things that Bill and Valerie have enjoyed, or are presently enjoying, in their laid-back retirement in and around Hawaii:

- They house-sit for their friends, the Goodsills, whenever they are away.
- Even though they swim regularly, they joined a gym to work out at least three times a week.
- Valerie sang with the Honolulu Symphony Chorus.
- They regularly go to the theater, to dance performances, and to museums.
- They took a basketry class sponsored by the Honolulu Academy of Arts and taught by Gail

Toma, a nationally recognized fiber artist.

- They bought a one-person inflatable kayak and now have a ball paddling it around their Hawaiian marina as well as at their cruising anchorages.
- In July 2001, they went back to their home on the mainland to "visit the doctor, dentist, audiologist, optometrist, dermatologist, financial advisor, get nails done and have a massage, visit, have dinner with various friends, etc."
- Bill maintains a website to share material concerning his interests in sailing and celestial navigation with others.
- While on the mainland, they found time for a four-day trip to the Sierra. They "stayed in an inexpensive motel in Mammoth, dined out in style most nights, and did day hikes back into the mountains to Red's Meadow, Mts. Ritter and Banner, Garnet Lake, Muir Trail. Great weather, great sights, great time!"
- After leaving the mainland, and before returning to Hawaii, they visited Alaska for two weeks.
- They are now back exploring the Hawaiian Islands, which could take a long time at the rate they are going.

> Home is the place where,
> when you have to go there,
> They have to take you in.
> — Robert Frost

You can read more about Bill and Valerie's fascinating adventures by visiting Bill's website (www.nav.org). It's one of the most interesting personal retirement websites (with great pictures from their travels) that I have found. Here you can peruse their past newsletters to find many more ideas on how to enjoy your retirement, particularly if you are considering living the laid-back island lifestyle. Indeed, Bill and Valerie may inspire you to buy a sailboat and make it your home.

9

Happiness Doesn't Care How You Get There

Retirement Is Not a Time to Sleep, but a Time to Awaken to the Beauty of the World around You

No longer forward nor behind
I look in hope or fear;
But, grateful, take the good I find,
The best of now and here.
— John Greenleaf Whittier

Not so long ago American filmmaker Marian Marzynski studied a Miami Beach retirement community and the way its residents were growing older. He formed relationships with several retirees and got to know their dreams, their pleasures, and their struggles. As the retirees pondered the meaning of their lives, Marzynski discovered that many held onto the past and some missed their productive years of work.

He made a few more observations while shooting the PBS documentary *My Retirement Dreams*. As would be expected, some retirees were bored, some were physically active, a few were expanding their minds, and a lot were waiting for destiny to show them the way. All things considered, Marzynski concluded that what makes the difference between happy retirees and unhappy ones has little to do with age or education. Just as significant was his

> Happiness is not a matter of events; it depends on the tides of the mind.
>
> — Alice Meynell

conclusion that a happy retirement has little to do with level of income.

Marzynski's conclusions aren't all that surprising. His conclusions support the premise of this book that how happy you will be in retirement will depend on whether you are willing to be happy. Clearly, happiness will elude you as long as you are thinking and doing what's wrong for you. And needless to say, it will come rather easily when you are thinking and doing what's right for you.

> The gradually declining years are among the sweetest in a man's life.
>
> — Seneca

To be sure, happiness in retirement, as in all stages of life, doesn't care how you get there. Not only doesn't happiness care how you get there; it doesn't even care if you get there at all. And you are sure not to get there if you rely solely on money, as do so many people in Western society. You are also sure not to attain true happiness if you wait for destiny or others to show you the way. If nothing else, satisfaction and inner peace will be missing.

Howard Salzman, one of the retirees featured in Marzynski's documentary, did not wait for destiny or others to show him the way to satisfaction and inner peace. A New York native, Salzman moved to Florida in 1955, where he worked for almost forty years as salesman, buyer, and manager. After he retired, he completed a degree in philosophy at University of Miami and Florida International University. Unlike some retirees, Salzman, seventy-one at the time, applauded the concept of retirement. To him, retirement has been an adventure — an occasion to celebrate, an opportunity to let go of the past, and a time to experience more peace of mind.

When Salzman was asked what had helped him enjoy his retirement years, he replied, "I never separated retirement from other events in my life — it just happened. There were very few shock effects. It simply evolved along the continuum of aging. One has to stay clear of the stereotypes of growing senility, lest you fulfill the stereotype. Human creativity makes life a good deal easier, for it carries with it tolerance and with tolerance comes compassion."

"Retirement is a time to make the inner journey," Salzman continued, "and come face to face with your flaws, failures, prejudices, and all the factors that generate thoughts of unhappiness. Retirement is not a time to sleep, but a time to awaken to the beauty of the world around you and the joy that comes when you cast out all the negative elements that cause confusion and turmoil in your mind and allow serenity to prevail."

If you are to, as Howard Salzman says, "awaken to the beauty of the world around you," you must put your life in synch with your deepest values and beliefs. You must pursue what you truly want out of retirement, and not what others want you to pursue, or what other retirees are pursuing. This is not an easy thing to do, particularly in modern Western society where we are subject to so many outside influences.

Erich Fromm in *Escape from Freedom* wrote, "Modern man lives under the illusion that he knows what he wants, while he actually wants what he is supposed to want." Indeed, in today's consumer society, advertisers and the media dictate what people are supposed to want. Many retirees consume this programming greedily instead of stopping to question what will truly make them happy. After all, it is much easier to try to fit in with the majority than to question what the majority is doing and then doing something different.

I always thought lots of leisure time was for losers, but looking retirement straight in the eye is probably the most challenging and satisfying thing I have ever done.

How do you fit into this picture if you are already retired? Probably the hardest thing about living a satisfying and prosperous retirement is to be true to your own dreams and refrain from going along with the masses. At the best of times, chasing after what everyone else is chasing is a zero-results game. To be like everyone else is to lose your true self.

Following the majority as they look for happiness in all the wrong places is about as pointless as installing a screen door on a submarine. Understand that happiness doesn't care how hard you worked in your career. Nor does it care whether you wear designer clothes, or how fancy your car is, or whether you get all of the other possessions you want. Moreover, happiness doesn't care how beautiful, talented, or intelligent you are.

Perhaps by now you are thinking that these are just crazy assumptions on my part. Be clear that I have not gone mad. On the

> The greater part of our happiness or misery depends on our dispositions, and not our circumstances.
> — Martha Washington

contrary, there is much scholarly evidence to support these statements.

Research by psychologists indicates that the things that most people assume would make life better — money, status, beauty, or social prominence — over the long run don't seem to matter all that much, if at all. For example, one research paper reported that physical attractiveness has at most a very marginal effect on how content people are in life. Another study concluded individuals may be pleased for a month or two after a big lottery win, but there is no relationship between the money and ultimate happiness a year later. Still other research has shown that social standing has no effect on true happiness.

Why waste time, energy, and money chasing after something you don't really need and may not even enjoy? Some things are important, and others are not. Some things appear to be important because people have been brainwashed by society, educational institutions, and advertisers to believe that they are important. Upon close scrutiny, most of these things have no relevance whatsoever to leading a happy and healthy lifestyle.

Far too few retirees in this world think for themselves. Instead of allowing their own creativity and inner wisdom to run their lives, they prefer to pay attention to what others are doing and thinking. You don't have to be one of those people. As an active, creatively thinking human being, you should realize that — contrary to popular opinion — you always have an alternative to following the herd. While the herd is moving in one direction, in fact, you can go in any one of several other directions.

It may appear easier to follow the herd than to think differently and do things on your own. You will always follow the herd at your peril, however. The more attention you pay to what the majority is doing, the more you will realize that the everybody-else-is-doing-it approach isn't the way to happiness and peace of mind. While it's tempting to join the majority, always remember that you have meaningful dreams and more important goals to pursue.

The way to wake up and make the best of your retirement is to regularly question the lifestyle that you are leading. For it to be your own, you must not wait for destiny to show you the way. Following are a list of questions you may want to ask yourself at least once a year to ensure that you keep on track for a happy, wild, and free retirement:

- Am I in control of my lifestyle?
- Do I make the most of my money to give me the best quality of life?
- What can I achieve in my retirement that would make me proud?
- What can I do that is unique?
- Do I have enough great friends in my life?
- Do I devote sufficient time to see my close friends?
- Do I watch too much TV?
- Does my lifestyle complement my partner's?
- Do I travel as much as I would like?
- Do my time commitments allow me to make a contribution to making this world a better place?
- Do my time commitments allow me to indulge in creative endeavors?
- Am I developing spiritually as a human being?
- Do I exercise enough, in my own enjoyable way?
- Do I complain too much?
- Am I as grateful as I should be for what I have in my life?
- Am I continually learning something new?
- Do I do something special for myself each and every day?
- Do I take enough time to meditate and keep my mind in tiptop shape?
- Am I living in the right country or in the right part of the country?
- What will make me feel better?
- Do I have everything I need to be happy, but don't realize it?

Answering these questions honestly is important because being truly and fully who you are requires knowing what's important to you, and only you. You have to make sure that your life's choices are your own. To quote e. e. cummings, "To be nobody-but-yourself — in a world which is doing its best, night and day, to make you like

> I like living. I have some problems with my life, but living is the best thing they've come up with so far.
>
> — Neil Simon

everybody-else — means to fight the hardest battle any human being can fight; and never stop fighting."

If you want to experience fulfillment and satisfaction, one of your most important retirement goals should be to be you and not anyone else. When Leonardo da Vinci was asked what his greatest accomplishment had been in his life, he replied, "Leonardo da Vinci." In this regard, Zen masters don't ask us to be something or someone we aren't; instead, they ask us to be more truly and more fully who we are.

Celebrate Your Eccentricity and You Will Be Set Free

There's nothing surer,
The rich get rich and the poor get poorer,
In the meantime, in between time,
Ain't we got fun.
— Gus Kahn and Raymond B. Egan, *Ain't We Got Fun*

Look closely around you. You will see many people with a lot less money than you. Yet some of these people are much happier than you. Your thoughts may be: "I am sane; therefore, these people must be crazy." Maybe. Maybe not. Perhaps it's the other way around.

Indeed, some of the happiest people you will see around you are labeled as eccentrics, people who others think are crazy, at least to some degree. So which do you want to be? An unhappy person who fits in with the crowd? Or a happy, fully functioning individual who can ignore the crowd and do your own thing?

"Eccentricity is not, as dull people would have us believe, a form of madness," declared Dame Edith Sitwell. "It is often a kind of innocent pride, and the man of genius and the aristocrat are frequently regarded as eccentrics because the genius and the aristocrat are entirely unafraid of and uninfluenced by the opinions and vagaries of the crowd."

The more you are out of step with society, the greater your chances for self-discovery, adventure, and happiness in

> We are all born charming, fresh, and spontaneous and must be civilized before we are fit to participate in society.
>
> — Judith Martin

this world. There is no better example to make my point than busker Ben Kerr of Toronto. He is one of the most intriguing individuals that I — and thousands of other people — have ever met. You can often find Ben performing his songs before hundreds of people either at the St. Lawrence Market or at the corner of Yonge and Bloor, in Toronto's busiest business and tourist district.

I first encountered Ben late October 13, 1993, when he called the John Oakley radio talk show on which I was a guest, discussing with listeners the joys of being unemployed. After a few words with Ben, I promised to meet him in person on the corner of Yonge and Bloor the next day and give him a copy of *The Joy of Not Working*. In exchange, Ben agreed to sing his song "I Don't Want to Be the Richest Man in the Graveyard."

Here are some of the things that I have learned about Ben since I met him that lucky day. Somewhere in his fifties at the time, Ben retired from his executive position at the Toronto Harbour Commission on March 31, 1981, because he wouldn't put up with the smoking-allowed policy the company had at that time. Soon after, he ran — physically — 3,000 miles from Toronto to Los Angeles to campaign for a no-smoking policy in office buildings.

> Freedom is always and exclusively freedom for the one who thinks differently.
>
> — Rosa Luxemberg

Before he left for Los Angeles, Ben wrote and recorded a song for his crusade. The song was called "Fire on One End (Fool on the Other)." It was recorded on the Emphysema Label in the CBC Radio studios in Toronto.

Upon his return home from Los Angeles, Ben pursued his passion — writing and singing songs. For over twenty years now, Ben has been a street musician, singing and playing his five-string guitar (the G string is missing). Toronto's harsh winter months haven't dissuaded Ben from hanging around outdoors to sing ballads about other people and songs about his own life. He claims that singing in the fresh, cold air exercises his lungs. Known to tens of thousands of people in his hometown, Ben is regularly voted as "best busker" in a survey conducted by Toronto's *Now Magazine*.

Here are some more of Ben's accomplishments during his interesting and enjoyable retirement:

- During his round-trip run to Los Angeles, Ben appeared as a guest on the Richard Simmons

Show where he promoted his no-smoking-in-the-workplace cause and aerobicized with Simmons and a number of fit, energetic women.

- Throughout his singing years, Ben has met many other international celebrities including Elizabeth Taylor and Richard Burton.
- Ben has written and sung songs for Mel Lastman, the mayor of Toronto, and Mike Harris, the premier of Ontario at the time.
- After Ben wrote a song about Frank Stronach, the CEO of the giant international Magna Corporation, Stronach took Ben to the racetrack — and signed him in as a guest in the exclusive clubhouse — to watch one of Stronach's prize racehorses compete.

> Only those who dare, truly live.
> — Ruth P. Freedman

- For years Ben has promoted his cayenne pepper cocktail (made with a tablespoon of cayenne pepper mixed in a glass of carrot juice), which according to him is better than Viagra and heals many addictions and illnesses. He has also written a book on the benefits of cayenne pepper called *The Cayenne Pepper Cocktail Does It All*.
- Ben has become one of the regulars on the Joey Reynolds Show, an all-night syndicated radio program based in New York that draws many other eccentrics, including Kenny Kramer (the guy who inspired Seinfeld's Kramer).
- In 1999, taking advantage of Greyhound's $269 Ameripass, Ben spent six weeks traveling across the United States visiting places such as St. Pete Beach, Florida; Weed, California; Las Vegas; and New Orleans. While in Las Vegas, Ben wrote a song called "There's Nobody Sweeter than Cindy from Las Vegas" and later sang it live on the Joey Reynolds Show.
- Also in 1999, Ben recorded two songs ("I'm Hitting It Big in Bakersfield" and "Appreciate What You Got before You Lose It") with The

Buckaroos (Buck Owens' backup band) in Bakersfield, California.

➤ Since 1985, every three years Ben has run for mayor of Toronto. He has never come close to winning, but he says he will win sooner or later because he plans to live forever. "The thing is, I'm going to win eventually," he declares.

Ben surmises that if he had decided to stay with the Toronto Harbour Commission until the traditional retirement age of sixty-five, he probably wouldn't be alive today. Yet today, in the words of *Health Perspectives* reporter Jerry Gillians, "Ben is as spry a senior as you will ever meet with energy and enthusiasm abounding."

When reporters ask Ben his age, he typically replies, "I am ageless, because age is a state of mind. I'm not too young or too old to do anything. When you are ageless, you never get sick, tired, or depressed."

In June 2002, Ben told me, "When I was a young lad, I used to look at 'old' people, and tell myself, 'When I get old, I'm not going to be like that.' I had a firm resolve in my mind back then that I would be happy, healthy, and financially independent in my golden years. And that's exactly what's happened. Today I can honestly say that I'm the happiest man in the world because I can do whatever I want when I want to do it."

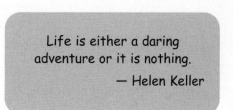

Life is either a daring adventure or it is nothing.

— Helen Keller

I hope that the story of this intriguing individual and his illustrious retirement will challenge you to make your retirement a lot more interesting and enjoyable. Most people go to their graves regretting things they haven't done. The easiest way to become one of them is by joining society's chorus instead of singing your own songs. As you can see, Ben dropped out of society's chorus long ago to sing his own songs, and he is much happier for it.

No doubt Ben Kerr fits the definition of a "true eccentric." Psychologist Dr. David Weeks and writer Jamie James, co-authors of the book *Eccentrics*, found that true eccentrics are much happier than the rest of the population. Moreover, they are healthier and tend to live much longer.

Contrary to the popular belief that people like Ben Kerr are crazy, Weeks and James concluded that eccentrics are much more intelligent than the general population. True eccentrics are highly creative, curious, idealistic, intelligent, opinionated, and obsessed with some hobby. These non-conformists give themselves the freedom to be themselves, a luxury that most people in society haven't learned how to enjoy. Eccentricity allows them to pursue hobbies and lifestyles that are their passions. Freed from the need to conform, eccentrics aren't bothered by what others think about them.

It follows that only those who can be eccentric can truly live. Thus, celebrate your eccentricity and you will be set free. Your self-development and movement toward self-actualization will be wondrous, mysterious, and fascinating.

If Money Can Buy Happiness, Then Why Aren't You Selling Some of Yours?

Mere wealth can't bring us happiness;
Mere wealth can't make us glad;
But we'll always take a chance, I guess,
At being rich, and sad.
— C. C. Colton

Many individuals in Western countries are looking solely to financial security and a lot of nice possessions to make them happy in retirement. Although most people don't know what exactly they want from life, they are absolutely sure that money in large amounts will provide it for them. They fool themselves, however, about how much happier they would be with much more money. After all, many wise people over the ages have warned us that money won't solve our problems. Yet most of us ignore this wisdom and strive for substantial material wealth regardless of the required sacrifices.

> The golden age only comes to men when they have forgotten gold.
> — G. K. Chesterton

No doubt fifty hundred-dollar bills can magically create two tickets for premium seats to a sold-out Super Bowl game. There is no evidence, however, that spectators attending the game in the stadium are any happier than individuals at home watching the game on TV. Moreover, there are millions of retirees who can be extremely happy without having to watch one minute of any football game, Super Bowl, or otherwise.

It's important that money and its relationship to happiness be put in proper perspective. Money is an important element for comfort and enjoyment of the finer things in life, but how much money retirees need to be happy is another question.

Money may eliminate certain modes of unhappiness but it certainly won't guarantee true happiness — even for a day. No one agrees with this more than University of Illinois psychologist and researcher Edward Diener, who specializes in what makes people happy. After conducting many studies over the last decade or so, Diener has concluded that money can add pleasure to people's lives, but it won't bring the true happiness that comes with self-respect, accomplishment, and satisfaction.

I can't figure out why all our friends our age are still working ten years after we retired and moved to Mexico.

Perhaps their incredible ability to delude themselves about the importance of both money and their work plays a key role.

Diener's conclusions are supported by Richard Layard of the London School of Economics. "Here's a shocking fact. Despite our huge increase in affluence, people in the West have grown no happier in the past fifty years," declared Layard in 2003. "If people are asked how happy they are, their replies indicate no increase in happiness. This is true of Britain, the United States, Europe, and Japan. Even in the so-called golden age up to the 1970s, there was no increase."

"The picture is different in poor countries," adds Layard, "where happiness has risen when people have got richer. If you are near the breadline, absolute income is a matter of life and death. But things are different in the West. Since the Second World War, people have become richer. They travel more, they live longer, and they are healthier. But they are no happier."

As a matter of course money is an important element for our survival, but how much money we need to be happy is another matter altogether. As well as anyone, Benjamin Franklin expressed the folly in trying to achieve happiness through money. "Money never made a man happy yet nor will it," observed Franklin. "There is nothing in its nature to produce happiness. The more a man has, the more he wants. Instead of its filling a vacuum, it makes one."

Perhaps you have been really broke at some time in your life. I am not talking about a time when you considered selling the cabin cruiser or the cottage to help you through a downturn in the economy as you continued to bask in luxury. I am referring to a situation when you were so broke that you might not have been able to think of a word or phrase to describe it. "Hard up" or "short of funds" just wouldn't do.

> A man is rich in proportion to the number of things he can afford to let alone.
>
> — Henry David Thoreau

If you have experienced this mode of being broke, undoubtedly you imagined that you would be really happy when you could elevate yourself to the financial position that you enjoy today. Your happiness today, however, is probably far from what you imagined it would be. Perhaps your happiness hasn't increased a bit, despite your wealth having increased considerably. You may even be unhappier and more miserable now that you have greater wealth.

Money is important for retirement in that it is a means of survival, a foundation for comfort, and a tool to accomplish some of your life's goals. It can't guarantee happiness or health or love, however. And regardless of how much you have set aside, money cannot buy creative fulfillment.

"If you want to know how rich you really are," declared William J. H. Boetcker, "find out what would be left of you tomorrow if you should lose every dollar you own tonight." Think about it. This is the ultimate test of how rich you will be during your retirement years: How happy can you be and how much fun can you have regardless of how little money you have?

Luckily, there are many enchanting experiences in this world that money can't buy. George Horace Lorimer advised, "It's good to have money, and the things money can buy, but it's good, too, to check up once in a while and be sure you haven't lost the things money can't buy." The more you can detach yourself from money and possessions, the more your life will be enhanced by the things money can't buy.

> Having money is rather like being a blond. It is more fun but not vital.
>
> — Mary Quant

Generally speaking, you can't buy things you can't see. Yet some of the things that you can't see are fundamental to happiness. In this group you can list peace of mind, love, satisfaction, health, and spiritual enlightenment. Lots of rich people don't have these things and, regardless of how much money they have, they can't buy them. Even health can't be bought. Sure, money can help maintain your health, and can provide quality healthcare, but once you lose your health, you can't buy it back.

If you were to think about it for a while, you would realize that there are many more personal attributes contributing to happiness that are beyond the realm of money. Following is a list of thirty-seven elements of happiness that I challenge you to purchase on the open market:

Elements of Happiness That Money Can't Buy

Health	Longevity	Self-reliance
Personal creativity	Real friends	Achievement
Satisfaction	Loving family	Respect of others
Integrity	Reputation	Peace of mind
Good character	Sense of humor	Ability to enjoy leisure
Street smarts	Patience	Gratitude
Compassion	Empathy	Emotional stability
Greatness	Warmth	How to handle money
Generosity	Humility	Appreciation of money
Luck	Charm	Physical fitness
Self-esteem	Time	Spiritual fulfillment
Wisdom	True love	Courage
A good night's sleep		

If these are all elements of happiness, and they can't be bought, then it follows that happiness can't be bought. The question that I ask people who believe that money is the key to happiness is: "If money can buy happiness, then why aren't you selling some of yours?" Indeed, if money could buy happiness, the happy poor would be selling it to the unhappy rich of this world.

Granted, a lack of money for basic necessities will leave us unhappy and dissatisfied about our position in life. This fact doesn't mean that having a lot of money will leave us truly happy and satisfied, however. Money may get us to a neutral state, somewhere between unhappy and happy, and somewhere between dissatisfied and satisfied. Generally speaking, more money won't get us beyond that neutral state. After we reach the neutral state, happiness depends on things that money can't buy.

Fantastic as it sounds, a cool million dollars won't make the slightest difference in your life if you have been miserable on a moderate income. You can live in a sparsely furnished one-room studio apartment and be surrounded by abundance. Or you can live in a lavishly furnished $10-million mansion and be operating out of scarcity. After basic necessities are provided for, abundance is, above all, a state of mind.

> To be without some of the things you want is an indispensable part of happiness.
>
> — Bertrand Russell

Virtually everyone will agree at some level that money doesn't buy happiness, but deep down they haven't accepted it. Regardless of how old you are, you will show wisdom well beyond your age when you truly accept that money can't buy contentment and peace of mind. Ironically, the more that you believe that money will bring you happiness in retirement, the less money will do for your happiness.

In a materialistic world, prosperity is invariably associated with hoards of money and countless possessions. The happy retiree's prosperity, however, is prosperity in its original sense. Indeed, prosperity comes from the Latin word "spes," which means "hope and vigor." To the happy retiree, being truly prosperous means being positive and happy in the moment, regardless of level of wealth.

The feeling of prosperity is an emotional state available to you whenever you want it. It has little to do with your wealth or the economy. You can experience prosperity-consciousness in a bad economy, even though many well-off people experience poverty-consciousness in a booming economy. Clearly, the rich may get richer and the poor may get poorer; you don't have to do either to feel prosperous.

Most successful and happy retirees are so busy indulging themselves in interesting activities that they don't focus much time or energy on the issues of finances. Some may have to live frugal lives; nevertheless, they experience much more contentment and peace of mind than many people who have a lot more money than they do. Active retirees learned a long time ago that money is not a guarantee of a happy and successful life — whether it's in one's working years or in retirement.

> I have the greatest of riches: That of not desiring them.
>
> — Eleonora Duse

Whether people accept it or not — and most people don't — ultimately happiness comes from within. A happy retirement starts with having a great attitude about life in general. In this vein, Dr. Joyce Brothers observed, "Those who have easy, cheerful attitudes tend to be happier than those with less pleasant temperaments regardless of money, 'making it,' or success."

Summing up, if you want to feel rich and happy, just count all the things you have that money can't buy. Happiness is priceless. And priceless things can't be bought. Never forget this — unless you experience great delight and happiness from being terribly deceived. In this case, more power to you. Again, happiness doesn't care how you get there.

You Will Overlook the Silver Lining If You Are Always Expecting Gold

> Glad that I live am I;
> That the sky is blue;
> Glad for the country lanes,
> And the fall of dew.
> — Lizette W. Reese

For most of us, the ideal life is the life we do not lead. Indeed, it's the life someone else leads. In this regard, a French proverb proclaims, "What you can't get is just what suits you."

What makes many of us unhappy, to the point of extreme misery, is our unreasonable and false beliefs about how happy others are. We have some strange idea that most people in Western society are happier than we are. Yet this is far from the truth. As Joseph Roux reflected, "I look at what I have not and think myself unhappy; others look at what I have and think me happy."

It's all too easy to fall into the trap of thinking that practically everyone else has a much easier and happier life than you do. There will always be friends, relatives, neighbors, or celebrities who own bigger houses, drive flashier cars, wear more expensive clothes, or have more physically attractive lovers. How happy they are is another matter. If they are envious of people who have things that they do not have, they certainly aren't happy.

One of the most important factors for enjoying life to the fullest is an absence of envy of others. Someone once said that envy is the satisfaction and happiness that we think others are experiencing, but aren't. Many, perhaps most, people whom we envy aren't any happier than we are. Even many of the rich and famous don't make good targets for our envy. Singer and actress Barbara Streisand warned us, "Oh God, don't envy me, I have my own pains."

> Now is not the time to think of what you do not have. Think of what you can do with what there is.
>
> — Ernest Hemingway

To envy the rich and famous is rather ill-considered in light of the fact that many aren't happy. If you are going to envy anyone, envy the poor of this world who are happy. Being happy takes some doing on their part.

Another important point is that experiencing envy has practically no benefit. Envy is an extremely heavy burden to carry because it breeds contempt and hate. Someone once said, "Envy is like acid; it eats away the container that it's in."

No matter how hard you try, you can't be both envious and happy. Envy and unhappiness go hand in hand. Envy of even one person is a mistake. What's the point of admiring someone else's fortunes so much that you become dissatisfied with your own? Comparing your position with that of others can lead to disillusionment and frustration. You will end up thinking overly well of others and disliking yourself.

While you are playing the comparison game, why not play it both ways? Perhaps you would like to live in one of twenty countries, such as Sierra Leone and Afghanistan, where rampant poverty, lack of health care, serious malnutrition, constant violence, and perpetual crime contribute to a life expectancy of less than forty-eight years. Moreover, about 90 percent of the world's working population has no retirement pension, forcing most to work well into old age.

In this regard, Helen Keller advised us, "Instead of comparing our lot with that of those who are more fortunate than we are, we should compare it with the lot of the great majority of our fellow men. It then appears we are among the privileged."

The way to overcome envy of others is to relax and count your blessings more often. At least once a week think about the great things your country offers that other countries don't. When you feel deprived because someone has something you don't, keep in mind that billions of people in other countries would gladly trade places with you.

Gratitude for what you have will do wonders for overcoming envy and enhancing your well-being. Pay heed to these important words by an unknown wise person: "You will overlook the silver lining if you are always expecting gold." When you regularly take the time to appreciate the things you have — your health, your home, your friends, your music collection, your knowledge, and your creative ability — you won't have time to be envious of others.

Over the ages the wise people of this world have advised that we be grateful for what we have. Now there is scientific evidence that gratitude enhances our well-being. In 2003, researchers at the Universities of California and Miami reported that people who consciously remind themselves every day of the things they are grateful for show marked improvements in mental health and some aspects of physical health.

The results appear to be equally true for healthy college students and people with incurable diseases, according to the researchers, who published their findings in the *Journal of Personality and Social Psychology*. Compared with groups of subjects who counted hassles, such as hard-to-find parking spots, grateful people felt better about their lives and more optimistic. In other words, they were happier.

To be happy, you must be grateful for many things in life — and there are many if you really look. To identify more of the things for which you should be grateful, borrow an idea from Oprah Winfrey: Keep a gratitude journal. At the end of every day count your blessings and write down at least five wonderful things that happened to you that day.

I like retirement life. It's something to do when you don't want to work ever again!

Many people get a great deal of enjoyment out of life having very little and many people get very little enjoyment out of life having a lot. Your happiness will be determined, not by how much you have, but by how much you enjoy what you have. It is folly to look at what others have that you don't have, and to think yourself poor. Instead, look at the things

> Just think how happy you would be if you lost everything you have right now, and then got it back.
>
> — Unknown wise person

that you have which many others don't have, and think yourself rich.

Moreover, ten times as many good things happen to you as bad things. Thus, it behooves you to spend ten times as much time ranting and raving about the wonder of life as you do complaining about it.

To become aware that you have a lot of great things in your life, pay attention to the small things instead of the big ones. "Most of us miss out on life's big prizes. The Pulitzer. The Nobel. Oscars. Tonys. Emmys," stated an unknown wise person. "But we're all eligible for life's small pleasures. A pat on the back. A kiss behind the ear. A four-pound bass. A full moon. An empty parking space. A crackling fire. A great meal. A glorious sunset. Hot soup. Cold beer. Don't fret about copping life's grand awards. Enjoy its tiny delights. There are plenty for all of us."

Above all, try living by this motto: "Happy to have, but just as happy not to have. And happy to be, but just as happy not to be." There is no better way to retire happy, wild, and free.

Be Happy While You Are Alive Because You Are a Long Time Dead

Happy the man, and happy he alone,
He who can call today his own;
He who, secure within, can say,
Tomorrow, do thy worst, for I have lived today.
— John Dryden

In the book *The Little Prince* by Antoine de Saint-Exupéry, the little prince arrives from a foreign planet to visit the planet Earth. One of the strange people he encounters is a merchant who tries to sell him pills that allow people to quench their thirst and feel no need to drink anything for a week. The little prince asks the merchant why he is selling these pills. The merchant replies: "Because they save a tremendous amount of time. Computations have been made by experts. With these pills, you save fifty-three minutes in every week."

The little prince then asks: "And what do I do with those fifty-three minutes?" The merchant replies, "Anything you like." The little prince, in bewilderment, says to himself: "As for me, if I had fifty-three minutes to spend as I liked, I should walk at my leisure toward a spring of fresh water."

This story has a lot to say about how we use our time and approach life. In Western society, there never seems to be enough time. In this do-it-all society, many retirees — not only working people — drive fast, walk fast, dine fast, and talk fast. Time is so precious that people don't even have a moment to think about time. They have become so involved in controlling time that they have forgotten how to live the moment.

In some cultures, a moment can last the entire afternoon. Activities have natural starting and ending times not dictated by the clock. People don't limit their conversations to fifteen or thirty minutes. Conversations start when they start, and end when the end, regardless of the number of clocks in the immediate vicinity.

Sadly, many North Americans haven't had a truly leisurely conversation with any of their relatives, friends, or neighbors for years. Given that a research study found that most couples spend about eighteen minutes a week in real conversation, it follows that most people probably haven't had a leisurely conversation with their spouse for as long as they can remember. Put another way, they haven't experienced living in the moment with their spouse for years.

I am taking early retirement because life is too short to waste in traffic and working with people so industrious that they don't have a clue about how to be truly happy.

The value of living the moment isn't an overly profound concept, yet few of us do it. Most of us, in fact, walk around awake, but yet asleep, paying little attention to what is going on around us. Some philosophers go so far as to say that most of us are unconscious most of the time; some of us are even unconscious all of the time.

Some people die at forty-five, but they have experienced a heck of a lot more happiness in those forty-five years than others who have lived to be ninety or one hundred. The reason is that they mastered the moment while they were alive. In this regard, a Scottish proverb advises, "Be happy while you are alive because you are a long time dead."

The way to join the conscious and happy minority is to accept that now — and only now — can you ever experience happiness. Living in the moment is crucial for living happily because the present moment is all that you really have. Being in the now means accepting that you can never experience past or future moments.

In short, this is it! Believe it or not, the now is all that you have and all that you will ever have. Don't be discouraged, however. The now holds the key to freedom, happiness, and peace of mind.

Mastering the moment is important for enjoying leisure, and life in general. The degree to which you can get totally involved in your leisure activities will determine the quality of your life. Unless you can get totally involved, you won't get much satisfaction from whatever you are doing. This is true whether you are playing chess, talking to a friend, wading through a stream, or watching a sunset. Learn to spend all your leisure activities in the now and you will experience happiness and a sense of peace in this world.

> If you have one eye on yesterday, and one eye on tomorrow, you're going to be cockeyed today.
>
> — Unknown wise person

Have you ever been so possessed by energy that it carried you away from your normal concerns into a state of indescribable bliss? If you have, you were mastering the moment and undoubtedly experienced numerous feelings that you normally don't experience in everyday life. Howard E. A. Tinsley and Diane J. Tinsley, professors of psychology at Southern Illinois University, concluded that individuals experiencing leisure activities to the fullest experience:

- ➤ A feeling of freedom
- ➤ Total absorption in the activity at hand
- ➤ Lack of focus on self
- ➤ Enhanced perception of objects and events
- ➤ Little awareness of the passage of time
- ➤ Increased sensitivity to body sensations
- ➤ Increased sensitivity to emotions

To be fully present, give any activity that you normally look at as a means to an end your fullest attention, so that the activity becomes an end in itself. For example, when you have a shower, pay close attention to the sound and feel of the water, as well as the scent of the soap. Moreover, truly feel the sensations in your body as the water connects with it as one. When you experience bliss and peace of mind, you are truly experiencing the shower.

Doing one thing at a time, instead of two or three, is crucial for mastering the moment. Doing something physically and thinking about something else at the same time are contradictory. You aren't fully taking part in the activity if you are thinking about something else. Key to mastering the moment is sticking with an activity, instead of quitting halfway through. Any activity or task should be worthy of your total attention, and of completion, if it is worth doing at all.

You can transcend time by doing your own thing at your own speed. Again, forget about what the masses are doing. Even if practically everyone else seems to increase the pace of life every day, you don't have to try to keep up. Take control of your physical and psychic space instead of allowing the distractions of the modern world to influence your lifestyle.

To make your days longer, don't rush; slow down instead. In a somewhat magical way, you will have more time when you start living every moment for all it is worth. Once you slow down, you will no longer fight time; you will master it. Full involvement and appreciation of any activity, whether it is writing your first novel, walking in the park, talking to your neighbor, or taking a shower, will make the whole world slow down for you.

> If you are not happy here and now, you never will be.
> —Taisen Deshimaru

The next time you think that you don't have time to enjoy a sunset, think about it a little more. You will realize that the most important time to enjoy a sunset is when you don't have time for it. Taking ten minutes to watch the sun go down will do more to help you catch up with the world than rushing around for several hours.

Life is short. To make it last a little longer, slow down and let it catch up with you once in a while. A day in which you haven't laughed with the world and loved it for what it is makes for a day in which you haven't truly lived.

Without any doubt in my mind, the best book available to help you live the moment is Eckhart Tolle's *The Power of Now*. The book is tremendously well written and powerful in its message. Buy this book and you won't be disappointed. It has the power to change your life.

Living in the moment relaxes us and lowers our stress levels. Spend more time in the present and you will have fewer problems and fewer worries. Indeed, spend all your time in the present and you will have no problems and no worries. No doubt this is hard to do and few people ever get to this level. If you are able to do this, however, you will become one of the truly enlightened individuals in this world, experiencing perpetual peace of mind and happiness that others experience sporadically, if at all.

Retirement, more than any other time in your life, is an opportunity to enjoy the moment for all it is worth. In fact, only by living in the moment can you make retirement the best years of your life. The thing to remember is that happiness has no past and no future. It is what it is right now. Experience it while you can. Happiness not enjoyed today can't be saved for the future. It is lost forever.

> As you walk and eat and travel, be where you are. Otherwise you will miss most of your life.
> — Buddha

It's Better to Live Rich than to Die Rich

Here lies a miser who cared for himself,
Who cared for nothing but gathering wealth.
Now where he is and how he fares,
Nobody knows and nobody cares.
— Anonymous gravestone in Lemmington, England

In a letter written on April 23, 1754, to Madame du Deffsand, the French philosopher and author Voltaire stated: "I advise you to go on living solely to enrage those who are paying your annuities. It is the only pleasure I have left." Hopefully, you won't end up like Voltaire, living for the sole purpose of trying to extract as much money from your annuities as possible before you die, and not experiencing enjoyment out of anything else.

A better strategy is to live to enjoy all your money before you die. This section is especially dedicated to retirees who have a lot of assets and a healthy ongoing income, but don't know how to enjoy their money. You don't have to be financially well-off, however, to benefit from this section.

During the first century A.D., Roman philosopher Seneca remarked, "We are always complaining that our days are few, and acting as though there would be no end of them." That being the case, things haven't changed much since Seneca's time. People today realize that life is short, but some people act as though they are going to live forever. This is especially true with regards to how they hoard money instead of spending it.

All things considered, it's better, in the words of Henry David Thoreau, to live rich than to die rich. Several other wise people have warned us about the folly of not enjoying our money. "To die rich," stated spiritual teacher Jiddu Krishnamurti, "is to have lived in vain." Errol Flynn declared, "Any man who has $10,000 left when he dies is a failure." And Thomas Fuller pronounced, "He is not fit for riches who is afraid to use them."

For some strange reason, many retirees don't like to see their net worth decline, even when they have less than ten years to live, and ten times as much money as they need to live in style for their remaining years. The fact is, most people who are well-off when they retire never even come close to running out of money before they check out for good. Given that most aspects of a happy, wild, and free retirement can't be bought, there is no rational reason for retirees to have their net worth increase.

Riches are to be used and not to be hoarded. After all, what is the ultimate purpose of money, but to spend it? Some people will point out that another purpose for money is to invest it. You invest so that you have more to spend later. Saving for retirement is prudent. When you are retired already, however, and have a good retirement income guaranteed for the rest of your life, saving a good portion of it so that your assets keep increasing, while sacrificing your enjoyment of life, is no way for a prosperous person to live.

It's a tired cliché, but "you can't take it with you." Sure, it would be nice to be able to respond, "If I can't take it with me, I'm not going." The fact is, you are going to die sooner or later. And it could be a lot sooner than you think, as it was for my friend Gabriel Allard, whom I talked about in chapter 1. What's the point of being wealthy if your life runs out long before your money does?

> Money is only useful when you get rid of it. It is like the odd card in Old Maid; the player who is finally with it has lost.
>
> — Evelyn Waugh

Wealth is having money; prosperity is enjoying it. Sadly, wealthy people can actually be worse off than poor people. Due to their poverty consciousness — a disease of sorts — some of the rich continue to live as if they were poor.

At the extreme, I can give no better example than seventy-nine-year-old Gordon Elwood from Oregon. He was known to drink outdated milk, live in an unheated house, use a bungee cord to hold up his secondhand pants, and eat free holiday meals at the

Salvation Army. Upon his recent death, it was learned that through self-denial and a shrewd understanding of investments he amassed a fortune of $9 million. At least there is a good side to this story: Elwood left all his fortune to social agencies, including the Salvation Army, which he had so loyally patronized.

As odd as it may seem, some people actually find making money easier than spending it. Spending it is a chore that makes them extremely uncomfortable. Giving his thoughts about hoarding money, sixteenth-century French writer Michel de Montaigne stated, "Once you have decided to keep a certain pile, it is no longer yours, for you can't spend it."

Clearly, financial satisfaction is more important than financial immortality. Financial longevity is important until the day you die; after that it's useless. You may want to argue that you have to leave money for your adult children. This is hogwash. Your adult children can take care of themselves. Don't you have any faith in their creative ability to make a living and fend for themselves?

Buying this new Porsche in my later years has proven that I can only be young once, but I can be immature forever.

Unfortunately, many people put together great fortunes but never get around to enjoying any of their money in their retirement years. Their children may not want an inheritance and yet these retirees insist on living like paupers so that they can leave as much money as possible for their estate. This is nothing short of insanity.

There is some good news in this regard, however, and it comes from Britain. Many of the new generation of British retirees aren't too keen on leaving their children or grandchildren any inheritance money according to a 2002 survey conducted by the insurance company Eagle Star. Indeed, almost three-quarters of retirees would rather spend all their savings on having a good time than setting it aside for their children's inheritance.

"While in the past retirees felt a responsibility to live sensibly," points out Phil Ost of Eagle Star, "this research shows the new breed of over-fifties is really relishing the opportunities and rewards retirement brings. They have planned and saved for these years, so spending savings that could otherwise be put toward an inheritance for their children seems to be a sound way in which to fund these lifestyles."

The new, happy-go-lucky British retirees use their savings to shop, socialize, and travel. Virginia Johnson, a retired child-and-family-court adviser, announced, "I spent my youth bringing up four children and now I would like to do the sort of things I thought I would do when I was a teenager, before things took a different path."

Johnson, a resident of Derby who recently trekked across Malaysia and Crete, is planning to spend the £100,000 equity in her Midlands cottage on herself. "I consider myself still young at fifty-five," Johnson told a reporter with *The Observer*, "and envisage travelling and enjoying myself to the full until I'm well into my eighties. I have some ideas about my pension but I'm thinking first and foremost about this next stage in my life."

Not only does Johnson like to travel, she socializes at least three times a week. "I don't think my children want me to leave my money to them," Johnson concluded. "I have worked hard to help them create their own independent, successful lives and now they are happy and settled, I want to enjoy myself."

Like this new segment of British retirees, you shouldn't be frugal in an attempt to leave money for your adult children to enjoy after you die. Indeed, if you have been retired for some time and are not enjoying your money, you should start taking every opportunity to spend the kids' and grandchildren's inheritance before it's too late! As financial writer Sandra Block advises, "Leaving a lot of money to your heirs doesn't guarantee tears at your funeral."

> A good folly is worth whatever you pay for it.
>
> — George Ade

Perhaps you have just retired, or are about to in the near future. As a celebration of your retirement, why not start it off by doing something special that you have longed to do for years? This can be anything from living in Greece for six months to taking yourself and all your grandchildren to Disneyland for a week or two.

If you are the type of person who doesn't enjoy enduring the good things in life, then give me a call. Like the great con artists of this world, I can make myself available to help liberate some of your money, and show you how to enjoy it. No amount will be too onerous for me. You can be assured that I will enjoy it and you can come along for the ride to see how it's done. High on my list of pleasures is a trip to Europe with a stop in Monte Carlo to dine at one of the world's most expensive restaurants where the average tab is $3,500 per person.

Given that you have worked many years to create an independent income, it follows that you should be doing everything possible to spend most of it. Spending most of it serves the purpose of reminding you why you were engaged in wealth-building during your working life — so that you could enjoy your money when you are retired. The key is to not outlive your money, and at the same time, to not have your money outlive you. To be sure, it's difficult to time it so that you achieve both.

> It is impossible to overdo luxury.
>
> — French proverb

Psychologically, the answer is to plan as if you are going to live to be 120 years old and live as if today could be your last day. Financially, this becomes a little more difficult. The answer is to have a good balance between how much money you are spending and enjoying today, and what you have in reserve to carry you through to the end.

As a matter of course your ultimate financial goal should be to spend your last cent just before you die. As Stephen Pollan, author of *Die Broke*, points out, the ideal is to have your last check, which is written to the undertaker, bounce. If you can time this perfectly, more power to you. In this case, your will should state: "Surprise! Having been of sound mind, I spent all my money while I was still alive."

There may even be a better way: Whether true or not, I once heard a story about a man who died with a lot of debts to his name. In his will he designated his six largest creditors as his preferred pallbearers. "If they have carried me this far," he wrote, "they can carry me all the way."

Helping Others Can Make Life More Worthwhile and You Happier than You Have Ever Been

The most deep-rooted of all human needs is the need to live for something more important than mere survival. We all want to make a difference, to leave a mark on this world that is still here when we are no longer here. For some retirees, volunteering to serve those less fortunate than they are is the one single thing that gives their lives purpose. Making the world a better place to live helps them earn self-respect and the respect of others.

Volunteering is often viewed as serious leisure by many retirees. It provides work-like activities that require goal-setting, discipline, responsibility, and teamwork. Above all, volunteering makes retirees feel needed and productive. On the other hand, certain retirees refuse to volunteer because they don't feel good working at something for which they receive no pay. Unfortunately, these mercenaries don't see the great benefits that come from volunteering.

Ex-president Jimmy Carter, who was quoted earlier, is arguably the most famous volunteer in America. Carter had this to say about volunteerism and the art of giving to others: "It's not something that's special for former presidents; it's the kind of chances or opportunities that are available to every person in America. There are hundreds or maybe thousands of opportunities that we have to expand our lives and to do something that might benefit other people, but in the long term we get more benefit from it than the people we're trying to help."

Thousands of groups across the United States offer community service opportunities for people aged fifty and over with diverse backgrounds, skills, and interests. For individuals who are new to volunteering or are seeking new opportunities, VolunteerMatch, the Web's largest database of volunteer opportunities, is a good place to start. Volunteers enter their ZIP code on the www.volunteermatch.org website to find local opportunities posted by nonprofit and tax-exempt organizations.

> No one is useless in this world who lightens the burdens of another.
>
> — Charles Dickens

By helping others, you too can make life more worthwhile and yourself happier than you have ever been. Just as work did before you retired, volunteering can take your mind off life's little annoying problems. You won't have as much time to focus on those everyday aggravations that creep into our lives if we let them. A recent research study indicated that retirees who volunteer live happier and longer than retirees who don't volunteer. Volunteering retirees have less stress, are healthier, and reap physiological benefits from regularly giving of themselves to others.

In another study, researchers at the University of Michigan found that seniors who performed volunteer work had a 67 percent lower risk of dying over a seven-year period than those who did no such work. Marc Musick, a research fellow at the university's

Institute for Social Research, said, "We are social animals and if you think of volunteering as a type of social interaction, it can make a big difference for older people."

Indeed, volunteering offers many retirees the opportunity to do something creative and out of the ordinary. They have the opportunity to get out of the house and rub shoulders with a wide range of people. Volunteers can shop around for activities that complement their skills and there is usually training available for those who want to try something new.

What acts of commitment and contribution would you like to engage in that will add value not only to your own life but to the lives of those around you? You don't need to make a big difference on a global level. You can make a big difference through a commitment to help others in your community, volunteering for a charitable organization or even on a one-to-one basis.

The best choice of a volunteering assignment is one in which you learn new knowledge and skills while you are helping others. You not only give to others but you get something invaluable in return. The more you give, the more you will receive.

> It is only in the giving of oneself to others that we truly live.
>
> — Ethel Percy Andrus

Givers are the greatest beneficiaries according to Claus Wedekind, one of the researchers in the Department of Biology at Bern University. The benefit is not a direct, reciprocal one, but generous people win out over the long term. This is due to the fact that giving is a trait that confers respect and status within society. Helping someone has an impact on an individual's image within a community. By being regarded more favorably by others, the generous are in a better position to survive and be happy in society.

Indeed, most retirees profess that their volunteering experience gives them much more than they put in. "Everything I need to know in life, I've learned from an Ottawa soup kitchen. I've only brought to it my time and energy and whatever personality traits I possess," declared Douglas Cornish of Ottawa. He has volunteered at the soup kitchen every Saturday for over ten years. "It's changed me and made me a little better," wrote Cornish in his *Globe and Mail* article "Lessons Learned in a Soup Kitchen."

Cornish mentioned that working in the Ottawa soup kitchen had accentuated five of his personal qualities — patience, persistence, compassion, understanding, and friendship. "Collectively these qualities might be called 'character'" is how he put it. In the world outside the soup kitchen, these five qualities always provide Cornish "with a very good rate of exchange."

> The miracle is not that we do this work, but that we are happy to do it.
>
> — Mother Teresa

In short, helping others while volunteering for a charity creates feelings of achievement, responsibility, growth, and recognition. The result is satisfaction and happiness that no amount of money can ever buy. American comedian and civil rights activist Dick Gregory agreed when he reflected about his life, "One of the things I keep learning is that the secret of being happy is doing things for other people."

Forget How Old You Are — This Becomes More Important the Older You Get

Age, many of you retirees, soon-to-be retirees, and wannabe retirees will be happy to hear, is not all it's made out to be. It's how you look at it. As a matter of course retirement is often associated with old age, even though it shouldn't be. The fact is, however, if you are retired long enough, sooner or later some people will think of you as an older person. Whether you perceive yourself as having entered old age will depend upon your attitude more than anything else.

"He who is of a calm and happy nature will hardly feel the pressure of age," Plato told us, "but to him who is of an opposite disposition youth and age are equally a burden." After all these years, experts are still trying to prove Plato right. In a study reported in the August 2002 issue of the *Journal of Personality and Social Psychology*, researchers claim that elderly people can actually think themselves into the grave a lot faster than they would prefer. Indeed, people with negative views about aging shorten their lives by 7.6 years as compared to their counterparts who have a more positive view of life.

Surprisingly, a positive view about aging can have a greater effect than good physical health. The researchers, led by psychologist Becca Levy of Yale University, reported, "The effect of more positive self-perceptions of aging on survival is greater than the physiological measures of low systolic blood pressure and cholesterol, each of which is associated with a longer lifespan of four years or less."

"Our study carries two messages," concluded the researchers.

"The discouraging one is that negative self-perceptions can diminish life expectancy. The encouraging one is that positive self-perceptions can prolong life expectancy."

The lesson here is that you shouldn't waste too much time and energy worrying about getting older. "Never think oldish thoughts," advised James A. Farley. "It's oldish thoughts that make a person old."

Talk to active elderly people with a joie de vivre, such as Ben Kerr mentioned earlier in this chapter, and you will learn that they are young at heart and don't perceive of themselves as old. Sure, they realize that they are physically limited to some degree, but psychologically they don't see age having much to do with their true selves. This applies whether they are in their sixties or nineties.

To be sure, many upbeat retirees usually feel extremely uncomfortable when in the presence of people their age, primarily because the majority of people their age think and act old. Simply put, active and happy elderly people don't want to waste their retirement years listening to people their age complain about the problems of being old.

"There is a fountain of youth," declared Sophia Loren. "It is your mind, your talents, the creativity you bring to your life, and the lives of the people you love. When you learn to tap this source, you will have truly defeated age."

I just learned that our new neighbor Mr. Klipson makes love to his wife twice a day. With Viagra, you could do the same.

Give me a little time. I haven't even met her yet!

By virtue of their positive thinking, many happy and active seniors have expanded the concept of middle age into the seventh decade. Take, for example, Robert Allen of Vacaville, California. Although he is officially seventy-five years old, he told a Vacaville newspaper reporter that he has a difficult time thinking of himself as a senior citizen.

Consider what and how much Allen has done at his age and you will see why he is young at heart. Robert is a founding member of the Vacaville Museum Board of Directors, where he cultivates a collection of native plants and teaches local school groups. He has also worked for the restoration of Pena Adobe Park and the development of the Vacaville Cultural Arts Center. Recently, he designed the panels for the kiosks in the new downtown Creekwalk. In 2001, he worked on the tedious task of organizing archive collections of old photographic negatives for the Vacaville Heritage Council.

To keep his musical side in tune, Robert regularly sings in the West Valley Chorale made up of singers from his hometown Vacaville and nearby towns of Dixon and Davis. Robert told the Vacaville newspaper reporter that he stays young by following the advice of his ninety-seven-year-old mother, Dorothy Allen: "To grow old, you have to be willing to take chances."

Robert Allen is not unusual in his approach to staying middle-aged for four decades or more. According to a 2002 study by The National Council on the Aging (NCOA), in this day and age one-third of Americans in their seventies consider themselves middle-aged. Among respondents age sixty-five to sixty-nine, nearly half (45 percent) said they considered themselves middle-aged.

> Age only matters when one is aging. Now that I have arrived at a great age, I might just as well be twenty.
>
> — Pablo Picasso

Thinking young can help you to stay busily and happily involved in your later years. "The most successful old-old people are those who have an important connection, a hobby, or something that gives them a zest for life," remarks Kevan H. Namazi, gerontologist at University of Texas's Southwestern Medical Center in Dallas. Being productive well into your later years will enhance your self-esteem and contribute to intellectual stimulation and social interaction. Moreover, you will enrich the lives of others while enriching your own at the same time.

Here are a few examples of individuals who kept themselves active and creatively alive in their later years:

- Martin Miller of Indiana at ninety-seven was working full time lobbying for the rights of senior citizens.
- Mary Baker Eddy was eighty-seven when she followed her personal mission — creating a new newspaper with a religious influence. She called it the *Christian Science Monitor*.
- Somerset Maugham wrote his last book at eighty-four.
- Giuseppe Verdi was still composing operas in his eighties.

> George Bernard Shaw was writing plays in his nineties. At ninety-three, Shaw wrote *Farfetched Fables*.

> Architect Frank Lloyd Wright, a pioneer in the modern style and considered one of the greatest figures in twentieth-century architecture, was eighty-nine when he designed his last building.

> How about Leopold Stokowski? Stokowski founded the American Symphony Orchestra at eighty and recorded twenty albums in his nineties. At the age of ninety-six, Stokowski — an eternal optimist no doubt — signed a six-year recording contract.

> You're never too old to become younger.
> — Mae West

These people appear to be somewhat remarkable, and in a way they are. They are not unusual, however. Hundreds of thousands of people in their seventies, eighties, and nineties have an incredible zest for life and show great vigor, enthusiasm, and physical ability for living. Like these active and happy retirees, you shouldn't let how old you are dictate when you enter old age. Indeed, one of the secrets to happiness is to forget how old you are — this becomes more important the older you get.

Don't Leave This World with Songs Unsung That You Would Like to Sing

An elegant sufficiency, content,
Retirement, rural quiet, friendship, books,
Ease and alternate labour, useful life,
Progressive virtue, and approving Heaven!
— James Thomson

Think about this quietly and carefully: Years from now, as you review your life, what may you regret not having done? Clearly, it won't be to have worked longer and harder at your career. And it won't be that you didn't watch more TV. Whatever it is, shouldn't you be doing it now?

To be sure, you don't want to leave this world with songs

unsung that you would like to sing. Nor do you want to end up on your deathbed pleading, "Lord, give me one more shot and I'll give it all I got." Thus, you must start singing these songs today if you are already retired. If you are working but contemplating retirement, the sooner you retire, the sooner you will have the time and freedom to sing the songs you have wanted to sing.

In an interview on CBC radio, a number of individuals, all over sixty years old, were asked what advice they would give themselves if they had life to live over. Here are six of their most important suggestions:

> - Take the time to find out what you really want to do with your life.
> - Take more risks.
> - Lighten up and don't take life so seriously.
> - Be more patient.
> - It's best to suffer from the Peter-Pan syndrome. Relive your younger days. What were your dreams when you were young?
> - Live the moment more.

Ultimately, successful retirement life requires that you be in control of your mind. To be sure, you are definitely not in control of your mind if friends, relatives, society, the media, and advertisers strongly influence your view

> You can't turn back the clock. But you can wind it up again.
>
> — Bonnie Pruden

of what makes for a happy retirement. The key is to spend significant time regularly evaluating and reevaluating what success means to you — and only you.

Resist the temptation to respond to people who call you selfish for doing your own thing. Anyone who calls you selfish is trying to get something out of you, or wants you to be the way they would like. This, of course, makes them a lot more selfish than you. It was Oscar Wilde who said, "Selfishness is not living as one wishes to live, it is asking others to live as one wishes to live."

The surest sign that you are on the right track to a happy, wild, and free retirement is that you have clearly defined success in a way that is different from the definition of any other individual on Earth. Indeed, the most important definition of success — and whether you have attained that success — will always be in the eye of the beholder.

Being true to yourself is important. Upon close examination of your life, you may determine that some of the things you presently want — things that you are pursuing with great zeal — may be a lot less important to your happiness than you thought. On the other hand, some of the things that you are presently neglecting may be essential to your peace and contentment. If you want your life to change for the better, you may need to change your relationship with money, material possessions, time, leisure activities, and even people.

The French have a saying, *"L'homme absurde est celui qui ne change jamais."* (The absurd human being is the one who never changes.) I couldn't agree more. If you aren't getting much out of life emotionally and spiritually, then you must look at what you bring into life. Clearly, to get more out of this world, you must make some changes in your life.

While making life-altering changes to create a fulfilling lifestyle isn't always easy, millions of retirees have shown it is possible. They have gotten their emotional acts together and accomplished what the majority have not. It is no wonder that these people live happier and fuller lives.

You must be absolutely clear about what really counts. And you must be even clearer about what doesn't count. Only then can you make the most of what matters most and make nothing of what doesn't matter at all. Do something every day to make your life less complicated. You will find that life's a breeze when you work as hard at simplifying it as you now do at complicating it.

Never be discouraged because others have more money or better health than you. You can always make up in creativity what you lack in good fortune. Playing the game of life is like playing poker. Playing three aces badly won't get you as far as playing a terrible hand well.

The defining moment for the amount of happiness you experience in retirement won't be when you become a multi-millionaire. In fact, the defining moment will be when you realize that, regardless of how much money you have to your name, you couldn't be any happier in the present moment. Some people are able to reach this state with a net value of under $20,000. Others never reach this state, despite having acquired millions.

> In a completely sane world, madness is the only freedom.
>
> — J. G. Ballard

If you are not as fulfilled as you would like to be, perhaps you are playing it too safe. The one thing we should never regret are our mistakes. And the one thing we should regret is not having made more. Always waiting for the river to run dry before you cross it is no way to live your life. Only by facing some risks along the way will your journey be worth making.

Some days you may be so bored that an invitation to the opening of a new garbage dump will excite you. Remind yourself who is responsible for your boredom. To repeat the words of Dylan Thomas: "Somebody is boring me; I think it is me."

Handling boredom is actually quite easy. Get busy doing the things you love, or something that you have always wanted to do. Your willingness to be accountable for your boredom is the creative force that will make it go away.

You are not retiring from life; you are only retiring from a job. I must repeat the importance of variety. Florida retiree Douglas Spangler, a former university administrator, claims, "For me, writing, photography, travel, and several other interests fill my days to the point that I can't imagine how I found time to also work before I retired."

The secrets for living a full, rewarding, fulfilled, and enlightened life are not really secrets. These principles have been passed down through the ages but the majority of humans tend to discount them and follow principles that don't work. "In the end these things matter most," revealed Buddha. "How well did you love? How fully did you live? How deeply did you learn to let go?"

Master, I have come all this way to find out how to retire rich and famous in America.

Why? No matter how much wealth and fame you attain, the size of your funeral will still pretty much depend on the weather.

According to a Hindu proverb, "True happiness consists in making others happy." As far as possible without surrender, be a kind, gentle, generous, and loving person. Share whatever happiness you experience with others. In this way you will multiply the happiness that comes into your life.

Generally this is not understood by most humans: We are always free to change our futures by being more alive and creative in the present. Happy, successful people don't expect mysterious forces to make tomorrow worth living. They themselves make it that way by what they do today.

According to the Buddha, "What we think, we become."

Therefore, always think and act as if you and your life really matter. Surprisingly, after awhile you won't be able to tell the difference.

Don't do things because you feel you have to do them. Do things because you want to. The difference in the results you attain will be beyond belief.

It is folly to strive for total comfort, however. Be creative, active, and productive in leisure activities that require some risk, challenge, and discomfort. Comfort is a double-edged sword. A little will increase health and happiness; too much, and it will destroy both.

You may hope for but you won't be happy with an entirely easy life. When you always do the easy and comfortable, life turns out difficult and uncomfortable. When you do the difficult and uncomfortable, however, life becomes easy and comfortable. Think about this carefully; it applies to many areas of your life.

> Enjoy every day as if it was your last and one day you will be right about it.
>
> — Graffiti

In your search for Shangri-la, don't overlook the possibility that paradise may be where you are right now. Everyone seems to want to be somewhere they aren't. Choose to be where you are right now and you will be happier than 90 percent of humankind.

Again, retiring happy, wild, and free is about attitude. Alter your thoughts and behavior and you will not only change yourself, you will change the world around you. Whatever psychic energy you put into the universe will be reflected back to you. The more positive energy you put into imagining and creating a happy, wild, and free retirement, the more it will manifest itself in the real world.

Happiness, it seems, doesn't like people who are desperate for it. The desperate pursuit of happiness is one of the chief causes of unhappiness. Thus, stop trying so hard to be happy. Slow down in your pursuit of happiness and it is more likely to catch up to you. When happiness forgets about you, see what treasures you can find in your unhappiness. It won't be long before happiness remembers who you are, and sneaks back into your life again.

Everything keeps its best character by being put to its best use. This applies to both people and things. Thus, pursue retirement goals in harmony with your character and values. Anything short of this and you will be cheating yourself out of many hours of happiness and satisfaction each and every day.

Do the simple things that are important for your happiness.

Spend time with people whom you like best. Get involved in the activities that you enjoy most. And totally avoid the people and activities that you like least. This strategy is so obvious, but few people use it.

Strive for personal freedom. Otherwise you will be imprisoned a good portion of your life. As indicated in the first chapter, you will have attained freedom when you can get up in the morning when you want to get up; go to sleep when you want to go to sleep; and in the interval, work and play at the things you want to work and play at — all at your own pace.

For independent-minded individuals, freedom contributes to much happiness. But freedom isn't the ability to do what others are doing. On the contrary, freedom is the ability to do what the majority in society are afraid of doing on their own. Only when you are able to be creative and different — even wildly eccentric — will you be free.

Don't lose touch with the craziness within yourself. Often one gets a reputation for mental stability simply because one doesn't have enough courage to make a fool of oneself. Is it more important to live with zest or to have people think nice things about you? The point is, if you want to be truly alive, forget about what people think.

> Sail away from the safe harbor. Catch the trade winds in your sails. Explore. Dream. Discover.
>
> — Mark Twain

To a large degree freedom entails nonattachment to what others can't do without. Zen masters tell us that people become imprisoned by what they are most attached to: Cars. Houses. Money. Egos. Identities. Let go of your attachment to these things and you will be set free.

Showing gratitude for what you have — to God or otherwise — should be a daily ritual. The more gratitude you express for the things you already have, the less you will need or want. Develop a new appreciation for the things you take for granted, such as the fresh smell of coffee, a gentle wind blowing in your face, and the purring of your cat. And never tire of watching a sunset or smelling the roses.

Resist accepting society's way of living as the right one. Your primary duty is to be yourself. Invent a lifestyle that expresses who you are. In the end, there is no right way of living. There is only your way.

Regardless of your age, try to reconnect with your childhood tendencies. To enjoy life in later years you won't need a second childhood if you haven't lost your first. A variety in relationships and interests will go a long way to making life rich and satisfying.

Always keep in mind that happiness is a mode of traveling and not the destination. Zen masters tell us that we corrupt the beauty of living by making happiness the goal. They say happiness is the practice of living in the moment; it's in everything we do.

Remember that a successful retirement is not possible unless you involve yourself in something that is vital and purposeful. Retiring happy, wild, and free means being engaged to the full level of your mental and physical ability. If you dream about writing books, write books. If you dream about traveling to Thailand, hop on an airplane for Bangkok. And if you dream about being a visual artist, then start painting pictures. Otherwise, you will find that the ache of unfulfilled dreams is the biggest pain you ever experience.

> Keep a green tree in your heart and perhaps the singing bird will come.
>
> — Chinese proverb

As the Western saying goes, "Get a life." Not just an ordinary life. Get a great life. Get a focused, satisfying, balanced life instead of one filled with nothing but watching TV and other passive activities. Spare lots of time for family, friends, and leisure. Most important — don't forget to spare time for yourself.

Nothing that is human should be foreign to you. Make the small pleasures in life your biggest priorities. The wise people on Earth realize that the simple pleasures — nature, health, music, friendship, etc. — are the most satisfying.

Have some perpetual small enjoyment in which you indulge daily. Never miss it, regardless of how busy you are. This will do wonders for your well-being. Indeed, it will do more for your happiness than acquiring the biggest and best of possessions.

To be sure, retirement life is a game in many ways. Ensure that you laugh and have fun, even when the score is not in your favor. This way, you will always end up winning at the most important game you will ever play.

Consider each day you haven't laughed, played, and celebrated your life to be a wasted day. You were given three special gifts when you were born: the gifts of life, love, and laughter. Learn to share these gifts with the rest of the world. And the rest of the world will play happily with you.

Your goal should be to make your stay on Earth as close to a heavenly experience as it can be. Indeed, Zen masters tell us that there is no sense to waiting for Heaven. Zen says that life lived today is Heaven.

Put another way, this is it! Today — this is all you get. Take it or leave it. And you can't leave it. Therefore, make the best of it. This way, if you get to Heaven, you will be well prepared to enjoy yourself there.

Freedom and happiness are easier to attain than you think. Take your lesson from children. Don't fret about the future. Don't regret the past. Live only in the present. The happiness you have at any moment is the only happiness you can ever experience. Reminisce about your great yesterdays, hope for many interesting tomorrows, but, above all, ensure that you live today.

When it's time for my retirement, I would like to have the arrogant bloke on the back of this bicycle pedal me around for a year or two.

It's essential that you identify the resources most important for your present-day happiness. When money is lost, a little is lost. When time is lost, much more is lost. When health is lost, practically everything is lost. And when creative spirit is lost, there is nothing left.

The rest of your life begins right now. It can be more than it has ever been. Your goal should be to enjoy everything in life that you can. It is a mistake not to. Let it be a wondrous life. Life is all around you. Live it to the fullest, with all your senses. Listen to it. Look at it. Taste it. Smell it. Feel it.

Always be true to yourself. Do not blindly believe what you are told about what brings happiness, even what is reported in this book. Find out for yourself what brings joy and contentment to your world. Your inner voice will tell you what will bring you peace of mind.

Above all, ask yourself what would give you true happiness. Listen to your answers carefully. Then do what you have to do to attain it. You cannot afford not to. Many years from now you will regret the things that you didn't do much more so than the ones you did do.

Again, retirement life is a game. Happy people are the players. Unhappy people are the spectators. Which would you like to be?

> Life is long if it is full.
>
> — Seneca

About the Author

Ernie Zelinski is best known as the author of *The Joy of Not Working,* an international best-seller that has sold over 200,000 copies and has been published in 16 languages. Ernie has negotiated over 80 book deals with publishers in 23 countries for his 12 books.

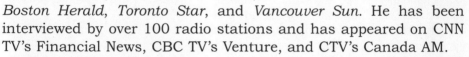

Photograph by Greg Gazin

Feature articles about Ernie and his books have appeared in major newspapers including *USA TODAY, National Post, Oakland Tribune, Boston Herald, Toronto Star*, and *Vancouver Sun*. He has been interviewed by over 100 radio stations and has appeared on CNN TV's Financial News, CBC TV's Venture, and CTV's Canada AM.

Ernie has a B.Sc. in Engineering and a Masters in Business Administration from the University of Alberta. He speaks professionally on the subjects of book marketing, retirement, and applying creativity to business and leisure.

Ernie is uniquely qualified to write *How to Retire Happy, Wild, and Free,* given that he opted for semi-retirement when he was only thirty years old and close to financial bankruptcy (with a net worth of minus $30,000). Yet today Ernie is a prosperous writer, entrepreneur, and connoisseur of leisure who maintains a three- to four-hour workday and doesn't like to work at all in any month that doesn't have an "r" in its name. Ernie is presently writing four other books including *Real Success WITHOUT a Real Job*.

Ernie would be pleased to receive letters from readers. If you have any questions or comments, write to:

Ernie Zelinski
VIP Books
P.O. Box 4072
Edmonton, Alberta
Canada, T6E 4S8

E-mail: vip-books@telus.net

For more information visit *The Joy of Not Working* Website at:

www.thejoyofnotworking.com

An International Best-Seller
by Ernie Zelinski

THE JOY OF NOT WORKING:
A Book for the Retired,
Unemployed, and Overworked —
21st Century Edition

Ernie Zelinski could change your view of the world forever. Ernie has already taught more than 200,000 people what *The Joy of Not Working* is all about: learning to live every part of your life — employment, unemployment, retirement, and leisure time alike — to the fullest. With this revised and expanded edition, you too can join the thousands of converts and learn to thrive at both work and play. Illustrated by eye-opening exercises, thought-provoking diagrams, and lively cartoons and quotations, *The Joy of Not Working* will guide you to enjoy life like never before.

Available at fine bookstores
and at www.tenspeed.com

Visit *The Joy of Not Working*
Website by Ernie Zelinski

This is a content rich website that provides inspiration to help you attain real success without a real job and much more including:

- ◆ An e-book version of *The Joy of Not Working*
- ◆ Other free e-books including the *Graffiti for the Soul* Series
- ◆ Special quantity prices for *How to Retire Happy, Wild, and Free*
- ◆ Over half of *How to Retire Happy, Wild, and Free* that you can e-mail to your friends
- ◆ Real life success stories from readers
- ◆ What's new to help you retire happy, wild, and free

www.thejoyofnotworking.com